Our Tropical Possessions in Malayan India

OUR TROPICAL POSSESSIONS

IN

MALAYAN INDIA.

P. Carpenter, del

SINGAPORE AT S

THE CITY WESTWARD

80

OUR TROPICAL POSSESSIONS

IN

MALAYAN INDIA:

BEING A DESCRIPTIVE ACCOUNT OF SINGAPORE, PENANG,
PROVINCE WELLESLEY, AND MALACCA; THEIR
PEOPLES, PRODUCTS, COMMERCE,
AND GOVERNMENT.

BY

JOHN CAMERON, Esq., F.R.G.S.

WITH ILLUSTRATIONS.

LONDON:
SMITH, ELDER AND CO., 65, CORNHILL.
1865.

CONTENTS.

——•◦•——

a 3

OUR TROPICAL POSSESSIONS

IN

MALAYAN INDIA.

a

OUR TROPICAL POSSESSIONS

IN

MALAYAN INDIA.

administration is a high and important trust, which if
boldly, and yet wisely conducted, will go further to
preserve the predominance and permanence of British
interests—commercial and political—in the Eastern
Archipelago, and the adjacent native continental States
—if not, indeed, in China itself—than any other means
which the Imperial Government can employ. Founded
under the rule of the old East India Company, and
fostered from its infancy by a policy which, if faulty
in many other respects, was at least well suited to
protect and encourage a settlement ere it attained
inherent strength enough to stand by itself, the Straits
Settlement has grown to an importance incompatible
with such tutelage. It remains to be seen how the
progress of its maturer years will be advanced or
retarded by the wise or unwise government of English
statesmen.

Hitherto but little has been given to the world
concerning it, and to the great bulk of untravelled
Englishmen it is known only as a distant Indian
station, where manufactures are sold and produce
bought under the sweltering heat of an equatorial sun.
Indeed, an existence there is viewed as an exile of the
worst description, to be compensated only by the
wealth which it is reputed to bring. But those who
have endured that exile can tell a far different tale of
the condition of life in the tropical garden ; and those
at all acquainted with the high roads of Eastern trade,
have but to view the position of the island of Singapore
on the chart, to become sensible of its importance to
such a nation as Great Britain ; an importance which

8 ð

OUR TROPICAL POSSESSIONS

IN

MALAYAN INDIA:

BEING A DESCRIPTIVE ACCOUNT OF SINGAPORE, PENANG,
PROVINCE WELLESLEY, AND MALACCA; THEIR
PEOPLES, PRODUCTS, COMMERCE,
AND GOVERNMENT.

BY

JOHN CAMERON, Esq., F.R.G.S.

WITH ILLUSTRATIONS.

LONDON:

SMITH, ELDER AND CO., 65, CORNHILL.

1865.

millions and a half sterling, and its exports over five
millions and a half. Penang and Malacca, sharing
soon after their incorporation the liberal policy inaugurated at Singapore, have prospered with it, though
not to the same degree. The gross imports of
the three settlements may be represented in round
numbers by eight millions and a half, and the exports
by eight millions and a quarter. These facts have
at last forced their way, if not into the notice
of the world at large, at least into that of the
British Government, the great arbiter of the fate of
aspiring dependencies, and it has, I believe, been
concluded that a possession of such a gigantic commerce should no longer remain "the dependency of a
dependency;" nor has it been thought wise, that
a place so valuable, in a strategic point of view, to a
nation aspiring to paramount influence in the East,
should remain to be administered under the circuitous
routine of the Bengal Government.

The tropical colony, then, comprises the island
of Penang, (or Prince of Wales' Island, including
Province Wellesley,) the town and territory of Malacca,
and the island of Singapore. The East India Company
in 1786 came into possession of Penang by treaty
with the Rajah of Quedah, a native state on the west
coast of the peninsula; and fourteen years later the
slip of land opposite Penang, now known as Province
Wellesley, was ceded to the Company by the same
prince.

Malacca was conquered by the Portuguese under
Albuquerque more than 350 years ago, and about 100

years afterwards fell by conquest into the hands of the Dutch, who retained it until 1795, when we took it from them. It remained in our possession until four years after the conclusion of the treaty of Vienna, and in 1818, was re-delivered by us to the Dutch in conformity with the terms of that treaty; but seven years afterwards it came finally into our possession in terms of the celebrated treaty with Holland of 1824. As for Singapore, it has never changed European owners. In 1819, Sir Stamford Raffles, then Governor of Fort Marlborough, or Bencoolen, in Sumatra, who had been long impressed with the importance of the position, came over and took formal possession of the then nearly uninhabited island, on terms which will be treated of hereafter.

The three settlements lie along the northern boundary of the Straits of Malacca. Penang is an island situated at its north-western entrance, or in about latitude 5° 24' north, and longitude 100° 21' east, and is about 13½ miles long, having an extreme breadth of 10 miles, containing an area of very nearly 70,000 acres. Province Wellesley is on the mainland of the peninsula, immediately opposite Penang, the water dividing them being about 8 miles broad at the narrowest point; it runs north and south 25 miles, varying in breadth from 4 to 11 miles, and containing an area of 15,000 acres. Malacca is a much larger tract of territory, distant from Province Wellesley some 260 miles along the coast of the Malayan Peninsula, in a south-easterly direction, the intervening territory belonging to the native states of Perak and Salangore,

both under the English protection; it has a frontage
to the straits of 43 miles, its extent inland varying
from 10 to 28 miles. The town stands in latitude
2° 16′ north. About 100 miles south-east from
Malacca, at the eastern entrance of the straits, the
island of Singapore juts out from the native state of
Johore, and forms the heel of the peninsula. It is
25 miles long by 14 broad, and contains an area of
206 square miles. The position of the town is in
latitude 1° 17′ north, longitude 103° 51′ east.

Of the island of Singapore—the youngest but
most important of the three incorporated settlements—I mean first to treat separately, leaving my
notice of Penang and Malacca to a later part of this
volume.

The very early history of Singapore can possess
but little interest to English readers as compared with
its present condition, and I shall consequently be
as brief on this head as possible. As will be seen,
when I come to treat of the native races of the settlement, the aborigines of the peninsula and adjacent
islands were composed of wandering and very thinly
scattered tribes, who never built permanent villages.
As early as the year A.D. 1160, the pioneers of
the Malays came over from Sumatra, and driving
out the few scattered tribes of the aborigines, planted
a considerable colony on the island, which they named
Singhapura. The kings of Java, anxious to possess
so prosperous a settlement, made repeated attacks
upon it, but were invariably driven back, until the year
1252, when treachery at last led to the defeat and

expulsion of the sturdy settlers. It appears that their prince or chief, captivated by the exceeding comeliness of the daughter of his bandahara or viceroy, took her to wife, much to the disgust of his other mistresses, who, not long after her marriage, accused her of infidelity, and so worked upon the jealousies of the prince that he ordered her impalement. The bandahara, assured of his child's innocence, earnestly entreated that, if his daughter must suffer death, it might not be so shameful a one. His request, however, was disregarded, and so was formed the first traitor in the camp of the islanders. The bandahara secretly invited the Javanese to the conquest of the place; they came, and the gates of the citadel admitted them by night; an obstinate struggle succeeded, but the Javanese were victorious, driving the Singaporeans from the island to seek a new colony on the mainland of the peninsula. This they did at Malacca, and in the end became the founders of the Johore Empire.

Singapore appears not to have prospered in the hands of its Javanese conquerors. It never rose to any pre-eminence under them, nor was it ever sufficiently powerful to take part in the many struggles that afterwards ensued between the Portuguese and the surrounding native principalities. Indeed, the most probable conjecture seems to be, that a century or so after its acquisition it had been abandoned, at least as a stronghold, by the Javanese, and left to a few peaceable fishermen and tillers of the soil, who neither attracted the cupidity nor provoked the jealousy of other states, nor possessed any sentiments of ambition in themselves. In this condition the island appears to have remained until the middle of the sixteenth century, when the descendants of its original founders, who had grown in power and opulence, were expelled from Malacca by the Portuguese under Albuquerque.

From the time that the Malay pioneers had been driven by the Javanese from Singapore to plant their new settlement at Malacca, they had prospered in no ordinary degree; and had not only brought under their dominion a considerable portion of the south-western coasts of the peninsula, but had extended their sovereignty over many of the islands south-ward of the Straits of Singapore. When, therefore, after many fruitless attempts to overcome their Christian foes, they were expelled from the centre of their government at Malacca, they moved further south, gathered together the remnants of their possessions, and founded the kingdom of Johore, which embraced the southernmost extremity of the peninsula, from Point Romania on the east to the Cassang river on the west, and also included Singapore and many of the islands to the south of the Straits, such as the Carimons, Bintang—of which Rhio is the capital, &c. I do not propose here to follow the chequered fortunes of the kingdom of Johore, but, from what has been stated, the singular circumstance can be noted, that the island of Singapore, though for whole centuries afterwards it remained an impenetrable jungle with but a few fishing villages on its shores, was neverthe-less the original settlement of the adventurous and, in many respects, noble race, that, like English colonists in more modern instances, have laid the foundation of a great empire on but a very small beginning.

From the time of the foundation of the Johore empire in 1512, till more than three hundred years afterwards when Sir Stamford Raffles founded a British settlement on it, Singapore was esteemed but of very little importance. The great empire itself had been much shaken by continued encounters with native as well as European foes; and, in some cases, internal dissension and disturbances had still further weakened its unity. The Dutch had just taken possession of Rhio for 4,000 guilders a month, and were busy with their intrigues to obtain supremacy over the entire kingdom of Johore. Sir Stamford Raffles, however, was not to be outwitted by native vacillation or Dutch cunning, and he was far more wise in his selection of the future English station than were the Dutch, when they chose Rhio. He must have clearly seen that, on the high road of China commerce, Singapore could not fail under a liberal and enlightened policy, and in the possession of such a nation as Great Britain, to grow up to an importance that would wither the efforts of any rival power in its vicinity. But he had no small difficulty to encounter. He was desirous to secure not a virtual possession only, but a legal one—legal in the eyes of the people themselves, as well as of European nations. This was not a very easy task at the time. In 1818 Major Farquhar, then resident of Malacca, had made a treaty with Sultan Abdul Rahman Shah, providing for mutual liberty of

navigation and commerce in the ports and dominions
of Johore, and securing a right to build a factory on
the island of Singapore. A few months afterwards,
however, the Dutch, when Malacca was delivered up
to them in terms of the treaty of Vienna, sent an over-
powering force to Rhio, where Abdul Rahman Shah,
with whom our treaty was made, resided; they declared
this chief to be their vassal, and treated with contempt
all the negotiations he had made with us; extorting
a treaty from him for themselves, which altogether
excluded British trade from his ports and possessions.
But Sir Stamford Raffles was not deterred from the
pursuit of his original intention towards Singapore,
and in 1819 he proceeded there with Major Farquhar,
and hoisted the British flag, placing the latter gentleman in charge of the new settlement. It appears that
soon after landing, Sir Stamford was visited by the
Tumongong or viceroy of Johore; this powerful chief
was far from friendly to the progress of the Dutch
in these parts, and readily lent himself to carry out
the wishes of Sir Stamford Raffles to obtain for the
British a legal and indefeasible title to the new settlement. He stated that the legitimate sovereign of
Johore was Hassan Shah, the elder son of the late
sultan, and not Abdul Rahman Shah, with whom our
first treaty had been made, and whom the Dutch
had acknowledged as the legitimate successor simply
because he was more conceding in his disposition.
Assured of this fact, Sir Stamford Raffles secretly
despatched a packet to Rhio where Hassan Shah
was living in obscurity, and had him brought over

to Singapore in the night-time. As soon as he landed, Sir Stamford Raffles called together the Tumongong of Johore and Bandahara of Pahang, the two hereditary elective officers of the empire, and had him proclaimed Sultan. A treaty was now drawn up, to the effect that British jurisdiction should extend over a limited part of the island, from Tanjong (or Cape) Mallang on the west, to Tanjong Katong on the east, and as far inland as the range of cannon shot. It was not until five years afterwards that final arrangements for the entire cession of the island to the British were made; when a treaty was concluded on the 2nd of August, 1824, between Mr. Crawfurd, on the part of the Company, with their Highnesses the Sultan and Tumongong of Johore, whereby " the island of Singapore, together with the adjacent seas, straits, and islets, to the extent of ten geographical miles from the coast of Singapore, were given up in full sovereignty and property to the East India Company, their heirs and successors, for ever;" the Company agreeing to pay the Sultan the sum of 88,200 Spanish dollars, together with a yearly stipend during his life of 15,600 Spanish dollars; and to the Tumongong the sum of 26,000 dollars, together with a yearly stipend of 8,400 dollars. By this treaty, too, the Sultan and Tumongong bound themselves to enter into no alliance, and make no treaties with any foreign power or potentate, without first obtaining the consent of the British thereto.

As will be gathered from the sequel, owing to a want of energy and a want of strength of character in

the family of the Sultan, it has gradually lost both
power and fortune; while, on the other hand, the
Tumongong's family, being distinguished by great
ability and determination, had steadily acquired wealth
and influence, until seven years ago, when, by a treaty
between the Sultan and Tumongong, recognized by
the British authorities at the time, the entire
sovereignty of Johore was conceded to the family of
the latter.   The transaction had certainly not the
approval of a very large majority of the European
community at the time; and it was said that the local
government authorities pushed matters on somewhat
indiscreetly.   To the present day, the question of the
rights of the Sultan as against those of the. Tumongong is not unfrequently the subject of argument in
the newspapers.   But it seems clear that the Tumongong's authority is now far too firmly established to be
overturned; and it would even appear that from the first
the Tumongong had more voice in the government than
the Sultan, especially in all that regarded Singapore,
the soil of which appears to have been his property.

    Singapore was not associated with Penang till
1826, but ranked for the first four years after its
settlement as one of the dependencies of Fort Marlborough (Bencoolen), of which Sir Stamford Raffles was
Governor, and after Sir Stamford left for Europe, was
constituted an independent residency under the Bengal
Government.   Bencoolen—which had been in the
Company's possession since 1685—was of but minor
importance, possessing almost no attractions in a commercial point of view.   It was valuable chiefly for its

pepper produce, which was a monopoly in the hands
of the Company; and it was to the servants of the
Company there that the celebrated message about
white pepper came out from the directors. It appears
that at the time white pepper found a much more ready
sale in the home market than black, and the directors,
ever watchful of their interests, wrote out to Bencoolen
in their usual magniloquent style, directing their
servants to " pay more regard in future to the planting
and cultivation of white pepper, and not to increase
the number of black pepper plants." But both black
and white pepper are from exactly the same plant,
the difference of colour only arising from the method
of preparation, the latter being allowed to ripen on the
vine, while the former is plucked when green. It is
said that the directors were always very tender to their
Bencoolen establishment after they found out their mistake, about which they never provoked a discussion.*

* It was not very long after this that a somewhat extraordinary
accident happened to the treasury chest at Bencoolen. A considerable
discrepancy appeared between the amount to the credit of the public
account and the specie actually on hand; in fact, several thousand
dollars were wanting. Every effort was made to detect either error in
the accounts or defalcation on the part of the inferior officers in the
department, but neither the one nor the other could be established; and
I believe that, in the end, the blame was laid upon the white ants—a
most destructive insect, but one which had never before been known to
extend its ravages to bullion. Still, however, it was left to the conjecture
of the directors whether the dollars themselves or only the chest that
contained them had been demolished, and they must have concluded the
former, for they expressed no remonstrance, but despatched by first
return opportunity a small parcel of steel files; and when the Bencoolen
Government wrote home to ask for what purpose the files had been sent
out, the directors answered that they were to be used against the teeth
of the white ants, should these insects again prove troublesome to the
money chest.

But when Sir Stamford Raffles came back from the administration of Java, where he had so distinguished himself, Bencoolen was constituted a Presidency, merely to confer upon him the appointment of Lieutenant Governor; and it was very fortunate that the appointment was made, and that Sir Stamford Raffles held the independent powers he did; for had a reference been made before Singapore was taken possession of, as would have been necessary on the part of any inferior authority, the answer could not have come back in time to prevent the Dutch from completely shutting us out of the Johore territories.

Colonel Farquhar was appointed by Sir Stamford Raffles as first Resident, and continued to administer the internal affairs of the settlement for the first four years of its infancy. Great outcries continued to be made by the Dutch against the legality of the settlement; and the Dutch Governor of Malacca produced a treaty of twenty-three Articles made with the Rajah of Johore before Malacca had fallen into the hands of the English in 1795, and which professed to place that country and all its dependencies, including Singapore, under the control of Malacca. That such a treaty was made actually appears to have been the case; but Sir Stamford Raffles defeated its application by referring to the terms of the cession of Malacca to us in 1795, when the Dutch, with a cautious and scarcely honest policy, having in view to limit our ascendancy as much as possible, took care to declare that all the Malayan States connected with them were *free* and *independent*. The deception must have come back rather forcibly upon themselves. These bickerings with the Dutch did not cease till the completion of the treaty with Holland in 1824, which gave us back Malacca, confirmed our possession of Singapore, and ceded us supremacy over all territories north of the Straits of Malacca, while it secured Rhio and Bencoolen and the supremacy of the native States south of the Straits to the Dutch.

The left or eastern bank of the Singapore river was the first selected for the site of the town. Colonel Farquhar built a residency bungalow on the ground in front of where the Court House now stands, with a number of smaller bungalows stretching eastward, along the present esplanade, for the accommodation of the other officers of Government. The cantonments for the military lay further back at the foot of Fort Canning.

As traders and merchants poured in, a plan of the town was drawn up, and the first allotments sold. This embraced the greater part of what is now called Campong Glam, as well as the lands fronting the beach eastward of the Institution buildings. These early sales were in fee simple, and contrary to the policy of the Company, who never gave away an absolute property in the soil, generally granting leases of 99 years; the reason being that they might, at any moment, order all residents to leave their possessions. As soon as Sir Stamford Raffles discovered his mistake, he called together the purchasers, and discharging them from the payment of their purchase-money gave them 99 years' leases of the land they had bought without any payment whatever.

In 1823, Colonel Farquhar retired to England, and Mr. Crawfurd, who had been a political agent of the Company, and had also held a high appointment during the occupation of Java, was installed by Sir Stamford Raffles in his place; and a few months afterwards, when Singapore ceased to be a dependency of Bencoolen, became Resident under the Government of Bengal. Both Sir Stamford Raffles and Mr. Crawfurd were literary men, and had commented on and criticized each other's political actions; but in June, 1823, when about to retire to England, and in handing the reins of government over to his old opponent, Sir Stamford Raffles said, " Mr. Crawfurd, there is no one to whom I could entrust the government of this infant settlement with so much pleasure as to yourself." Shortly after Mr. Crawfurd's accession, it was resolved, at the request of the merchants, who had grown a very considerable body, to build the town upon the western side of the river, where the mercantile portion of it is at the present day. At one corner of what is Commercial Square now, stood a large stony mound, and the rest was a mangrove swamp; but the swamp was filled up by excavations from the mound, and so in time was formed the level plateau on which the buildings now stand.

From the time of its settlement, Singapore had been maintained as a free port; whereas at Penang the impost of five per cent. duties was continued till the date of incorporation. With this advantage, added to its favourable geographical position, it is no wonder that Singapore grew and prospered, while the older colony remained stationary, if, in fact, it did not in some respects retrograde. The merchants of the latter place made sad complaints, but they were always met by the fact that the government of this island already cost the Company some 60,000*l.* a year over and above the revenue. The government of Singapore, it is but fair to observe, was also carried on at a heavy loss.

In 1825, Malacca was again handed over to the English, and in the year following, Penang, Singapore, and Malacca were incorporated as one settlement; Mr. Fullerton, a Madras civilian, and formerly member of council of that presidency, was sent out as governor, and as Penang was still by far the largest of the three stations, he made that the seat of government. Mr. Prince, and afterwards Mr. Murchison, both old Bencoolen servants, were Resident Councillors at Singapore; Mr. Crawfurd having, previous to the incorporation, gone home to England, where he still lives one of the best and most active friends that the settlement possesses. In 1827, Sir John Claridge came out as first Recorder of the incorporated settlements.

At this time, the Company pursued very nearly the same jealous policy as the Dutch still do in Java, and no one, merchant or otherwise, was allowed to come out to India unless under what were termed "Free Mariner's Indentures." But Sir Stamford Raffles had never paid regard to this form, and had offered the greatest inducements to every one to come and settle freely in Singapore. Mr. Fullerton,

2

however, on one of his first visits to Singapore, issued letters addressed to all the residents, asking by what right they continued on the island. Only one or two possessed the required "indentures," and the others pleaded the invitation of Sir Stamford Raffles. The matter was referred to Calcutta, where it was allowed to drop; but Mr. Fullerton lost his popularity by the measure, as it was believed some personal pique lay at the bottom of it. Neither does Mr. Fullerton appear to have been fortunate in getting the machinery of government to work smoothly. On one occasion of the circuit of the supreme court to Singapore, Sir John Claridge, the Recorder, absolutely refused to proceed with the accommodation placed at his disposal by Mr. Fullerton, who as distinctly refused to furnish better; and the difference ended in Mr. Fullerton bringing down the court establishment, and holding the session at Singapore himself. These proceedings were afterwards referred home, and it is just to say that the Recorder was severely reprimanded. Mr. Fullerton, who had been eminently successful in the settlement of the land question at Madras, also made a great mistake by introducing here a tax upon cultivation similar to that which had succeeded in raising the revenue there. This drove many of the Chinese gardeners away from the island, and caused others to retire back into the jungle to be out of reach of taxation.

The condition of the Straits was far from satisfactory. The revenue had not increased, while the expenditure had steadily progressed till it approached an annual deficit of about 100,000*l.*; and several expensive works had been commenced, including the erection at Singapore of Fort Fullerton; when, in March, 1827, Lord William Bentinck, the Governor-General, suddenly made his appearance armed with powers from the directors to remodel the system of government. Mr. Fullerton was at Malacca at the time, and he there received intimation from Lord Bentinck that if he proceeded to Anjer, one of the Company's ships would be at his service to convey him to India or England. The civil and military establishments were both greatly reduced, and it was at first contemplated to dispense with the office of Governor; but this was not carried out; a reduction in the stipend was made, and Mr. Ibbetson, who had been Resident Councillor at Penang, was appointed to the office. One of Lord Bentinck's observations on landing at Penang was, that he "could not see what the island was like, for the number of cocked hats which were in his way." We can readily believe that this was a pointed observation, when we remember the then population of the island, and reflect that its expenditure was nearly treble what it is now.

Great improvements were made about this time, 1830, in the appearance of the town of Singapore. The buildings around Commercial Square were nearly completed; and on the other side of the river, the court-house, which still forms one of the ornaments of the town, had been erected, and the land now forming the esplanade, which had been marked out by Mr. Fullerton in building lots, was made a reserve,

on the condition that all the buildings fronting
it should be of an ornamental style of architecture.
This one act of liberality on the part of the Company,
by introducing among the residents a spirit of rivalry
in elegant building, has done a great deal to give the
town its present fine appearance.

Mr. Ibbetson retired from the governorship in
1833, after being three years in office, and was
succeeded by Mr. Kenneth Murchison, who had
been Resident Councillor at Singapore during Mr.
Fullerton's time, and also at Penang during the
governorship of Mr. Ibbetson. He did not bring any
very great ability to bear upon the affairs of the island,
and his administration was distinguished for its singular
immunity from anything in the shape of excitement.
In 1837, after four years' term of office, he proceeded
to the Cape on his way home, and the acting governorship was handed over to Samuel G. Bonham, Esq.
(afterwards created Sir S. G. Bonham). Mr. Bonham had been Resident Councillor at Singapore during
Mr. Murchison's time, and had displayed abilities
of no ordinary degree, so that his confirmation to the
appointment of Governor was looked forward to with
general favour. This, however, was for a time post-
poned, and, indeed, rendered doubtful, by a somewhat
untoward event.

Mr. Church, who had held the office of police
magistrate and Assistant Resident Councillor at Penang
during the five years previous to 1835, and was consequently higher in rank than Mr. Bonham, retired
in that year from the service, and proceeded home

He had not been long there, however, before he
repented of his resignation, and petitioned the Company to be allowed to rejoin, and this was allowed
him on the condition that he should be placed at the
bottom of the list for promotion.. Mr. Church thereupon proceeded to Calcutta, *en route* to the Straits,
and while there waited upon Sir Charles Metcalfe,
then acting Governor-General of India, who asked
him the period of his previous service. Mr. Church,
unfortunately for himself, as it afterwards turned out,
was by no means communicative on the point of his
late resignation, and Sir Charles Metcalfe, judging
that he was older in the service than Mr. Bonham,
sent him on to the Straits with powers to relieve that
gentleman of the acting governorship. This, on ·his
arrival there, he did, and continued to administer the
government for a few months; but it was not long
before matters were cleared up, and as soon as this
was the case, positions were reversed. Mr. Bonham
was confirmed as Governor, and Mr. Church received
the appointment under him of Resident Councillor.
Singapore now, for the first time, was made the
permanent residence of the Governor.

The period of Mr. Bonham's administration was
in many respects an important one, extending, as
it did, from 1837 to 1843. Singapore progressed
with rapid strides in commercial importance; and it
also came, for the first time, to be acknowledged as
of the greatest strategic value. The China war broke
out, and for nearly three years it formed the gathering
point as well as, in a great measure, the point of

supply, of the fluctuating forces engaged in this
struggle. It is described as a brilliant sight, the
departure thence of the first great force for China.
It was in April, 1839. For upwards of three months
the vessels of war and transports had been flocking
in, both from England and from India; and at last
the array was complete. There were thirty-six transports and twelve men-of-war, and they left the harbour
in two divisions at the firing of the same gun, each
division led by a steamer. Admiral Maitland was in
command of the fleet.

Mr. Bonham was a most liberal man, and all
through the China war he kept open house. The
expense of this hospitality was enormous, but it was
borne uncomplainingly, and when the Company afterwards passed to his credit the sum of 80,000 rupees,
they did about as little as they could have done.

In 1843, after six years of able administration,
Mr. Bonham proceeded to Europe, and was a few years
afterwards sent out to China as Governor of Hong Kong,
which island had then recently been ceded to us.
Colonel William John Butterworth (afterwards Major-
General Butterworth, C.B.) succeeded to the governorship of the Straits. He had previously been assistant
quartermaster-general of the Madras army, but had
proceeded to the Cape on furlough in 1841. Here
he met Lord Ellenborough, who was on his way out
to assume the governor-generalship of India; and so
favourable was the impression he made upon the future
Viceroy, that, when he came back to India, the
governorship of the Straits having been lately vacated,

by Mr. Bonham, he received the offer of the appointment, and accepted it.

Colonel Butterworth's tenure of office was a very long one, extending over nearly twelve years, and witnessed considerable progress in the material prosperity of the island. The country lands which had hitherto been locked up by the Company, under the impression—derived, it is believed, from some reports made by Mr. Ibbetson—that in the monopoly of their cultivation there lay a rich mine of wealth, were now thrown open to the public; those within a certain radius of town were disposed of at ten rupees per acre, and those beyond it at five rupees per acre. This, in a few years, added considerably to the exports of the island, and Singapore promised soon to possess a valuable trade in local products. How it has come to pass that these expectations have been disappointed may be learned at another part of this volume. An improvement which closely followed, was the appointment of a municipal committee to look after the affairs of the town.

The close of Colonel Butterworth's administration was marked by two rather important events. The one was the outbreak of the first Chinese riot in 1854, and the other was the conclusion of a treaty between the Sultan and the Tumongong of Johore already alluded to, by which the former ceded to the latter the sovereignty of Johore. The first was an event entirely beyond the influence of our Government; but the second, which transferred a dynasty, certainly from weaker to more powerful hands, but, nevertheless,

from an ancient family of rulers to a family of subor-
dinates, was thought by many to be the result of a
scarcely fair exercise of the Governor's power in favour
of a personal predilection. However, Colonel Butterworth has altogether earned well the esteem in which
his memory is now held by the people of Singapore.*

In the latter part of 1855, Edmund Augustus
Blundell, Esq., of the Civil Service, succeeded Colonel
Butterworth. He had been for a long time commissioner of the Tenasserim provinces, and would most
probably have been appointed to the governorship of
the Straits twelve years before, had it not been for
Lord Ellenborough's attachment to Colonel Butterworth. During Mr. Blundell's administration the
great rebellion in India broke out, and with him it
was that Lord Elgin was staying when he issued the
famous order which deflected the troops of the China
expedition at Anjer and sent them back to India.
The news of the Indian revolt reached Singapore in
the afternoon; all that night Lord Elgin remained
pacing up and down his room in the Government
bungalow that stood where Fort Canning stands now,
holding various interviews with the naval and military
officers of the expedition, and next morning at daylight a steamer was despatched to the Straits of Sunda
with the order which, it is believed by many, saved
the British empire in India.

---

* Major-General Butterworth died about two years after he returned
home. He had received his commission of Major-General just as he
was stepping on board the vessel which was to convey him from the
island which he had governed for twelve years.

The only two other events worth chronicling in Mr. Blundell's time were the breaking out of a somewhat protracted riot among the Chinese, and the handing over of the East India Company's ancient authority to the Crown.

In 1859 Colonel Cavanagh received from Lord Canning the appointment of Governor of the Straits. Colonel Cavanagh had twice distinguished himself in India; he had been actively engaged in the Punjaub war, where he had had the misfortune to lose a leg, and at the time the mutiny broke out he was town-major at Calcutta. For his skill and discretion in the latter capacity, which at such a time as that of the mutiny involved a rather important trust, he obtained good praise. When the mutiny had been suppressed, the office of town-major was abolished, and Colonel Cavanagh accepted the vacant office of Governor of the Straits, very much in the light of a temporary appointment. The agitation for the transfer of the settlement to the Crown had already commenced, and as Lord Canning was one of those most favourable to it, he was particular, when making the appointment, to explain its probably short-lived nature.

Colonel Cavanagh's term of office, however, has, contrary to expectation, extended quite as long as that of most Governors of the settlement, being only exceeded by that of Mr. Bonham and that of Colonel Butterworth. It has also witnessed a very marked progress in commercial prosperity, and has not been chequered by any local or national misfortune. It has witnessed the uncontested imposition of a stamp-tax, and the successful resistance of a measure to burden the port with tonnage dues.

Of the eight Governors whom the settlement has possessed since its foundation, few have probably been more painstaking than the present. He possesses in a singular degree the ambition and the perseverance to make himself well acquainted with even the most minute affairs of his government; and men of much longer residence are scarcely better informed as to the character and peculiarities of the population, as to the capabilities of the soil and the extent of its cultivation, or as to the elements of the settlement's commerce. This is amply evidenced by the administration reports now issued annually, and which embrace a much wider range of subjects than they did in previous years. But the limited power which has hitherto been entrusted to the local government of the Straits is little calculated to develope administrative ability to the full. And, though surrounded by important interests and events, the Governors have but too often found that they can interfere neither with dignity nor effect. It is to be trusted, that when the settlement comes under the more direct control of the Imperial Government, its Governor will be vested with full powers as his Majesty's representative and plenipotentiary for the Malay Peninsula and the Indian Archipelago.

CHAPTER II.

SCENERY: SINGAPORE FROM SEAWARD.

Surpasses in Loveliness that of Ceylon and Java—Green Islets—The Old Strait—Lake Scenery—Ancient Piracy—Native Craft—Wood Rafts—Singapore Harbour—Eastern Approach—Approach from Westward—Mount Faber—P. and O. Company—Projected new Dock—H.M.'s Dockyards—Present Dock—Shipping in the Roadstead—Men-of-War—Chinese Junks—Coolie Horrors—Malay Prahus—Small Boats—Coral—The Town Frontage—Fort Fullerton—Public Buildings—Old Residences—St. Andrew's Church—Background—Fort Canning.

A GREAT deal has been written about the natural beauties of Ceylon and Java, and some theologians, determined to give the first scene in the Mosaic narrative a local habitation, have fixed the Paradise of unfallen man on one or other of those noble islands. Nor has their enthusiasm carried them to any ridiculous extreme; for the beauty of some parts of Java and Ceylon might well accord with the description given us, or, rather, which we are accustomed to infer, of that land from which man was driven on his first great sin.

I have seen both Ceylon and Java, and admired in no grudging measure their many charms; but for calm placid loveliness, I should place Singapore high

two hundred years the entire population of Singapore
and the surrounding islands, and of the sea frontage
of Johore, subsisted upon fishing and pirating; the
former occupation only being resorted to when the
prevailing monsoon was too strong to admit of the
successful prosecution of the latter. Strange stories
are told of these pirating days, and old grey-headed
men still may be heard to gloat over the prowess they
displayed and the victims they despatched ere what
they account English over-sensitiveness put a check
upon the system. It seems, however, that they them
selves had always a lurking consciousness that the
practice of piracy was scarcely justifiable according to
strict rules of right and wrong; and they invariably
did their best to obliterate every trace of their
crimes, by systematically destroying all those whom
they robbed. The idea was simple and primitive
but it was effectual in serving its purpose, and the
individual pirates, did they afterwards find it to their
advantage to pursue an honest walk in life, had no
fear that their old sins would be brought in judgment
against them.

By the constant vigilance of our authorities at
Singapore, and by the combined action of the Dutch
and the native princes of the surrounding States
piracy on an extensive scale in this neighbourhood
has been now put an end to, and we hear very seldom
of any case where a combination is attempted. Still
however, solitary instances of piracy, accompanied by
the most cold-blooded and brutal murder, continue to
obtrude themselves upon our notice, and take their

place on the criminal calendars of the settlement; and it is distressing to reflect that justice is in most cases defeated, owing to the unreliable and often contradictory nature of native evidence.

Of the numberless prahus, sampans, lorchas, pukats and tongkangs, therefore, that in these days give life to the waters of the old strait, and between its numerous islands, nearly all have honest purposes, fishing, timber-carrying, or otherwise trading. A very extraordinary flotilla of a rather nondescript character may be often seen in this part of the straits at certain seasons of the year. These are huge rafts of unsawn, newly-cut timber; they are generally 500 or 600 feet long, and 60 or 70 feet broad, the logs being skilfully laid together, and carefully bound by strong rattan-rope, each raft containing often 2,000 logs. They have always one or two attap-houses built upon them, and carry crews of twenty or twenty-five men; the married men taking their wives and children with them. The timber composing them is generally cut many miles away, in some creek or river on the mainland, so that they have to perform long voyages ere they reach a market—either Singapore or the Tumongong's saw-mills already referred to. Sails are used when they are crossing from one coast to another, but not otherwise, as it is found more expeditious to haul them along. For this purpose a windlass is erected about ten feet high, with a bench behind it on which some ten or twelve of the crew sit, driving, or rather treading, the barrel round with their feet by projecting cogs. Attached to the barrel of the windlass is a strong rattan-rope, about the eighth of a mile long, with an anchor at the end, which is run out by a small boat to its full stretch, and the anchor dropt. The winding on the windlass then commences, and goes on till the anchor is reached, when it is weighed and again sent out. This is necessarily a very slow means of progression, and impracticable in certain conditions of the weather, and these voyages often occupy months; but if the raft is successfully brought to market, its price amply repays the venture, and renders one voyage in six months a satisfactory return.

But though the old strait displays more wildness of tropical scenery, it can scarcely be said to exceed in loveliness the side which faces the present thoroughfare of shipping. The harbour of Singapore is formed of an extensive bay on the southern coast of the island about equidistant from its extremities. The approach from the eastward is comparatively tame in appearance, cocoanut plantations extending along its coast for miles, with here and there a little fishing village standing out in relief; yet the contrast between the dark foliage of the trees and the snowy whiteness of the sandy beach is very pleasing. It is at the western entrance, through New Harbour, however, that the greatest measure of beauty is to be found. This is the side from which Singapore is approached by those who come from home to take up their sojourn there; and no wonder that they enter their new home predisposed in its favour, for the scene is one very rarely to be surpassed in the world, certainly not in the English

but in larger furrows; these are the pineries belonging
to the Tumongong, and from which Singapore is
chiefly supplied with this its staple fruit.   On the very
summit of Mount Faber stands a flagstaff, from which
vessels approaching from the west can be seen at a
distance of sixteen miles; it also repeats the signals of
the town flagstaff at Fort Canning, and so great is the
commerce of the Straits, that from sunrise to sunset
they are both plentifully decked out in bunting.

On the top of this hill are two mortars, and lower
down is a battery of two 56-pounder guns, with barracks
attached, forming part of the far-famed fortifications
of Singapore.   It is difficult to say whether the two
gaping mortars on the top of the hill, or the two
lonely guns below, convey the greatest feeling of
desolation and decay.   The very sepoys that guard
the latter—for they don't man them—seem touched
with the melancholy of neglect.

The P. and O. Company's wharves, at which their
steamers lie, are situated at the head of a small bay,
with the island of Pulo Brani in front.   This bay is
completely shut in on all sides from the view of the
Straits, and is distant from town by water or by road
about 2½ miles ; it is commonly designated New
Harbour, but the name equally applies to the whole
of the land-locked passage between the south shore
of Singapore and the small islets lying off its western
extremity, about 3 miles in extent, and of which the
P. and O. Company's wharves only occupy a small
frontage.   It is not, properly speaking, a harbour
at all; for vessels rarely ride at anchor there, the

narrowness of the channel, and the strong tides that
run through it, rendering this unsafe; they only
come there to discharge their cargoes, which, from
the deepness of the water, they are enabled to do
at the wharves. Though there are wharves belonging
to two other companies in New Harbour, still those
of the P. and O. Company are the most extensive,
and the coal-sheds and other premises attached to
them are of great extent, and must represent a large
amount of capital. The coal-sheds of this company
are all built of brick, and tile roofed, and they are
capable of containing—as, in fact, they often do contain—about 20,000 tons of coal. The wharves are
strong and substantial, and have altogether a frontage
of about 1,200 feet. What with these and the warehouses attached, I should judge that the marketable
value of the P. and O. Company's premises at New
Harbour alone (for they have coal-sheds in Singapore
besides) is very little under 70,000*l*. I have often
thought if the shareholders in this company had an
opportunity to inspect the company's establishments
east of Suez, that they would be somewhat slower of
parting with their shares at the modest premiums
they do.

The mail steamers never come into the roadstead
now, but land their passengers and cargo at these
wharves. Most of the passengers, whether their
ultimate destination be Singapore or not, land, and
drive up to town to inspect for themselves the
beauties of a place the approach to which is so
lovely; those who remain on board, however, may

3—2

find entertainment in the feats of swarms of small
Malay boys, who immediately surround a steamer
on her arrival, in toy boats, just big enough to float
them, and induce the passengers to cast cents or
other small coins into the water, for which they dive
down, and in almost every case succeed in recovering.
I may mention here, in case I should not have another
opportunity, that almost all the ships visiting Singapore
have their bottoms examined, and some have had as
many as twenty or thirty sheets of copper put on
by Malay divers.   One man will put on as many as
two sheets in an hour, going down, perhaps, a dozen
times, and when such vessels have afterwards had
to go into dock, not a fault could be found with the
manner in which these odd sheets had been fixed.

On 'leaving New Harbour to come out into the
roadstead, the scenery loses considerably in effect by
several long mud and coral reefs which run a long
way out from the shore, and are dry at low water.
It is on this part of the coast that the projectors of
the Tanjong Paggar Dock Company have determined
to construct their works.   Opinion seems to differ
to a great extent as to the suitability of the position
in respect of the tides, the nature of the bottom, and
otherwise.   The balance of local authority, however,
seems to be in its favour.   Five years ago there was
no dock whatever in Singapore, though as far back
as fifteen years, specifications and estimates for one
on the island of Pulo Brani, fronting the P. and O.
Company's premises in the New Harbour passage,
were prepared, and received the approbation both of

the Government and the merchants; but from a want of combination, the scheme was left to progress slowly by the private efforts of the projector, till four years ago, her Majesty's Admiralty took possession of the site and the works which had already been constructed there, no grant for the land ever having been obtained by the persevering projector. Still there are certain claims resulting from this appropriation by the Government, which should not be overlooked. In 1857 a private proprietary undertook an enterprise similar to that which had so long hung fire on the hands of the public. And at the western extremity of New Harbour, that is, at its entrance, a dock 400 feet long was dug out of the rock, and furnished with the necessary appliances to take up and repair at once two vessels of 800 tons each. This dock, called the New Harbour dock, has been in operation four years; but, as has generally been found at ports situated in the fair way of a large traffic, the facilities for docking have increased the demand, and at times vessels requiring repairs have to lie as long as six weeks waiting their turns to get into dock. The new company proposes to provide the additional accommodation, and should it succeed in doing so, the result, whatever it may be to its own shareholders and to the proprietors of the old dock, cannot fail to be beneficial in the highest degree to the Straits.

On rounding the eastern exit of New Harbour, the shipping and harbour of Singapore at once bursts on the view, with the white walls of the houses and the dark verdure of the shrubbery of the town nearly, if not altogether, hid by the network of spars and rigging that intervenes. It is truly a noble sight the shipping that rides throughout the year in the road-stead of Singapore ; for the box-shaped, heavy-rigged East Indiamen that thirty years ago carried the then moderate freight of the island, have been exchanged for the beautifully modelled clipper or frigate-built ships of the finest building yards in Great Britain and America; their tall, slim, raking spars reaching in the view from seaward high above the hilly background of the island.

Neither is the harbour without a good supply of steamers ; there is scarcely any time during the year when there are less than half a dozen steam-vessels in the port, and not unfrequently there are twice that number. Of these, not a few are war vessels—British, French, Russian, Austrian, Spanish, American, Dutch, and, I may also say, Confederate and Chinese, for here has harboured the renowned *Alabama*, and on Singapore waters has been borne almost all of the notorious Anglo-Chinese fleet under Captain Sherard Osborn ; it may also, in these days, be worth recording that it has harboured an Italian merchantman commanded by the famous Garibaldi. The greater number of the steamers, however, are those which belong to private firms or companies, and are engaged in trade between India, China, Java, Siam, Borneo, &c. ; and among them there are probably as fair specimens of naval architecture as are to be found afloat. The opium steamers, those belonging to Messrs. Jardine, of China, and to the Messrs. Cama, of Bombay, especially, lack nothing

either in beauty of model or effectiveness of machinery
which money can secure. The boats of the Peninsular
and Oriental Company, too, that carry the mails are
some of them fine ships to look at; and it is but
justice to say that those of the Messageries Imperiales
are the largest, swiftest, and finest-fitted of any
steamers that have yet been placed on the route
between China and Europe for the purpose of passenger
traffic.

But it is not so much from the fine character of its
foreign merchantmen that the harbour of Singapore is
chiefly remarkable; it is rather from the extraordinary
variety of nondescript native craft that swarm in its
shoaler waters. Most peculiar and most striking of
all are the huge Chinese junks, some of 600 or 700
tons measurement, which during the greater part of
the year lie anchored there. Though the largest of
these junks must measure quite as much as I state,
yet the great majority are much smaller; but it is
singular that in shape, and generally in rig, all are
nearly similar. Indeed, the very sampans, or two-
oared China boats, used to convey native passengers
and luggage to and from the ships and the shore, are
identical in shape. All have alike the square bow and
the broad flat stern; and, from the largest to the
smallest, on what in a British vessel would be called
her " head boards," all have the two eyes embossed
and painted. John Chinaman's explanation of this
custom, according to general account, " no got eyes
no can see," is but little complimentary to the good
sense of his utilitarian and sensible nation. I rather

incline to the belief that these " eyes," as they are
called, are significant of the new moon, and represent,
as such, some principle in the Buddhist religion.
About the months of March and April the greatest
number of these junks are to be seen in harbour.
They come down from China towards the close of the
north-east monsoon, and remain till the opposite or
south-west monsoon sets in to enable them to return,
for they never attempt to make headway against a prevailing wind.   During these two months as many as
fifty large junks, besides many smaller ones, lie at
anchor in the eastern corner of the harbour. Some
are painted red, some green, some black, and others
yellow; each colour, I have been told, being the badge
of the particular province to which they severally
belong.   The ornamental painting is confined chiefly
to the stern, which generally bears some elaborate and
fantastic figuring, conspicuous in which can invariably
be traced the outlines of a spread eagle, not unlike
that which is borne on the reverse of the American
dollars.   The rigging of these craft consists, when in
harbour, of little else than a few coir or rattan ropes
rove through the tops of the three bare spars or masts,
the centre one standing up about perpendicular, the
one forward leaning at about an angle of 15 degrees
over the bows, and the after one leaning at about the
same angle over the stern.   It is difficult, while looking at these junks, to imagine how they can manage
in a sea way; and yet they must at times encounter
the heaviest weather along the Chinese coast in the
northern latitudes. It is true that when they encounter

gale they generally run before it, but yet, in a typhoon, this would be of little avail to ease a ship. There is no doubt they must possess some good qualities, and probably speed with a fair wind in a smooth sea is one of them. Not many years ago, a boat-builder in Singapore bought one of the common sampans used by the coolie boatmen, which are of exactly the same shape as the junks, and rigged her like an English cutter, giving her a false keel and a shifting weather-board; and, strange to say, won with her every race that he tried for at the regattas. I don't know why the experiment was not improved upon; I suppose the unsightly and unsailorlike aspect of the craft was the chief deterrent.

Passing through between these junks about sunset is a singular spectacle. Amid the beating of gongs, ringing of bells, and discordant shouts, the nightly religious ceremonies of the sailors are performed, consisting chiefly in the burning and scattering about of gilt paper, the swinging to and fro of lanterns and lighted torches; one's boat, too, as it passes close to them during these ceremonies, not unfrequently receives a shower of the rare condiments which are scattered on the sea as an offering of their worship.

But many of the junks which lie quietly at anchor there, could, if they had the power to speak, tell sad tales of human suffering. The chief trade of not a few of them is the traffic of human freight; and it is unfortunately of such a generally remunerative character as to leave but little hope of its voluntary abandonment. The demand for labour, and the wages

paid in Singapore, are so considerable, as to induce a
large number of junks yearly to sail from China with
men, picked up, and stowed away on board, under
what misrepresentations it is very difficult to say, and
on arrival they are kept on board till a bargain for
their employment is effected.   It appears that no
passage money is demanded from these emigrants
before leaving China, but that they are made to pledge
so many years of their labour on the condition of
bare sustenance only.   Large premiums, at least five
or six times the mere cost of passage, are at once
offered by the gambier and pepper planters of the
island for the transfer of these contracts; and when
the bargain is struck the coolies are hurried off to
some isolated clearance in the midst of the jungle,
before they can have communication either with the
authorities, or with their own countrymen in town.
It is not, however, by the endurance of cruelty or of
unreasonably long terms of servitude, when the men
are arrived, that the laws of humanity are in much
danger of violation.   One or two years at most, and
the new arrivals become acquainted with their rights
as English subjects, and with the knowledge how to
enforce them.   The danger is in the overcrowding of
the vessels that bring them; in this, the poor fellows
have not even the protection that is secured to the
African slave, in so far that by their death, though
there may be a loss of profit, there can be none of
capital to the shipper.   The men cost nothing, and
the more the shipper can cram into his vessel the
greater must be his profit.   It would be a better

speculation for the trader whose junk could only carry
properly 300 men, to take on board 600—and lose
250—on the way down, than it would be for him to
start with his legitimate number and land them all
safely; for, in the first case, he would bring 350 men
to market, and, in the other, only 300. That this
process of reasoning is actually put in practice by the
Chinese, there was not long ago ample and very
mournful evidence to prove. Two of these passenger
junks had arrived in the harbour, and had remained
unnoticed for about a week, during which the owners
had bargained for the engagement of most of their
cargo. At this time two dead bodies were found
floating in the harbour; an inquest was held, and
it then transpired that one of these two junks on her
way down from China had lost 250 men out of 600—
and the other 200 out of 400. The bodies upon which
the coroner's inquest was held, were two of the sickly
passengers who had died after arrival, and whose
corpses the owners, forgetful that they were now in
harbour, had tossed into the water as doubtless they
daily had the bodies of their companions on the
voyage from China. It is needless to say that no
Europeans are in any way engaged in this traffic.

But the Chinese junks are not the only remarkable
craft that are borne on the smooth waters of Singapore harbour. There are the prahus, pukats and
tongkangs, besides some completely illegitimate ships
in the shape of old European hulls, which their
Chinese owners, with a strange persistency in their
national distinctions, have had cut down, patched and

rigged to look as near the junk genus as possible. They are far from pretty, and doubtless the reverse of manageable; but there is possibly something flattering to the vanity of the Chinaman in thus reversing the legitimate order of affairs, and, as it were, turning back civilization to the old barbarian channels.

The Malay prahus are the craft of the native inhabitants of the Straits, and therefore peculiarly interesting. Though slightly similar in shape, they are never so large as the Chinese junks, seldom being over fifty or sixty tons' burden. They have only one large mast, or rather tripod, made of three large bamboos lashed together at the top, but some two or three feet asunder at the bottom; across two legs of the tripod small pieces of bamboo are lashed, making a sort of ladder up to the block at the head, through which the haulyards of the large single sail are rove. This sail is in the shape of an English lug-sail, but with much more width than depth, and with a yard both at top and bottom; it is generally made of coarse grass-cloth, very light and gauzy, and rolled round the lower yard, through the forward end of which a cross-bar or handle is placed, by turning which the sail can either be set, reefed or furled, with great ease from the deck. These prahus would doubtless from their build sail well were it not for the top-hamper they carry near the stern, which, though composed of the lightest material, nevertheless renders any attempt to make headway against the wind impossible—it is not unusual for one of them to have the deck only three feet out of the water forward, and for

the top of the housing at the stern to be at least
fifteen feet in height. Another peculiarity they possess is that they are steered by two rudders—one on
either quarter.

In addition to the ships and native craft that are
crowded together in the harbour, there are hundreds
of small boats of all descriptions constantly pulling
about, selling fruit, provisions, birds, monkeys, shells,
and coral. The birds and monkeys generally find a
ready sale; the former are of beautiful plumage, and
the latter are a very small tractable species; but the
shells and corals which are daily hawked about by
these boatmen are of the rarest and most lovely
descriptions. The corals are especially beautiful, and
probably in no other part of the world could a finer
collection be made; they are of all tints and hues,
green, purple, pink, blue, mauve, and in shape often
resemble flowers and shrubbery; a whole boat-load
of them can be obtained for a dollar and a half, or
two dollars,—and I have often wondered that among
the curiosities which are picked up and carried away
from Singapore more of these beautiful specimens are
not included.

As the outer shipping is passed, the town of Singapore comes distinctly before the view. But the
word town, in its usual acceptation, fails to convey
the appearance which Singapore presents to its harbour. However dense and crowded together some
of the native divisions may be, this does not show
from seaward, and the houses and buildings appear
beautifully interspersed with patches of garden and

clumps of trees. The town has a frontage to the bay
of not much less than three miles, and is divided at
its centre by the Singapore river, on the western side
of the entrance of which stands Fort Fullerton, with
the black muzzles of nine 68-pounder guns peeping
from its grassy embrasures, and showing a pretty little
bungalow behind surrounded by shrubbery. From
Fort Fullerton westward to a deep turn of the bay,
a fine stone sea-wall has been constructed with a long
range of elegant godowns in course of erection, the
land on which they are being built having not long
been reclaimed from the sea. Further to westward of
this, but in a recess of the bay, the line of native
houses commences, gradually becoming broken by the
intervening patches of cocoanut and fruit trees, until
Fort Palmer is reached, where four guns guard the
town's extreme western limit.

The eastern side of the river, however, presents
the most picturesque view to the harbour. This is
the non-mercantile half of the town, and the one upon
which all the public buildings are erected. Close to
the river, facing Fort Fullerton, stand the court-house
and town-hall ; both large, fine edifices, and ornamental
in design, but which are only partly visible from the
seaward, through some splendid drooping Augsana
trees, which were planted nearly forty years ago, and
have now grown to fifty or sixty feet in height, with
evergreen wide-spreading branches, clad in their season
with fragrant golden blossoms, and casting a dense
shade for many yards around them. Farther to the
eastward commences a succession of handsome lofty

mansions, which years ago, while the present suburbs
of the town were yet jungle, constituted the residences
of the merchants and Government officials. They are
all large buildings, generally kept snowy white with
pillared porticoes and balconies, and green-painted
latticed doors and windows ; to each also is attached a
compound or garden of fair dimensions, tastefully laid
out with trees and shrubs. Few of these houses are
now in use as private residences, some of the best are
taken up for hotels, and one is used as the masonic
lodge. The line of these old beach residences is first
broken by the noble pile of St. Andrew's Church, one
of the largest cathedrals in India, which, begun in
1855, has only this year been completed. Close to
the church is Raffles Institution, a fine square, massive
clump of buildings, with some stately old trees around
it. Further to the eastward, and about a mile from the
river, the native houses commence, but they are shut
out of view to a great extent by the projecting promontory of Tanjong Rhoo, which leads away to the
cocoanut plantations which I described before as lining
the eastern approach to the harbour ; and here a white
obelisk, standing out from the dark shade of the trees,
marks the eastern limit of the harbour.

The background is no less lovely than the front of
the picture ; peering over the red tiled roofs of the
houses just described are an endless succession of little
knoll-like hills, covered with nutmeg and fruit trees of
all varieties, and each crowned by a white walled
bungalow. But most prominent in the background is
the hill on which Fort Canning has been constructed,

and which rises up abruptly about a quarter of a mile inland from the beach; it is almost pyramidal in shape, covered from its base up to the ramparts with beautiful green turf, and crowned with a cluster of thick foliaged trees, through which the garrison buildings can barely show their white walls and red roofs. Here, too, is erected the town flagstaff, kept pretty constantly busy signalling the daily arrivals in the harbour.

Such is the appearance of the island and town of Singapore, as it is viewed from seaward. As I have stated before, the entire circle of its coast presents an endless panorama, most beautiful where its wild forests are untouched, picturesque where are clustered together the leaf-built houses of its native villages, and most interesting and little less lovely where stands its European capital. For forty-five years have the hands of man been busy accumulating wealth on its bosom, and yet scarce a scar is visible. Nor do I believe that in twice that number of years will the island present a less charming picture than it does now.

CHAPTER III.

SINGAPORE: THE TOWN.

Ancient Tradition—Crowded Streets—Commercial Square—Verandahs
—Vigour of Nature—The River—Crowd of Boats—Busy Wharves
—Proposed Pier—Native Part of the Town—Native Shops—Chinese
Trades—Opium Shops—Manner of Smoking—Chinese Barbers—
Itinerant Vendors—Street Scribes—Dangerous Driving—River
Bridges—Eastern Division of the Town—St. Andrew's Cathedral
—Court House—Town Hall—Night View.

AMONG the traditions that are handed down to us
concerning the early inhabitants of the island of Singapore, there is one which deserves to be distinguished from many of the others, in so far that some substantial record is left behind, which will at least serve to perpetuate its memory, if it cannot materially assist its authenticity. On the western entrance of the mouth of the Singapore River, near that portion which is now built over by Fort Fullerton, stood, as late as 1835, a large stone, with some strange characters carved or impressed on it, the deciphering of which has defied the utmost ingenuity. Sir Stamford Raffles was so much occupied with the desire to learn the meaning of these hieroglyphics, that he caused, it is said, an abundant supply of muriatic acid to be poured over the stone, with the view to clear off any crustaceous matter that

4

might have accumulated on it, and bring out more
clearly the characters it bore. Unfortunately, however, the experiment failed, as has every more recent
attempt either to decipher the letters or to arrive,
through them, at a true knowledge of the date of their
inscription; and we are still left to the old legend
regarding them. It has been differently told, but the
most common account is, that a powerful chief—of
what country is not very clear—coming to attack the
Malays shortly after they had formed their settlement
at Singhapura, landed at this point of the island,
and proceeded up the hill to the Malay encampment.
He was met, it appears, on his approach, by the
greatest Sampson among the Malays, named Badang;
and, after some altercation, it was agreed that instead
of engaging in a general combat, a trial of strength
between the foreign chief and the Malay Sampson
should decide the fate of the invasion. A large piece
of rock was lying close at hand, and it was decided
that whoever could handle this stone with the greatest
ease, was to be declared the victor. The invader tried
first, and he succeeded in raising the stone as high as
his knees, and then let it fall; on which the Malay,
seizing it in one hand, balanced it high in the air,
took a steady aim, and shot it right out to the mouth
of the river, crushing to pieces the boat from which
the invader had landed. Others, who agree in the
first part of the story, as I have told it, maintain that
instead of the stone, the Malay giant seized the
invading chief himself, and hurled him back upon his
boat, and that the stone was afterwards conveyed

there to commemorate the deed. In any case the invading force, fearing that they would be immolated if they had to combat with a race of men like Badang, beat a precipitate retreat.

I have begun my chapter with this tradition because it is the only one I know of related by the Malays which serves to fix the exact locality of their very early settlement on the island. And it is singular that the spot marked out by this stone, where tradition says the invading chief disembarked 600 or 700 years ago, is but a few yards from the present landing-pier by the site of Fort Fullerton; and as the Malay encampment, according to the story, was but a stone's throw distant, it in all probability stood just where the modern town stands to-day. But the scene which is presented to the traveller on landing now forms a striking contrast to that which moved the cupidity of the invading chief, and tempted him to try his strength with the Malay giant. In place of the little pathway that must have led through the jungle to the Malay village, composed, probably, of a cluster of attap-covered huts, are now the busy thoroughfares of a great commercial emporium. The first thing that strikes the stranger on landing as remarkable is this appearance of bustle and activity, heightened by the motley character of those who compose the crowd. The street leading from the landing-place to Commercial Square, the great business centre of the town, is a rather narrow one, with a constant stream of Chinese, Malays, Klings, Parsees, and Mussulmen, pouring one way and the other.

4—2

Their costumes are as varied as their nationalities.
From the simple white rag of the nearly naked Kling,
to the heavy flowing dress of the Mahommedan
Hadjee, almost every shade of colour, and every variety
of habit which it is possible to imagine, are here
mingled together. The neatest style of dress is probably that of the better class of Chinese; the most
picturesque, and, to them, most becoming, is the
Malay costume.

But the place itself is no less Oriental in appearance than its inhabitants, though considerably less so
here than at the native parts of the town lying further
back. Commercial Square, which, ever since the
settlement rose into importance has been the principal locality for the European houses of business, is
about 200 yards from the landing, but completely
shut in from a view of the sea. It is built round
a reserved piece of ground, turfed over with green
sod and tastefully laid out with flowers and shrubs,
which afford to the eye a pleasing relief from the
glare of the whitewashed walls of the square, while
the open space ensures good ventilation to the neighbourhood. The square itself is some 200 yards long
by fifty broad, and many of the houses, or rather
godowns (the latter term being used to denote mercantile establishments), which surround it, are of very
elegant design. They are all built of brick and plastered
over, but as both labour and materials have at no period
since the settlement of the place been costly, their construction and finish is good. Some of the finest now
standing are twenty or thirty years old. They are two

stories high, lofty, and with heavy, overleaning eaves; and the lower part of the front wall is composed of a series of arches or pillars inside of which a verandah runs from building to building. It appears that, in most cases, the early grants for town lands were in the nature of 99 and 999 years' leases, and imposed an obligation on the lessee to erect buildings with verandahs of a certain width for foot passengers. The clause seems, however, not to have been strictly insisted upon, and many of the verandahs were blocked up until about a year ago, when the municipal commissioners raised the point in the Supreme Court and obtained judgment in their favour. Since then, the verandahs have been kept tolerably clear, which, in the narrower and more crowded thoroughfares of the town, is a great advantage to pedestrians, there being no pavement. In the centre of the square is the telegraph-office, connecting New Harbour with the town, and at one end of it is the favourite stand for hack-gharries, which, with their drivers, form by no means an ornamental feature of the town. Four of the buildings fronting the square are occupied by banks, each with an English proprietary, and the everlasting chink of dollars to be heard on passing these establishments is almost deafening. All the cashiers in the banks, as, indeed, in mercantile establishments generally, are Chinamen, who count and, at the same time, test the genuineness of dollars with remarkable exactitude and rapidity, by pouring them from one hand to the other. By the ring which the dollars give in falling, they are able at once to detect

base metal and even light coin. These men keep
their cash accounts not in the English but in the
Chinese character, and it is remarkable that they
are never known to be incorrect.

Till within the last year, the European business
was almost entirely confined to this square, but a
good deal of it is likely to be deflected to the sea
frontage immediately in advance, where, upon land
recently recovered from the sea, a fine terrace of
godowns is being built, some of which are already
in occupation. These buildings are being constructed
as nearly uniform as possible, and though they are
not, individually considered, finer than some of the
old ones in the square, still, viewed together, they will
most probably form the finest part of the commercial
half of the town.

It is remarkable to witness occasionally in the
midst of the busiest parts of the town the struggle
made by nature to assert her presence. It is not
an uncommon sight to see ferns and creepers cluster-
ing about the tiled roofs of the older buildings, with
no other soil than the damp mould which time has
collected. I have witnessed a still harder struggle
on the part of nature; it was a small shoot of the
papaia-tree which had taken root in a soft and
probably earthy part of the plaster of the perpendicular wall of a godown. It grew up gradually, till
it appeared to have exhausted all the nutriment about
its root, and then it remained stationary for a long
time, and I even thought it was growing less in bulk.
About six months afterwards, however, to my surprise

mouth. It is here crossed by an iron girder bridge named after the late Lord Elgin. From the river entrance to this bridge, on the town side, a large range of godowns extend, forming a complete crescent. Those nearer the entrance are occupied by Europeans, but all the godowns further up are the property of Chinese; and though the whole range is pretty much of a character as far as the buildings are concerned, yet the Chinese division is the most imposing on account of the bright colours which adorn the walls, and the plentiful display of Turkey red cloth, which at all seasons, but especially during their feasts, forms the drapery of their verandahs. At night the view of these houses is still more interesting, all the verandahs and windows being lit up with many coloured Chinese lanterns, the effect of which is doubled by the reflection of the placid water that flows past their doors.

On the eastern bank of the river for a considerable way up there are no houses, the land having been reserved for Government purposes, but the green grass and the foliage which surround the public offices erected close by, form a very pleasing contrast to the thickly-packed buildings opposite.

The river is alive with boats of all sorts, Chinamen with their shoe-boats, Malays with their sampans, or fast-boats, and Klings with their tongkangs. The first two craft are used for the conveyance of passengers and their luggage; the last, which are far the most numerous, are employed in bringing up and down the river the cargoes of ships in the harbour. The latter

tain from ten to fifteen coyans* each, and so numerous are they, that they generally lie three or four
breast along the entire western bank of the river, from
its mouth to Elgin Bridge above. I have never counted
them; but should say that very seldom indeed are there
less than 500 of these small craft to be seen at one
time in this first reach of the river. To each of these
boats, taking one with another, there is a crew of not
less than three men, which would give a floating
population of at least 1,500 men; and the expression
is by no means improperly applied, for most of these
men live and sleep in their boats, and at night time
the effect of this part of the river is considerably
heightened by the innumerable lights which glimmer
from under the attap or kajang awnings of this little
fleet.

The crescent of buildings which I have described,
and which is about a quarter of a mile long, is termed
Boat Quay, from the fact of nearly the entire river
frontage opposite them being taken up with the loading
and discharging of cargo boats. Here it is, at present
at least, that three-fourths of the entire shipping business of the island is effected, and from morning till
night may be seen the landing of huge cases, casks
and bales of British manufactures, as well as machinery
and iron-work of all descriptions; and no sooner are
the boats which bring these emptied, than they are
filled up again with bales of gambier, bundles of
rattans, tin, bags or cases of sago and tapioca, bags

---

* A coyan is about two tons English.

of pepper, and boxes of spices. It is, indeed, impossible
sible to view these operations and not realise the
fact that Singapore possesses a commerce and commercial importance altogether disproportioned to its
size and population. Here alone there must be
landed and shipped not less than 30,000*l.*-worth of
goods per diem, throughout the entire year, and
this is allowing some 5,000*l.* or 6,000*l.*-worth more
to be landed and shipped from the private wharves
possessed by a few godowns on the western side of the
town.

It has frequently been a subject of complaint with
the merchants of Singapore that great loss is sus-
tained during the year by the damage occasioned to
merchandise from the severe handling it receives in
this process of lightering, and several plans have
been proposed to remedy the evil. One was to build a
series of wharves at the nearest point of New Harbour,
where ships can lie close alongside, and connect these
to the town by means of a tramway or railway.
Another was to construct a pile-pier running right out
from the busiest part of the town into deep water, to
enable ships of all sizes to come alongside and load
and discharge into trucks, which could afterwards be
conveyed on tramways to the various godowns. The
latter plan is one upon which Colonel Collyer, for some
years chief engineer, spent a good deal of time, and
which he reduced to shape. Either plan appears to me
feasible, and likely to prove profitable to the capitalists
who would undertake it, and valuable to the town.
The first has not very many engineering obstacles, and

the works connected with it could be made permanent; but the cost would undoubtedly be very great. The second plan, on the other hand, requires a very limited outlay, and though a considerable sum would have to be yearly spent in renewing the piles, yet similar undertakings in other parts of the world have, I believe, generally proved more successful than costly permanent erections. The water of Singapore harbour is never so seriously disturbed as to interfere with even the largest vessels lying safely alongside such a pier, and from the soundings obtained along the site proposed, the bottom was found to consist of soft mud, so that ships might without danger ground at low water, should a pressure of business ever require them to do so.

Above Elgin Bridge the river continues of the uniform breadth of about 200 feet, and is navigable by small boats for about two miles, and, as it feeds all the mangrove swamps in the suburbs of the town, many houses entirely removed from the course of the river itself have, at high water, the advantage of water communication with the sea, and timber and building materials are in this way often conveyed well out into the country where they are required for use. It is, however, a very insignificant traffic that takes place above this bridge.

The whole of the native part of the town, the chief business division of which lies behind Commercial Square, and the river frontage I have described, are very much alike in appearance. The buildings are closely packed together and of a uniform height and character. The style is a sort of compromise between English and Chinese. The walls are of brick, plastered over, and the roofs are covered with tiles. The windows are of lattice woodwork—there being no glass in this part of the world. Under the windows of many houses occupied by Chinese are very chaste designs of flowers or birds in porcelain. The ridges of the roofs, too, and the eaves, are frequently similarly ornamented, and it is no unusual thing to see a perfect little garden of flowers and vegetables in boxes and pots exposed on the tops of the houses. Underneath run, for the entire length of the streets, the enclosed verandahs of which I spoke before, and in a quiet observant walk through these a very great deal may be learned concerning the peculiar manners and customs of the trading inhabitants. The principal street for native shops leads from Commercial Square towards the country. For a quarter of a mile after leaving the square, but before crossing the river, this is a great thoroughfare. Being narrow, it is nearly always crowded, and the buildings fronting it are occupied entirely by Chinese and Klings.

The necessities of the European community have, doubtless, created many trades before unknown to these peoples; but still their shops are sufficiently characteristic of their nationalities, and no one could for a moment imagine, while viewing them, that he was in a European town. The Kling shopkeepers are principally sellers of European wares of the cheapest and most indifferent description, and exposed in the most extraordinarily confused manner; but there are

few who confine themselves to the sale of seeds
and spices, arranged in earthenware bowls, piled up
pyramid-shape in their windows.

The Chinese, who are in the proportion of ten to one
of the trading population, embrace a much wider field
of trade. These are warehousemen, tailors, carpenters,
coopers, blacksmiths, tinsmiths, gunsmiths, grocers,
butchers, opium vendors, and barbers. The warehousemen seem to take things most coolly, and may
be seen naked to the waist, lounging about upon
mats, and perched upon high bamboo stools. Their
goods are exposed to view, but they neither by look nor
gesture invite the passer-by to purchase. The tailors
are a hard-working and assiduous class; in one
shop there are often as many as forty men seated
on benches placed round three or four long tables.
They work with English needles and materials, but
use them in a different way—sewing, as it were,
from them. They stitch carefully and at the same
time rapidly. Many of these tailor shops are open till
midnight, but have relays of fresh workmen. The
night workmen have each a very primitive and very
effective sort of lantern, which I think might be
imitated with good effect at home. A small light only
is used, but the rays are completely reflected down
upon the table and cannot reach the worker's eyes—
indeed the room looks half in darkness, while the work
on which each man is engaged is strongly illuminated.
The method of sewing from the person may render
the use of this sort of lights more practicable, but yet
I think it could be adjusted to English use.

The carpenters' and coopers' shops present very much the appearance of similar establishments at home, except as regards the workmen and their tools. The Chinese carpenters are very clever, and will closely imitate any piece of furniture given them as a pattern, but I do not think they can at all approach European workmen in fineness of finish. Blacksmiths here are also very much like those at home in their way of working, except that they have a different and original sort of bellows. It is in the form of a square, air-tight box, with a closely-fitting piston, which by an arrangement of leather valves forces a stream of air upon the fire both as it is drawn out and pushed in. Tinsmiths and gunsmiths are much of the same genus. One of the chief occupations of the former of these, in the part of the town of which I speak, is in making small flasks into which the gunpowder that arrives here in kegs is refilled. In this sort of package it finds, I believe, a much more ready sale amongst the Kling and native buyers. A rather singular occupation in which I have seen the Chinese gunsmiths engaged, was the furnishing of some thousands of percussion-cap muskets with the old-fashioned flint-locks—the reason of this somewhat extraordinary change being that the islanders of the archipelago, to whom the muskets were to be furnished, could always find a piece of flint to use in their guns, but might be years before they could buy a box of percussion-caps.

The trades of grocers and butchers appear to be combined generally at the same shop, as rice, tea or coffee, flesh, fish, and fowl,—the two latter dead or

e, fresh or preserved—can be obtained. Pork is
chief, if not the only, butcher's meat consumed
the Chinese, and they make use of it very sparingly,
ging by the small pieces into which it is cut up and
osed for sale. I have often seen Chinamen con-
tedly returning to their houses in the suburbs after
ood day's barter in town, carrying on a piece of
ng about a quarter of a pound of pork and three
four small fish like sardines, out of which they
ald doubtless manage to make a good supper
l breakfast. One thing must be remarked to the
dit of the Chinese in their shopkeeping, viz., the
reme cleanliness they observe; but for this it
ald scarcely be possible to combine successfully
ether, as they do, the trades of butcher, fish-
nger, and grocer.

The opium shops present no particular appearance
n the street, as the windows and doors are usually
eened off. Inside there is very little remarkable
rer: a few benches with mats spread upon them,
l some few trays, containing little lamps and the
dinary smoking paraphernalia, resting on tables close

Whatever may be the headaches or the frightful
pressions suffered from the practice of opium-
oking, none of them are visible here: a quiet
hargy, unlike that of intoxication, seems to mark the
tures of the few men to be seen in these houses.
e process of smoking is somewhat different from
at might be conjectured by those who have not seen

The pipe is made of a short piece of Malacca cane,
out three-quarters of an inch in thickness, and

perhaps two feet long; towards the end, projecti
from the stalk, a metallic (often silver) knob—in
and shape like the handle of a room-door—is fixed;
through the centre of this knob a small hole is pier
communicating through the cane to the mouth of
pipe.   The smoker lies on his side on a mat, his he
pillowed up to the necessary elevation, with a tr
before him containing a small lamp, some silver pron
and a little cup of liquid opium of the consistency a
very much of the appearance of molasses.   With o
hand he holds the pipe to his mouth in such a positio
that the knob is near to the flame of the lamp; wi
the other hand he takes a silver prong, and dips th
point into the opium, twirling it round till a piece th
size of a pea is accumulated; this he then places clos
to the orifice of the pipe on the metallic knob, and
approaches both to the flame of the lamp. As soon a
the opium commences to burn, he inhales heavily,
rather breathing it in than smoking it. While inhaling
he continues to hold the pipe to the flame, and uses
the silver prong to keep the orifice from clogging. A
good many fresh supplies of opium are applied during
an ordinary smoke.   The smell of the smoke while
fresh is not unpleasant, but when stale it is much
worse than that of tobacco.

The Chinese barbers' shops are numerous throughout the town; and, singularly enough, they are marked
by variegated poles very much resembling those used
by the same trade at home, only that they are square
and not round.   They are generally entirely open to
the street, and the operations are gone through in the

most public manner possible. Hair-cutting is never part of these operations, for all the hair that China- men allow to grow on their heads is gathered up into a tail behind, which is never cut, its length and luxuriance being its chief recommendation. The tail, however, is opened out, combed, and replaited, and the head all round, as well as the face, is shaved. While this is being done, the customers sit poised upon stools, in view of all passers-by, gazing forward with the same blank stolidity that pervades the faces of those under operation in any barber's shop at home.

There is probably no city in the world with such a motley crowd of itinerant vendors of wares, fruits, cakes, vegetables, &c. There are Malays, generally with fruit; Chinamen with a mixture of all sorts, and Klings with cakes and different kinds of nuts. Malays and Chinamen always use the shoulder- stick, having equally-balanced loads suspended at either end; the Klings, on the contrary, carry their wares on the head on trays. The travelling cook- shops of the Chinese are probably the most extraor- dinary of the things that are carried about in this way. They are suspended on one of the common shoulder- sticks, and consist of a box on one side and a basket on the other; the former containing a fire and small copper cauldron for soup; the latter loaded with rice, vermicelli, cakes, jellies, and condiments; and though I have never tasted any of their dishes, I have been assured that those they serve up at a moment's notice are most savoury, and that their sweets are delicious. Three cents will purchase a substantial

meal of three or four dishes from these itinerant
restaurateurs.

Another remarkable feature of the streets, and one
which carries the mind away back to a very early
period in the history of our own country, is made up
of the letter-writers or penny-a-liners, who take up
their stalls at various parts of the town.   They are
always to be seen in the mornings seated composedly
at their desks in the verandahs or out in the streets.
On their desks or tables are piled several quires of
Chinese straw paper, and a small porcelain tablet contains their ink and writing-brushes ; pens of any kind
are unknown to them.   A large—perhaps the largest
—section of the Chinese population can write for
themselves, but all are equally endowed with this
amiable feature, that they never forget or neglect the
friends they have left behind them in China ; and these
letter-writers do a large business in making out for the
illiterate section epistles which invariably contain the
good wishes, and often convey the substantial money
gifts, of those who dictate them.   When not engaged
in taking down the thoughts of others, these penmen
generally employ themselves in copying out stock
pamphlets, or, it may be, composing original prose or
verse suited to the popular taste. But their productions
cannot be very deep, for they seem to write away with
great facility, even when not copying; and I have
never witnessed them in anything like what we term
the agonies of composition.   As a rule, they are not
more intellectual in appearance than their neighbours,
though I have remarked one or two who clearly bore

the print of letters on their features. The feast times are the busiest seasons with them, when they make out large placards on red paper to adorn the door-posts and lintels of their customers.

In driving through the narrow streets of Singapore, it is at times difficult to avoid running over some of the crowd. The danger of such an accident is increased by the circumstance that Chinamen are ordinarily very deaf—owing, it is believed, to their so frequently having their ears cleaned out by rough steel instruments—and are also very indifferent. If you nearly run over a Chinaman, and he escapes but by a hair's-breadth, the only way he indicates an appreciation of the danger he has escaped is by turning round to you with a good-natured, well-pleased grin on his face. Some of them will even pass on without raising their heads, as if no danger had been incurred. I shall not soon forget one occasion on which I had the misfortune to run over a Chinaman. It was in a four-wheeled Yankee buggy; the horse had taken fright and started off into a canter, and on turning a corner came right up against a Chinaman who was leisurely walking in the centre of the road. The shaft caught him about the shoulder and down he went; all I felt being the bump, bump of the two pair of wheels passing over his body. In a few moments the horse was pulled up, and on approaching the man I saw him still on the ground, but apparently busily engaged about something. When I got up to him I found that the wheels had passed over his waist, cutting his belt in two, attached to which had been a purse containing a

5—2

handful of copper cents, which were now scattered
on the ground, and the man was quietly gathering
them up, never having risen since he was run over.
He had two long skin wounds across his waist, but
they appeared to give him no anxiety whatever compared with the safety of his money.

There are three permanent bridges across the river.
One is the iron girder bridge before alluded to, and
which, though connecting two of the busiest parts of
the town, and sustaining a constant stream of traffic,
is barely seventeen feet wide. The bridge was sent
out from home, and no doubt the natives gather from
it a somewhat narrowed view either of English traffic
or English good sense. The other two bridges are
wooden, both higher up the river. One of these is
the renewal of a very old structure, and the other has
just recently been cut up for the first time. In addition
to these, a temporary foot-passenger bridge has been
thrown across nearer the mouth of the river, but it is
an eyesore to the town, and the sooner it is taken
down again the better, though some 3,000 dollars
were spent upon it.

The portion of the town which stands on the
western side of the river covers probably an area of
128 acres; but though it is the busiest it is by no
means the largest. On the eastern side are the
various campongs, or districts, bordering one on the
other, and which together occupy an area of 333
acres. These campongs are chiefly composed of
dwelling-houses used by the natives, of similar construction to those already described, and they scarcely

merit any particular notice. There is a Campong Bencoolen, Campong Rochore, Campong Kapor, a Campong Java, a Campong Bugis, and Campong Glam,—the first part of the island sold, and where the European merchants originally had their residences, but which has now chiefly passed into the occupation of the natives. Though the Campongs Java, Bugis, &c., were probably first occupied by the races whose name they bear, no such distinction appears now to exist.

The eastern division of the town is interesting rather for its fine European public buildings than for any peculiarity in the style of the native houses. The finest of these buildings is the cathedral, called, as a compliment to the nationality of the majority of the European residents, St. Andrew's Church. It is a fine edifice, and, as I have said in the previous chapter, has occupied eight years in the construction. Its dimensions are: length from extremes, 225 feet; breadth across at the aisles, but independent of the broad carriage porticoes, 56 feet; height to the ridge of main roof, 75 feet; and the spire, which is 40 feet square at its base, is 220 feet in height. Its style is taken from Netley Abbey; the interior is very handsomely fitted. The residents subscribed and got out an organ which cost 600*l.* Three fine stained glass windows, costing a large sum of money, were also procured for the chancel; one is inscribed " to the memory of Sir Stamford Raffles, the illustrious founder of Singapore ;" another to " Major-General Butterworth, who successfully governed these settle-

ments from 1843 to 1855;"* and the third is set
up "to the honour and glory of God, and as a
testimonial to John Crawfurd, Esq." But it is only
by close observers that these inscriptions can be made
out; the windows look very magnificent at a distance.
Though the new cathedral was named after the Scotch
saint, it has proved somewhat unfortunate for the
popularity of the Presbyterian worship, many of the
Scotch kirk-folks preferring the lofty arches of St.
Andrew's to the humble square walls of their own
chapel. There was such a great demand for seats
and such competition for choice places that a public
ballot was held for their disposal. It would be unfair,
however, to argue any great godliness from this eager-
ness to obtain places, for though all the forward seats
are now secured, it would be impossible to point to
any Sunday when they have been really well filled.

The court-house and the town-hall stand close
together on the east bank of the river. The former is
thirty-five years old, but not a bit the worse for its
age. It is a large graceful building with a fine display
of pillars and porticoes, and by its size and elegance
shows that as far back as the date of its foundation
the old Company had foreshadowed the greatness to
which Singapore would arise. It is now used as the
treasury, the land-office, and the resident councillor's
office; only a small outer building connected with it is

* Unfortunately, the artist who executed these fine windows has
made this last date 45. instead of 55; by which it would appear that
Colonel Butterworth had administered the government for only two
years instead of twelve; but I give it in the text as it ought to be. I
have, however, left the next epitaph exactly as it reads in the church.

propriated to the use of the Court of Judicature, and which is scarcely large enough to afford accommodation to its thirteen licensed practitioners.

The town-hall is of modern construction, having been commenced about four years since by public subscription of the merchants. It was to cost just 30,000 dollars, though when finished it was found that no less than 50,000 dollars had been spent upon it; but it is a pretty building, and the money has not been grudged. It is of a mixed style of architecture. The lower hall has been neatly fitted up as a theatre by the Amateur Corps Dramatique, and the upper hall is used for public meetings and other public purposes.

Close to both these buildings are some fine old trees which throw a grateful shade all around, and from this the esplanade extends in a broad belt of beautiful turf along the beach as far as the institution buildings. The esplanade contains about nine acres, and it is wonderful how green the grass keeps throughout the year. The institution buildings were erected by Sir Stamford Raffles, and are consequently older than any other public building in the place. The purpose of the institution is a most worthy one. It was endowed by the Company for educational purposes, and a yearly sum is still granted for its maintenance.

To the line of buildings fronting the beach on this side of the river, extending from the church for a quarter of a mile eastward, more perhaps than to any other feature, Singapore owes its pretty appearance, viewed from the harbour. These, as I have said before, though the finest of them are hotels now, were

once the residences of the early merchants, and
large and of elegant construction; they each co'
considerable space of ground and have compoun(
gardens around. It is a very fine sight from the l
to see these houses lit up at night, the bri
argand lamps in use shedding a flood of light i
the lofty white pillars and colonnades of the i
stories, while the lower parts of the buildings ai
by the shrubbery of the gardens in front.   Every
and window is thrown open to admit the cool
breeze, and gathered round their tables, or l
about in their easy chairs, may be seen the we
travellers or residents, with the strange and
grotesque figures of their native servants flitting i
with refreshments.   Indeed, on a fine starry i
standing there, on the sea-wall of the bay, witl
stillness around only broken by the gentle ripp
the wavelets at one's feet, it is not difficult
gazing on the houses, the lights, the figures, an
heavy-leafed shrubbery in front, to imagine oi
amid the garden palaces of the Arabian Nights.

(73)

CHAPTER IV.

INLAND SCENERY: JUNGLE—TIGERS.

Residences—Indian Bungalows—Roads—Dhobies—Fireflies—Nutmeg Plantations — Gambier Plantations — The Jungle — Parasites—Rattans — Pitcher Plants — Jungle Roads — Selita Bungalows—Monkeys — Deer — Hogs — Tigers—Yearly Victims—Concealment by the Chinese Planters—Small Number of Tigers—Few killed—First Tigers seen in Singapore—Swim across from Mainland—How they attack Man — Instant Death — An Escape — Tigers cowardly—Malay Adventure—Singular Attack in Province Wellesley—How they mangle their Victims—Means adopted for their Extermination—Their Habits—Tiger Pits—Late Incident at a Pit—The Reduction of Tigers a Consideration for future Government.

THE inland scenery of Singapore is exceedingly lovely, whether we view that portion of it which has been adopted for European residences, the districts which have been cleared for cultivation further in the interior, or that part, still by many times the largest, which has been left in its primeval forest and jungle. The town extends in very few points more than a mile from the beach, and, being remarkably compact, the country may be said to come right up to its walls. There are none of those intermediate, half-formed streets, with straggling houses here and there, separated by blank, barren, open spaces, which so often disfigure the outskirts of a town. Where the town ends, the country commences ; indeed, it would be difficult for a

piece of ground to remain long desert, for nature
would soon crowd it with her works, if man did not
with his.

The greatest number of European residences are
about two miles out, but some are twice that distance.
Those nearer town, where ground is more valuable, are
built tolerably close together, with perhaps one or two
acres to each; those at a greater distance are more
apart, generally crowning the summits of the innumerable little hills, which are such a geological peculiarity
of Singapore, and surrounded by ten or fifteen acres
of ground, either covered with patches of jungle, or
planted with nutmeg and fruit trees. It is difficult to
account very satisfactorily for the hillocky appearance
which pervades the entire island, except along its
south-eastern coast. In the case of the large hills, it
is clearly to be attributed to some internal upheaving
action, for in these the broken strata can be distinctly
traced. Most of the smaller hills, however, show no
indication of any stratum whatever, consisting entirely
of an accumulation of large boulders of sandstone,
rounded as if by the action of water, and cemented
together with red laterite—a hard gravel, believed to
be the decomposition of granite. It appears, too,
from the discovery of shells and other evidences, that
the sea covered at one time by far the greater part of
the island.

However, let their origin be what it may, these
little round hills or *bukits*, as they are termed by the
Malays, give a very singular and very pleasing appearance to the island. They average about 100 to 200

in height. Bukit Timah, which is the highest
int of the island, and almost in its centre, has an
ovation of 530 feet.   All those within a radius of
our miles from town are built upon, and generally
ear the names of their first European proprie-
ors.   The residences are built very similar to one
another, and generally of brick.   Bungalows, a term
often applied to any style of dwelling-house in the
East, are, properly speaking, only of one story,
- elevated some five or six feet from the ground upon
arched masonry.   A moderate-sized building of this
description might be 90 feet long, 60 or 70 deep,
usually a parallelogram in form, but sometimes varied
in shape to suit the arrangement of the rooms inside.
The walls from the flooring to the roof are seldom less
than fifteen feet high, which gives a lofty ceiling to
the apartments, and the roof is covered with tiles.
The most striking feature of these buildings, however,
is the broad verandah which runs right round the
house about eight or ten feet in width, resting on the
plinths of the pillars that, extending upwards in round
columns with neatly moulded capitals, support the
continuation of the roof which projects some four feet
beyond the pillars, forming deep overhanging eaves.
On to the verandah, which is surrounded by a neat
railing, all the doors of the bungalow open, and as
these also serve the purpose of windows, they are
pretty numerous ; they are in two halves, opening
down the centre like cottage doors at home, with the
lower panels plain and the two upper ones fitted with
venetians to open or close at pleasure.   From the

centre of the building in front a portico projects some twenty-five or thirty feet, and generally about twenty-five broad, covering the carriage way and a broad flight of stone steps leading from the ground to the verandah. The pillars and walls are chenammed to a snowy whiteness, the doors are painted a light green, the tiled roof in time becomes a dark brown, and the whole forms a very pleasing picture, especially in its contrast with the foliage around.

Those residences which are not bungalows have no peculiar local denomination. They are two stories high, and very similar in construction to the others.

The interiors of all the houses are lofty, for in addition to the side walls being seldom less than fifteen feet high, the ceilings of the principal rooms are alcoved. There are numerous columns and arches inside as well as outside, and the Chinese builders make very neat cornices to the doorways and ceilings. The rooms are never papered, but the entire plaster-work—ceilings, walls, and pillars—is kept beautifully white with chenam. The floors are matted, not carpeted, and the apartments not overcrowded with furniture. The wooden doors leading from room to room are usually thrown open, there being silk screens on hinges attached to each doorway, which, while they maintain a sufficient privacy, admit of a free ventilation throughout the house. From the ceilings are suspended a very liberal supply of hanging argand lamps, which, when lit up, give a brilliant effect to the rooms. Punkahs are used in the dining-rooms, but not in the sleeping apartments, as is the case in India.

The kitchen, stables, and servants' rooms are always built at a good distance from the house, and connected with it by a covered passage. There is little remarkable about these, except perhaps in the internal arrangements of the kitchens, which, though for the use of Europeans, are thoroughly oriental in their character. There is no fireplace, but in the centre of the room a table of solid brickwork is built with slabs of stone or brick tiles laid on the top; at one end of this a small circular chamber is built to serve as an oven; a strong fire is placed inside, and when the brickwork is thoroughly heated, the fire is raked out, and whatever dish is required to be baked placed inside and the aperture closed up, the heat given out from the bricks being sufficient to cook it in a short time. The rest of the table is divided into a series of little fireplaces, over which proceed the ordinary processes of cooking. Wood or charcoal only is used as fuel.

The grounds around the European residences are for the most part tastefully kept. A couple of gardeners cost eight or nine dollars a month, and to such good effect can nature be cultivated that the expenditure is seldom begrudged. The beauty of the hedges, which are either of bamboo or of wild heliotrope, and the greenness of the grass, are features not often seen in a tropical climate, but which are particularly noteworthy about Singapore. The grass is a very coarse, short, thick sort, and so vigorous is it of growth that a considerable body of men are maintained throughout the year at the public expense to keep the roads clear

of it. Few of the private gardens as yet yield much
fruit, owing to the fact of the greater part of the
grounds around Singapore not many years ago having
been laid out with nutmegs, a crop which made magnificent returns for many years, and then suddenly gave
way from some unknown disease or blight. Fruit
trees, however, are now growing up in their place.

The roads leading from one to another of these
residences, and from them to the town, are very
pleasant walks or drives, according as it may be morning or evening. Of those leading into and out of town,
Orchard Road and River Valley Road are the two chief.
The former is the approach to the greater number of
houses, and has the most traffic; it is, besides, probably the prettier of the two.   Shortly after leaving
town it follows the windings of a small stream of anything but pellucid water, in which the dhobies, or
washermen, are busy from morning till night, on
Sabbaths and on week-days, in shower and in sunshine, beating away at the soiled linen of the clothed
section of the population. The process is common in
India, but certainly quite strange to Europe. The men,
generally strong, stalwart Klings or Bengalese, naked
to a strip of cloth round the loins, stand up to their
knees in the bed of the stream with a flat slab of
stone in front of them. They seize the pieces of cloth-
ing one by one—if it is a shirt by the tail, if a pair of
pants by the legs—dip them into the stream, swing
them over their heads, and bring them down with their
whole force on the stone slab. This operation is continued with each piece till it is thoroughly cleaned. A

reat deal of damage is, of course, done to the clothes
by this process; it is especially fatal to buttons; but on
the other hand, it undoubtedly secures a matchless
whiteness.

Beyond these dhobie lines, Orchard Road runs for
about a mile in a straight line through a valley lying
between a series of little hills, from the summits of
which the residences I have described look down;
but it is only at intervals that these can be seen. The
road on either side is lined by tall bamboo hedges
with thick shrubbery behind, and broken only here
and there by the white portals at the entrances of the
private avenues leading from it, or occasionally by a
native hut or fruit shop. Many years ago, too,
augsana, wild almond, jambu, and weringan trees were
planted along both sides at equal distances, and these
have now grown up to their full proportions, closing
overhead, forming a complete shade to the road, and
giving the appearance of a very beautiful vista extending along its entire length.

The smaller roads which branch off from this, as,
indeed, all the others throughout the district, are
characterized by the fresh green appearance of the
hedges and the richness of the underwood behind
them, with here and there some fine old tree stretching its branches right across. There cannot be said
to be many wild flowers about, but the blossoms of
the trees more than make up for the deficiency, as,
in addition to their pretty appearance, they usually
give out very sweet perfumes. Some of the wild
creepers; however, that overgrow without apparently

injuring the roadside trees, bear clusters of large convolvulus flowers of almost every hue; others, again, bear little bunches of peculiar thick flesh-coloured blossoms resembling wax-work. There are also many orchids, which, though common here and of no value, would be much prized at home.

An improvement that still remains to be carried out on some of the roads leading to town is that of hedging off the mangrove swamps through which they here and there pass. These swamps, as I have remarked when describing the Singapore river, are filled and discharged by the rise and fall of the tide. At high water they look pretty enough, for the mangroves are covered over to above their roots, and display only their thick green bushy tops. At low-water, on the other hand, the muddy bottom is exposed and glistens half wet in the sun, with the dull, dirty roots of the mangroves standing naked out of the mud like the ribs of an inverted umbrella. Passing these swamps on a sultry night, especially at low water, and when there is no moon, the sight is a very peculiar one, certainly never to be met with in temperate climates. The bushes literally swarm with fireflies, which flash out their intermittent light almost contemporaneously; the effect being that for an instant the exact outline of all the bushes stands prominently forward, as if lit up with electric sparks, and next moment all is jetty dark—darker from the momentary illumination that preceded. These flashes succeed one another every three or four seconds for about ten minutes, when an interval of similar duration takes place; as if to allow the insects to regain their electric or phosphoric vigour. The Malays here and in many parts of the Archipelago have jewels made for night wear, set, not with pearls or stones, but with little round cages about the size of a pea, in each of which a firefly is imprisoned; the little insect, excited by the narrowness of its cage, gives out even more brilliant and more frequent flashes than when at large. The jewel could have no more pretty setting; it is also a very cheap and a very harmless one, as the firefly is set free before the night is over. I have read somewhere that these insects are impaled on little golden needles, as in the agonies of death they emit a more brilliant lustre. This must be a mistake, however, for I have found that the strength of the flashes they give out is in proportion to their vitality, and if this is in any way impaired, as by the loss of a leg or a wing, the bright flash becomes dull and often extinct. It is difficult to believe that the light of these insects is phosphorescent; it certainly has much more the appearance of electricity, for it is a sharp bright spark and not a dull lustre, and if not under the control of the animal is at least affected by its passions. If they are irritated, as by confinement, or if a branch of a bush on which they are clustered be roughly shaken, they will flash out much more rapidly and brilliantly than when enjoying themselves undisturbed.

About three miles out the residences are thinly scattered, and only one or two are to be found beyond the four-mile radius. But the jungle does not immediately commence where the residences end. So great

G

at the time was the mania for nutmeg plantations, and so likely did it seem that they would realize large fortunes to their owners, that many hundreds of acres were purchased in a distance of four or five miles from town, the jungle cut down, the land cleared, and planted with nutmegs procured at great expense from the Moluccas. Most of these plantations are now abandoned, the trees being dead or dying, and it is a somewhat melancholy sight to see acre upon acre of these skeleton trees, upon which many enterprising men have lost fortunes, with their bark bleached white, and their branches overgrown by tangled creepers.

But between these and the pepper and gambier plantations a belt of jungle intervenes, more or less broad. Properly speaking, there is no particular locality for the growth of pepper and gambier, the plantations being scattered all over the island. Chinamen, who are in all cases the planters, select the most retired spots they can find in the midst of the jungle, generally one or two miles away from the nearest road, and commence clearing all around till they have perhaps fifty acres free of jungle. Gambier requires little cultivation, and for its growth the roots of the old trees are never removed. Pepper on the other hand requires the utmost attention, and constant tilling and manuring of the soil. Wherever there is a gambier plantation, pepper is sure also to be found growing in a small corner of a few acres near the homestead. It is a very pretty plant, and is reared much as grapes are at home.

Doubtless it is the desire to obtain land without

urchase which drives the Chinamen so far into the
ungle; but what induces them to keep so far apart
om one another, with, in many cases, miles of
ungle intervening, I am at a loss to understand.
erhaps it is their desire that the coolies they have
r labourers, and whom they obtain by a species of
urchase from the trading junks, should have no
eans of comparing their condition, or the term of
eir servitude, with those of the men engaged by
ther planters. Or the reason may be, that the wall
f jungle which boxes in each plantation, and shades
ff more than an hour of the morning and evening
un, has a beneficial influence on the growth of the
lants; the proximity of a large tract of jungle, too,
known to conduce to a more equable temperature.*
Iowever this may be, the circumstance, as will pre-
ently appear, has much to do with the fearful mortality
early suffered in the island from tigers.

It is difficult to convey any adequate idea of the
ungle to those accustomed to the forests of the
emperate zones. In the back lands of Singapore it
onsists, in the first place, of a forest of gigantic trees,
omprising among others the daroo, tampenis, and
intaugor,† standing close together, like the stalks in

---

* In the preparation of gambier, as will be learned from my remarks
garding that product, a large amount of firewood is consumed, and
is would render the proximity of a forest desirable; but it certainly is
reason why whole miles of jungle should lie between the various
antations.

† I use the Malay names throughout, as I am unable to give the
stanical ones. In the Appendix, however, will be found a table of all
forest trees of the peninsula, with their peculiarities, and the uses to
hich they are adapted, first published by Colonel Low, who had civil
arge of Province Wellesley.

a wheat-field. their trunks varying in diameter from two to six feet. They are smooth and branchless for two-thirds of their height, and then spread out in a small but compact foliage of dark green leaves. The tops of these giants join together and form a dark shade. under which grow up trees of another tribe, short in stature. but more umbrageous in their development. Among them are the wild fruit-trees, the mangosteen. the durian. the mangoe, the jack-fruit, and the jambu. Beneath these again comes a growth never seen beyond the limits of the tropics ; strange hybrids between ferns, and palms, and plants, very few of which have even got Malay names.

But it is not so much the way the trees are crowded one upon another that gives the character to the jungle as the extraordinary manner in which the whole mass is literally woven together by a network of creepers and parasites. Chief among the former is the rattan,* pieces of which I have seen cut out from the jungle nearly an inch in diameter, and over 300 feet long; the ordinary rattans, though much thinner, are equally long. Among the parasites I have seen some as thick as a man's body twining spirally round the trunks of the larger trees, beginning at the bottom and after seven or eight turns reaching to the top, from which they not unfrequently drop down again in straight columns of uniform girth to the ground, where they become attached, and again start forth on a fresh mission.

Another peculiar and at the same time beautiful

* The rattan is a species of palm.

...ture of these jungles consists of the numerous
...hidaceous plants that drop from the elbows of the
...her trees, or, it may be, fix themselves on some
...ut of the creeper network that grows around them.
...nspicuous, too, are the varieties of pitcher-plants, to
...found probably in greater luxuriance in the jungles
...Singapore than in any other part of the world.
...hese plants have been so frequently described that,
...ough seen by but few, they are nevertheless well
...own to most people now-a-days, and a description of
...em here is therefore unnecessary. It is extraordinary,
...owever, where these singular plants place themselves.
...ome can be seen on the very pinnacles of the highest
...trees, while others, as if destined for man, cluster
...within an easy distance of the ground. They always
...ontain a good supply of pure, wholesome water,
...erhaps about a quarter of a pint to each cup. It is
...aid that the monkeys which crowd the jungle rely
...pon them entirely for their supply of water; whether
...this be so or not, they are always called monkey-cups
...by the Malays.

. Besides these obstructions, which of themselves
...nearly render the jungle impenetrable, there are the
...fallen trees of bygone ages piled one on top of the
...other or lying side by side, giving, in their decay,
...birth to a hundred different forms of vegetation. With
...respect to vegetable life in Singapore, I have noticed
...that the process of decay by no means keeps pace with
...the rapidity of reproduction. While beside you there
...still lie in good sound, solid consistency the trunks
...that must have fallen half a century ago, there is

flourishing above your head the **stalwart** growth of but twenty years. It has been remarked, too, that the vegetable mould of the jungle is very shallow, seldom being over a foot in depth, and geologists have concluded from this circumstance, I think erroneously, that, geologically speaking, only a very short time has passed since the surface of the island underwent its last great change.

There are but few who have had an opportunity of viewing the wild luxuriance of this growth to the best advantage, that is, in the thick of it; but there are many of the roads stretching either across or around the island, which at a distance of some nine or ten miles from town give a magnificent glimpse of the primeval jungle through which they have been cut. One of these glimpses can be obtained near the termination of the road to Changhi, which runs for about fourteen miles in a north-easterly direction across the island to a beautiful little sandy bay on the eastern entrance to the old strait where two bungalows have been built, one by the merchants and the other by Government, which are resorted to for a fortnight or a month at a time for a change of air and the benefit of sea-bathing. But it is on the road to the Government bungalow at Selita that the wildest jungle scenery is passed. This bungalow is about nine miles from town in a direct line across the centre of the island, and the road leading to it passes for some distance through the thickest of the old forest. At one point, about a mile from the bungalow, where the road winds through an elevated valley formed by two parallel ranges of hills, the scenery is particularly imposing. Even in the glare of noonday it is little more than a subdued twilight that reaches the traveller as he passes along. The tall forest trees start up from the very edge of the road, as straight and regular as the pillars of a colonnade, their branches often meeting at a height of 130 feet overhead, and what sunlight struggles into the road is admitted through the leafy tops of these, for the winding nature of the road shows no outlet in front or to the rear; all around is jungle, with here and there a cavernous rent, showing the almost pitchy darkness it encloses.

The bungalow at Selita is, I think, as worthy of a visit as any place around Singapore. It is a simple building in itself, constructed of wood, and covered with attaps, the leaves of a species of palm; but it is beautifully situated, and stands fronting about a square mile of cleared ground dotted over with the huts of Malay and Chinese gardeners and planters. There is also a small native village close by, and a police tannah, or station, but these are hidden from the bungalow by a row of weringan-trees, planted many years ago, and which have now grown up to a good height. About fifty yards behind stands the dark impenetrable jungle,* from out of which gushes a clear, sparkling brook of icy cold water that runs past

---

* On visiting Selita since the above was written, I was sorry to find that the convicts there had levelled some of the finest trees on the borders of this stream; and also that the jungle along some of the wildest parts of the road leading from town had been set fire to—acts of vandalism, prompted, I believe, by the suspected vicinity of tigers, but perfectly useless and unavailing.

the foot of the declivity at the back of the bungalow.
A cover of attaps has been built over this part of the
stream, and there are steps leading down from the
bank to the water's edge. The bottom of the stream is
strewn over with sand and pebbles, and a very delightful
bathing place thus secured. I have called the water
of this streamlet icy cold; it is so, of course, only
comparatively speaking, though its temperature must
be at least ten degrees below that of water ordinarily
exposed to the atmosphere; and this is scarcely to be
wondered at, as the stream here sees the light for the
first time, having hitherto meandered through the dull
shade of the jungle.

These Government bungalows here and throughout the other stations are a relic of the old East India
Company which should not be swept away, but maintained even at some cost. They were built for the
accommodation of the Company's servants while travelling through the country, but are freely placed at
the disposal of any one who makes application for their
use. The accommodation thus afforded to men of an
inquiring and perhaps scientific turn of mind, desirous
to visit the interior of the various settlements, cannot
fail to be amply repaid to Government by the further
development of the resources of the soil.

The denizens of the jungle here are not nearly so
varied in species as those on the mainland of the
peninsula. First, and probably greatest in number,
come the monkeys; of these there are several species,
but all of diminutive size; they are neatly formed,
gentle, and easily tamed. Formerly they used to be a

vourite dish with the Malays, but of late it has been
)und more profitable to capture them alive and dispose
if them to the residents in town or on board the ships
in the harbour. They are very numerous in some
parts of the jungle, and seem to go together in tribes.
At morning and evening they show themselves
oftenest, jumping about from branch to branch of the
tall forest trees, and chattering loudly. They will
often venture tolerably close to the traveller, and
thrusting out their little faces from between the leaves
of the lower jungle, give a series of their peculiar
grimaces with raised eyebrow and puckered mouth,
and then dart back into the thicket. I have seen a
flock of them follow a party of pedestrians for more
than a mile along some of the jungle paths, grinning,
jumping, and chattering all the way, not ill-naturedly,
but apparently in frolic. Down at Selita they were
very plentiful at one time. The convicts in charge of
the bungalow there had laid out a small patch of
ground with maize or Indian corn, surrounded by a
thick bamboo jaggar hedge, and this being just on the
confines of the jungle was a great attraction to them.
They used to come in flocks of forty or fifty, and while
the bulk were in the enclosure devouring the maize,
four sentinels were placed in position, one at each
corner of the hedge, and from whichever side danger
was seen to approach the flock invariably scampered
off in that opposite to it. The very young do not
attempt to run about on these occasions by themselves,
ut cling on to the bodies of the full-grown animals—
)t always those of their parents—and so are carried

about from place to place. The grown-up monkeys scarcely seem to like being burdened with the youngsters, and more than once I have seen them scuffling off thus encumbered, evidently not in best humour, thrusting and jerking in anything but a tender manner at the throats of the young ones in their endeavour to get free: but they seldom succeed in getting rid of their burthen, and when convinced of the uselessness of their efforts, carry them resignedly.

The wild hogs, which crowd all the swampy parts of the jungle, are precisely the same animal as is to be seen all over the world, but are usually black, and much smaller and more wiry than the common pig of Europe. There are two kinds of deer on the island, the ordinary elk and the moose deer; both are found in considerable numbers, and supply the natives with food. Alligators and boa-constrictors are likewise frequently to be met with; the latter are harmless to man, but destructive to poultry, and are often discovered near the henroosts of houses close to the jungle, either unable or indisposed to move after having gorged four or five fowls. Otters have also been captured in the creeks and rivers.

But the most remarkable animal of all, the one for which the jungles of Singapore possess a melancholy yet a world-wide reputation, is the tiger. There is a statement by which it is not unusual to convey to the minds of people at home an idea of the extent to which the island is infested by these monsters; it is, that on the average one man per diem falls a victim to them. No doubt, this is in most cases received very much as travellers' tales were as a rule received in olden times; for it must immediately occur to the listener that Singapore is an island of but limited dimensions, containing an area of only 200 square miles, and that it is crowded with a population which if spread out would give 500 men to each square mile; but the statement is no exaggeration. I am fully convinced that 365 men per annum have their lives dashed out by the crushing stroke of the tiger's paw.

In the first place, there are the indisputable proofs of at least forty cases in the year recovered in the mangled corses of the victims. Dating a year back from the period at which I now write, there have been recovered no less than forty-one bodies in all conditions of hideous dismemberment, leaving no earthly doubt as to the manner in which the poor fellows met their deaths. In the same period I find that eighty-five additional cases have been reported to the police, in which the bodies could not be found. This would give only a little over a third of the number I have set down; but the cases substantiated can never, under the peculiar circumstances, be expected to reach a larger proportion than this of the deaths that actually take place from tigers.

It must be borne in mind that the victims are almost invariably Chinamen, and that the distance from town of the localities where these deaths take place is seldom less than nine miles, and oftener fourteen. For the neighbours of a man who had been carried away by a tiger to come into the nearest police

... with a [self] necessitate the loss of a day's [work], and this also would probably be extended to two or three days before the body of the victim was recovered and laid in the grave. Now Chinamen, though of a [small] disposition to their own countrymen—at least to those of the same clan or [boey]—and willing to aid and assist one another to the extent of their power, are nevertheless strongly utilitarian, and reckon one living man more worth looking after than a thousand dead ones. They know by sad experience that a tiger having once seized his prey never leaves it till life is extinct, and that therefore all the time and money they may spend, if not in the search of the body, at least in reporting the matter to the police, is a needless waste for which they are not called upon either in aid of the living or respect of the dead. It is asserted besides, that Chinamen have a superstitious aversion to expose the dead bodies of their friends to people not of their own nationality and religion. It may very reasonably be believed, therefore, that even where there is no interested motives for concealment, many and many a poor Chinaman is carried away by a tiger, and his remains either left unsought for in the jungle, or, if sought for and found, quietly interred near the spot where he suffered.

But it is beyond all doubt that interested motives also combine to still further prevent our obtaining a knowledge of the true measure of mortality in the island caused by tigers. The men most exposed to danger are those who work on the gambier and pepper plantations close to the wall of jungle which sur-

'unds them. These are not independent labourers, 2t either the hired or half-hired and half-purchased rvants of the planter, who is forced from time to ae into the labour market to replace the men whose reements or whose terms of servitude are up. It his interest to obtain these new hands as cheaply as ssible, and, that he may do so, it is obviously rirable that his plantation should bear a reputation safety as well as for good treatment. The notoriety the island for tigers has spread far and wide, and a of the first inquiries made by new arrivals, as well by those some time in the country, is as to the edom of the locality from these monsters.   If, arefore, a labourer on a plantation should be carried ay by a tiger, it is only reasonable to imagine that a proprietor will do all in his power, first to ignore a fact, and if this be impossible, then to conceal it.

That a very extensive system of concealment is in a way practised was, not long ago, made tolerably parent, not certainly by direct evidence, but in a unner perfectly convincing to those at all acquainted th the habits of the people.   About a year ago, ien the reported cases of deaths by tigers had ached a very low ebb, it was found on examination at nearly all the victims who had suffered were wood-tters—men who are under no masters, but wander out the jungles collecting firewood where they can t it best to sell in town.   Scarcely a gambier or pper planter appeared to have lost a man, yet in umbers the labourers on the plantations were as a ndred to one of the woodcutters, and they were

exposed to equal danger. Inquiries were made, and
it was then well ascertained that concealment had been
systematically pursued by nearly every one of the
jungle planters, and that of the little graves which lay
around each homestead nearly one-half were filled by
the remains of such as had been killed by tigers.

But though there can be no gainsaying the fact
that these deaths form a serious item in the year's
mortality, the statement that a man falls each day a
victim is apt to carry with it a very erroneous impression as to the number of tigers actually in the
island. One not unnaturally jumps at once to the
conclusion that Singapore must be thickly infested with
them, whereas I believe that there are not now more
than twenty couples, if so many; and probably at no
time previously have they been so numerous; in proof
of which I may mention that the Government has all
along held out a reward of fifty dollars per head, and
latterly, as the evil grew worse, extended it to one
hundred dollars, with another fifty dollars from the
merchants' fund, for any tiger captured or slain, and
yet during the last four years there have only been ten
cases where the reward was claimed, and this though
a body of convicts are detailed for the purpose, and
though, if the vicinity of a tiger in any locality was
known for certain, there are not wanting those of the
community who would gladly lie in watch every night
in the week for the chance of a shot.

For many years after its settlement there were no
tigers at all on the island—at least none were ever
seen, and the Malays make no mention of their

arance antecedent to that. It was not till 1835
their presence first became known. Mr. Cole-
, the surveyor of the station, accompanied by a
of convicts, was in that year laying out a new
through a low swampy part of the jungle about
miles from town. He was in the act of taking an
rvation through his theodolite when a crashing
d was heard among the bushes close by, and a
tiger leaped right into the thick of the party, but
mately alighted on the theodolite, which was over-
ed and broken, and, doubtless alarmed by the
motion occasioned, the animal immediately sprang
the jungle again and disappeared. The convicts
man flew back to town, and the surveyor himself
wed as quickly as he could, leaving the theodolite
re it lay on the ground. It was a long time before
people in town could be brought to believe that a
really had been seen, and it was only on an
al to the broken fragments of the theodolite—in
nature of that made by Macaulay in his lays to the
ten image of Horatius—that unbelief was finally
come. After this no work was done near the
le but under arms, though it was some years before
next tiger showed itself.

If these animals were not indigenous to the island,
ay be asked, how came they there? and this
a question which for a time puzzled conjecture.
it was before long determined, and I think satis-
rily, in a rather singular manner. The old strait
lies between the back of the island and the main-
of the peninsula is a favourite fishing ground in

certain seasons of the year, and is then thickly spread over on the Singapore side with stakes and nets. Early one morning a party of Malay fishermen, who had set their nets overnight, proceeded to examine what luck they had had, and were surprised to find secured in their meshes a large female tiger. The animal had in its struggles to get free thoroughly entangled itself, and was completely exhausted, and nearly drowned. There was still some life left, however, and the Malays thought it wiser to despatch it before bringing it to shore. From the part of the net in which the animal was entangled, it was clear that it had been approaching from the mainland; it could not have swam off from the Singapore shores, for several rows of nets lying further in were uninjured.

This circumstance first directed attention to the probability that it was from Johore that Singapore was supplied with tigers, and it is said that since then they have on several occasions been seen swimming across the channel. It is beyond doubt that, once established on the island, they have since increased and multiplied,* but it is probable that considerable reinforcements are still from time to time received from the mainland.

What has induced these animals to leave the mainland of Johore, where the forests are undisturbed, for the limited jungles of Singapore, it is difficult to say, unless it be their horrible love for human blood. In Johore, game is plentiful; there are deer and wild hogs in much greater abundance than in Singapore

* This is certain, as cubs only a few days old have frequently been caught.

a host of other animals besides, that are unknown the island, among which are the buffalo, rhinoceros, elephant; indeed, as far as animal life is con—ed, it is beyond all doubt that the mainland is r in every species except man. On the island, ever, they have now established themselves, nor it seem at all probable that they will leave it as as a strip of jungle remains.

The manner in which they execute their destruction man is simple and uniform. Though ferocious, are cowardly to a degree, and while I have ired into the circumstances attending every death tigers for a number of years back, I have been able to find one case where the victim was not come unawares, and from behind. The animal moves idly and noiselessly through the tangled brushwood the jungle as near to its intended victim as possible, there keeps watch, it may be for hours, for a opportunity. This occurs when, if the poor be a gambier planter, he is intent upon stripping out-of-the-way branch of its leaves, and has his turned to the direction of the tiger. The brute steps forth slowly in a crouching attitude till seven or eight yards, when it gives one fierce well-directed bound forward, and down goes the dead, with the first stroke of the beast's muscular . In an instant the tiger seizes the body, gene—lly by the neck, and tossing it across its back, bounds to the jungle, where it is safe.

It is at all events some comfort to reflect that wever horrible the death may appear it is quickly

7

suffered.   There is every probability that the unhappy
victim loses all consciousness, and indeed every spark
of life, with the first fell stroke that knocks him down;
for in almost every body that is recovered the back
of the head is found completely smashed in, or the
neck is found broken, the impression of the animal's
paw remaining distinctly visible.   The force of this
blow must be something fearful.   I have been told by
a gentleman who had travelled a good deal in the
peninsula, that he has frequently come upon buffaloes
which had been killed and partly devoured by tigers,
and in many cases found the frontal bone of the skull,
which is nearly an inch thick, smashed in by this
crushing blow of the fore-paw.

Rescue, therefore, may be said to be impossible,
and I only know of one man having escaped from
them after being thus struck.   This was on the
Sirangoon Road about five miles from town.   The man
was walking slowly along, when from a little eminence
on the side of the road, the tiger sprang forth upon
him.   In springing from the bank, however, the tiger
had snapped some branches of a tree, and the man
was in the act of turning round to learn the cause of
the sound, when the animal alighted upon him.   Either
disconcerted by this motion or thereby missing its
aim, the fore-paw of the tiger struck the man's cheek,
tearing off the flesh and skin down to his waist; but
the blow did not stun him, and he had sufficient
presence of mind to draw his parang, or large knife,
and make a cut at the animal, on which it retreated
back into the jungle.

I believe that face to face a tiger will not attack a
man being, unless he displays a thorough want of
rve; the Malays are also of this opinion, but express
differently. They say that "if you will only speak
a tiger, and tell it that it can get plenty of food in
.e jungle beside you, the animal will be persuaded,
id leave you unmolested." Unfortunately, few get
ie chance to speak to the tigers in this way, because,
i I have stated, they almost invariably steal up
ihind those they intend to attack. I have, however,
iard the following account told by an old Malay of
i attack which he prevented by an appeal to the
itter nature of the animal. He was returning home
ter a visit to town to his house at Selita, along that
irt of the road which I have described as being the
ost thickly surrounded by jungle. He had his little
iild, a boy of seven or eight years old, slung behind
m, and both were contentedly chewing away at
gong,* when the father on lifting up his eyes saw a
ger crouching down right in front of him, and
)parently preparing for a spring. Calling to mind
ie old saying, he gasped out a few sounds and
und that they appeared to arrest the tiger, but being
ixious not to risk the life of his son, he moved
owly backward to a tree which he remembered to
ive passed a few yards behind. The tiger advanced
)on him step for step as he retreated. When the old
an's back touched the tree, he told his son to climb up.
his the boy did, and the father relieved of anxiety on

---

* Indian corn.

7—2

his account, drew his wood-knife and commenced an advance, arguing all the while with the keenest logic—sharpened no doubt by the occasion—that it would be infinitely better for both to part without quarrelling. This advance and retreat continued for about fifty yards, when the tiger, either persuaded by the logic, or daunted by the bravery of the man, turned tail, and bolted into the jungle.

Mr. Vaughan, in his notice of the Malays, tells of a remarkable instance which fell under his observation. "Several men had been killed at a village in Province Wellesley by the same tiger, and for many nights he had been heard prowling about the houses regardless of cattle and dogs that fell in his way. He was evidently bent on catching one of the inhabitants. Finding at length that the villagers kept close, he actually sprang at the door of a house at night, burst it open, seized a man from his bed and walked off with him. At daylight he was traced by his foot-prints into the jungle, and the body of the man was found partly devoured. A native who was a famous shot was in the neighbourhood, and he proposed that the remains of the poor fellow should be kept in the house, as the tiger would be sure to return for a second meal. This was done, and over the door of the house a strong platform was erected, on which the native took his station with his gun. Sure enough the tiger a little after nightfall returned to the house, and was shot through the head."

But it is seldom that any account can be rendered of encounters with tigers, beyond that which is to be gathered from the mangled remains of the victims. These are presented to the beholder in every variety of dismemberment and mutilation. A leg, a foot, an arm, and sometimes the head, is gone. From two recently recovered bodies the heads only were missing, and the other parts apparently untouched. In some cases the chest is torn open and the heart and lungs devoured, while in a few the body has been found perfect, but sucked completely dry of blood—a gash and the mark of the animal's fangs on the throat showing where the suction had been applied. The thigh, however, appears to be the part best liked by the tigers, and in the greater number of bodies recovered both thighs are eaten to the bone, while below the knee the leg is untouched. It is a horrible spectacle, the view of one of these mangled corpses, and raises up in the breast of the beholder a feeling of malignant hatred against these brute murderers.

No extensive or combined action has as yet been attempted for the extirpation of these monsters; nor does it appear very clearly how such could be effected. If the island could be cleared and kept free of jungle, no doubt the tigers would immediately desert it; but such a proceeding on the part of Government is completely impracticable, even if it were advisable. It would cost many times the year's revenue of the settlement to cut down and burn all the jungle on the island, and when this was done, it would annually take tens of thousands of pounds to keep it down. The only means by which we can look for a reduction of the jungle is in a more extended cultivation of the soil; but agriculture unfortunately, though stimulated by the present high prices of produce, and by the very easiest terms of land tenure, has of late years been decidedly on the decline. It is to the rifles or traps of those, induced by the reward offered or by the love of sport to undertake the hunt, that the destruction of tigers is left; even the convicts who are detailed for the service go out on the understanding that they will obtain the stipulated reward only if successful.

Of the ten tigers destroyed during the past four years' eight have been shot and the other two captured by means of traps. There is nothing exciting about tiger shooting here, and consequently few join in it from pleasure. Covered huts are built on two or three of the trees around the spot where it is thought the tiger is most likely to appear, and in each of these a man with one or two loaded pieces beside him keeps watch, one by night and one by day, till the tiger appears or is known to have shifted his quarters. It is usual to tie a bullock or some dogs to a stake in the centre of the guarded trees as a lure to the tiger. Watches of this sort often continue for weeks—and dreary, uninteresting, uncomfortable affairs they are—and after all the chances are ten to one that no tiger shows itself. It frequently happens, too, that the tiger actually carries off the bait uninjured, owing either to the watchers being asleep or to their ill-directed firing. There is an American here, an old backwoodsman, who has for many years devoted himself to the destruction of these animals; he is known as Carol, the tiger hunter; but he has had but poor sport of it in Singapore, having only upon two occasions succeeded in obtaining the reward—though I believe he has killed many tigers in Johore.   He is of eccentric habits, but is kindly treated by the Chinese planters throughout the island and by the Malays in Johore, and seems content with the hunter's life.

I have learned something of the habits of the tigers of Singapore from this hunter.   I do not suppose they will be found to differ from those of the same animal in other parts of the world; but, being gathered from the personal observation of this man in the jungles of Singapore and the Malay penin- sula, I may as well relate them.   The tigress goes with young for about two months; towards the close of this period she separates from her mate, and seeking the shelter of a fallen tree in the loneliest and grassiest part of a thicket, or sometimes in a cave amongst the rocks, she brings forth from two to five cubs.   On leaving the lair she always covers her little ones up carefully—sometimes she places them in the hollow of a decayed log, and at others scratches a hole two feet deep in the ground, and depositing them there covers them over with loose soil through which they can breathe.   All these precautions are taken to save her progeny from their most inveterate enemy—the "tiger- father," who hunts about for the place of concealment, and if he discovers it, immediately devours every one of the cubs.   Carol estimates that seven out of every ten cubs born meet their death in this unnatural manner; and so, he says, in the notes he has fur-

nished to me, " has Providence limited the too rap
increase of this scourge of creation." Alligato
show a similar disposition, and in even a more aggr
vated degree, for besides the males eating up all t
eggs they come across, the females also prey upon t
contents of one another's nests—so that a very sm
proportion indeed of the eggs are ever hatched.

The method of trapping ·tigers is simple. A ɪ
is dug about four or five feet square and some fifte
deep, in what is thought to be the track of the anim
and covered over with dead branches, grass, and fer
A large number of these pits are scattered over tl
country, each owned by the man who dug it. It
a labour which is so seldom rewarded that it
left almost entirely to the convicts, who are sure
their rations whatever luck they may have. No wat
is kept over these pits ; the men to whom they belo
go round and examine them every second day, a
it is only when a tiger is snared that there is a
approach to excitement. So great is the terror whi
these animals implant, that though secure in the p
much caution is observed in approaching them, a
among the natives he is still thought a brave m
who fires the death-shot.

It has sometimes happened that a tigress has h
her cub fall down one of these pits, and in such cas
there is no small measure of excitement, for t
tigress keeps hovering about the spot, lying for hot
perhaps in the jungle, and then suddenly boundi
out and leaping backwards and forwards over t
pit to see that her cub is alive ; but so rapid is h

...tion that a shot has very little chance of taking
...ct. A case of this sort occurred only a few months
...o.* Several men had been carried off within four
...five days from the same district, and a number of
...sh pits were dug. In a few days it was discovered
...at a well-grown cub had fallen into one of them,
...nd as the object was to kill the mother if possible,
...he cub was allowed to remain in the pit uninjured,
...nd a body of police were sent for. On the following
...morning about ten native peons armed with muskets,
...&c., arrived, under the charge of the deputy commissioner and two European inspectors. They proceeded
cautiously to the mouth of the pit, and were looking
down at the cub, when suddenly, with a fierce growl,
the mother-tiger bounded from the jungle right into
the midst of them, tearing the sides of the pit, and
forcibly scattering those around it, but directly attack-
ing none. For a moment all were petrified, for
the animal was actually brushing up against them.
It would have been well had they remained so, for
immediately the first surprise had passed away, an
ill-directed, random fire was commenced by the native
peons, the effect of which was certainly fatal, but fatal
in the wrong quarter. The tigress retreated reluctantly
to the jungle, apparently scatheless, and it was found
that one of the peons had received a shot through the
body, from the effects of which he died the same
evening; the deputy commissioner had himself received
a ball through the sleeve of his coat.

---

* In January, 1864.

Discouraged by the untoward result of this first encounter, no near approach was made to the pit again that day, and though the tigress showed herself frequently, she escaped the few scattered shots that were fired at her. The brute's stubborn affection for its young, however, was destined to prove fatal to it. On the third day the police, who apparently had had enough of it, gave up the direction of affairs to a person of some experience, who, approaching to within a few yards of the pit, threw into it a large piece of wood, causing the cub to howl out loudly. On hearing the cry of its young, the tigress bounded fiercely to the mouth of the pit, and ere it could change its position, received in its breast the charge of a well-directed rifle. The cub was afterwards taken out and brought into town alive.

It is a good many years since the attention of the House of Commons was directed to the mortality reported to be then caused by tigers in Singapore. It was asked, could it be possible in an island of such limited area and with such a numerous population, that men, at the rate of one per diem, were destroyed by these jungle monsters; and inquiries were directed to be made of the Indian authorities. The then Governor, Colonel Butterworth, was written to on the subject, and his answer, I believe, was, that he could not affirm to so extensive a destruction, but that he thought at least 200 lives were each year lost in this way. Since the period that that question was put and answered, the evil has been gradually growing worse, till, at the present moment, the mortality stands higher than ever it did before.   It becomes, indeed, a serious consideration whether this increase is to go on or not,* and the subject, altogether a singular one, must be earnestly taken in hand by the future Government.

---

* I have thought that a few thousand dollars of the public money might be well spent in the construction of additional travellers' bungalows in the various jungle districts, to be thrown open to the use of the residents when not required for Government purposes.   They would not fail to be frequently made use of, and would be likewise sure to draw around them numerous native houses, and thus eventually become the centres of little agricultural hamlets.   Besides the stimulus thus given to the culture of the soil, the measure would, I am sure, have a wholesome effect in diminishing the number of tigers.

CHAPTER V.

POPULATION: ABORIGINES—MALAYS—CHINESE.

Population Tables—Aboriginal Tribes—Their Country—Their own Traditions—Driven to the Interior by the Invasion of the Malays—Customs—Feasts and Marriages—The Chase—Their Dwellings—Features—Disposition—Superstitions—Contact with the Malays. —THE MALAYS: their Origin—Number in British Settlements—Mahomedans—Hamlets—Domestic Relationship—Appearance—Comeliness of the Women—Dress—Want of Industry—Pursuits —The Tumongong and Sultan.—THE CHINESE: their Industry—Secret Societies—Obstruction to Justice—Opium Smoking—Gambling.—NATIVES OF INDIA: Klings—Bengalese—Other Asiatics —Half Castes—Progress of the Population, past and future.

THE population of Singapore may be set down roughly at 90,000 souls. The last census, necessarily in such a country a very imperfect test, made it 84,000. The population of the united British possessions in the Straits, that is, of Singapore, Penang, Province Wellesley, and Malacca, together, may be estimated at 290,000 souls, and the following table will give, at a glance, a tolerably correct idea of what elements the native part of it is composed. The numbers may be slightly above or below the truth, but I believe that the relative proportions are sufficiently accurate, having reduced them from the last reliable accounts

own to the present time by the rules which seemed
ı each case best to apply :—

Races.	Singapore.	Penang and P.W.	Malacca.
Aborigines	.....	.....	900*
Malays	13,500	72,000	55,000
Chinese	58,000	39,000	12,000
Natives of India	12,700	14,000	1,200
Other Asiatics	6,500	1,700	2,500
Totals	90,700	126,700	71,600

Europeans and their immediate and unmixed
descendants do not, I think, number 800,† nearly
two-thirds of whom are stationed at Singapore.

By far the most interesting of the races set forth
above are the aborigines, and they possess a claim
upon our attention quite independent of their being
n element in the population. They inhabit various
districts in the peninsula; those towards the north
f the province of Ligor are called *Karians*; towards
Kedah, Perak, and Salengore, *Samangs*; those between
Salengore and Mount Ophir, *Mautras*; those from
Mount Ophir to the coast, in the province of Malacca,
Jacoons; and those in the territory of Johore, immediately behind Singapore, *Bumas*. Besides these,
there are several other tribes; but those I have

* This item is considerably in excess of what has been set down in
other tables; but Father Borie, the French missionary near the town
f Malacca, told me that his flock of Jacoons numbered 450, and I judge
that altogether there are at least twice that number within British
territory.

† This figure does not include the military stationed at each settlement, nor the seafaring population, which is constantly coming and
going from the ports.

named appear to me the chief divisions into which
the aborigines have subdivided themselves.

The aborigines of Singapore have long since ceased
to exist as a distinct race upon the island, though,
doubtless, their blood flows in the veins of many
of the Malays now there. But we have not altogether
lost sight of them. It appears that not very long
after the Malays came to settle down at Singapore,
or about the beginning of the thirteenth century, a
large body of the aborigines—indeed all those who
had not become connected by intermarriage with the
invaders, crossed over to the coast of Johore, and
there rejoined the wild races of which they were
doubtless originally a section; and travellers into the
country of these people have encountered a tribe
named after a river in Singapore, and whose rude
traditions allude to the period when their ancestors
had crossed over the Straits to the mainland of the
peninsula. It seems to me, however, a very useless
task to attempt while treating of these people to keep
distinct the various tribes into which they are broken
up, or to attach much weight to the slight differences
of features and of language which are to be met with
among them. There can be little doubt that to all
intents and purposes they are the same people.

These tribes, then, that formed the aboriginal
inhabitants of Singapore, and of the most southern
portion of the Malay peninsula, including Malacca,
wander about the hills and valleys of the country of
which they were once lords paramount, very much
as they did in olden times but with this difference,

they have now altogether forsaken the coast line,
retreated to the fastnesses of the interior before
gradually encroaching inroads of the Malays. The
more lonely the spot of their encampment the better
suited to their taste. Scattered over a wide extent of
country, it is very difficult to form anything likely to
be a correct conjecture as to their numbers; but it is
generally believed that, including all the tribes in all
parts of the peninsula, they do not exceed 7,000 or
8,000 souls, and of this number only a very small
proportion are on British soil. That they are on the
decline seems certain, but it is not a rapid decline.
So great is the vigour of tropical nature, that the
jungle presents a barrier almost irresistible to the
progress of cultivation; and to them the jungle will
continue to afford a home and means of subsist-
ence.

The accounts they give of their origin are amusing,
though somewhat conflicting; but none of them indicate otherwise than that they are indigenous to the
soil. Among one tribe it is stated, and with all
gravity, that they are descended from two white apes,
Ounka Puteh, who having reared their young ones
sent them into the plains, where the greater number
perfected so well that they became men; those who
did not become men returned once more to the mountains, and still continue apes. Another account less
favourable to the theory of progressive creation is
that God, having in heaven called into life a being
endowed with great strength and beauty, named him
Batin. God, desirous that a form so fair should

be perpetuated, gave to Batin a companion, and told him to seek a dwelling upon earth. Charmed with its beauties, Batin and his companion alighted and took up their abode on the banks of the river of Johore, close to Singapore, increasing and multiplying with a rapidity and to a degree now unknown; and from these two, they say, all the tribes of the peninsula are descended. To the present day the name Batin is given to their kings or chief leaders.

Another tribe of the aborigines give the following account of their origin, and of that of the country they inhabit.* " The ground, they say, on which we stand is not solid. It is merely the skin of the earth (kulit bumi). In ancient times God broke up this skin, so that the world was destroyed and overwhelmed with water. Afterwards he caused Gunong Lulúmut with Chimúndang and Béchnák to rise, and this low land which we inhabit was formed later. These mountains in the south, and Mount Ophir, Gunong Káp, Gunong Tonkat Bangsi, and Gunong Tonkat Subang on the north (all mountains within a short radius), give a fixity to the earth's skin. The earth still depends entirely on these mountains for its steadiness. The Lulúmut mountains are the oldest land. The summit of Gunong Tonkat Bángsi is within one foot of the sky, that of Gunong Tonkat Subang is within an earring's length, and that of Gunong Káp is in contact with it. After Lulúmut had emerged, a práhu of pulái wood, covered over and without any opening, floated on the waters.

* Related by Mr. Logan in his paper on the Binnas.

this God had enclosed a man and a woman whom
had made. After the lapse of some time the
was neither directed with nor against the current,
driven to and fro. The man and woman, feeling
at rest motionless, nibbled their way through it,
on the dry ground, and beheld this our world.
first, however, everything was obscure. There was
neither morning nor evening, because the sun had not
been made. When it became light they saw seven
bádo trees, and seven plants of rumput sámbáu.
They then said to each other,—'In what a condition
are we without children or grandchildren?' Some time
afterwards the woman became pregnant, not however
her womb, but in the calves of her legs. From the
right leg was brought forth a male, and from the left
a female child. Hence it is that the issue of the same
womb cannot intermarry. All mankind are the descendants of the two children of the first pair. When men
had much increased, God looked down upon them with
pleasure, and reckoned their numbers."

Somewhat similar to this is the account given by
the Mantra tribe behind Mount Ophir; they say that
their fathers came originally from heaven in a large
and magnificent ship built by God, which was set
floating on the waters of the earth. The ship sailed
with fearful rapidity round and about the earth till it
grounded upon one of the mountains of the peninsula,
where they declare it is still to be seen. Their fathers
disembarked and took up their abode on the new
earth, some on the coast, some on the plains, and
others on the mountains; but all under one chief

8

called Batin Alam. They further relate, with
regard to the invasion of the Malays in the
thirteenth century, that a long time after the
their first Batin, who had lived an extend
period, they were attacked by a people call
selves Battacks, who came in boats from the
slaughtered great numbers of them. This
however, the descendant of Batin Alam, was
and courageous man, who, gathering togeth
remains of his people, built a large ark in
he conveyed them to a land of safety, and
returned alone to avenge the destruction of the
and liberate his country from foreign yoke. He
it is said, at Malacca, where the news of his
spread about like lightning, and the Battacks
together in great numbers once more, as they
drive out the enemy; the enemy, however,
but one man, had become invulnerable the
of reprisal was near. Meragalange, their
chief, threw himself among them, and they
never able to arrest or to wound him;
towards his enemies he said to them, "If
arms respect my person, tie your arms in the
throw them into the air, and if they come
admit myself to be your prisoner for ever;
contrary, your arms obey the laws of nature,
down upon the earth, and if mine only have
to fly, you will obey my laws as your own.
The challenge was accepted, and when put
test, the arms of Meragalange alone could fly,
flew, by themselves, cutting down the neighb

...reaks, and then returning to the astonished Battacks, ...them in pieces. All perished with the exception ...one only who, having submitted himself, saved his ... Free possessor of the country, Meragalange ...turned to where he had left his people, and brought ...all back in safety to their own land.

But about half a century after this, when Meraga-...ge was dead, the Battacks came across once more, ...drove them finally back from the coast line.

The inference to be drawn from each of these ...ditions seems to be pretty much the same, namely, ...these inland tribes, known among the Malays now ...the Orang Utang or Orang Bukit, according as ...are found on the plains or among the hills, are ...aborigines of the soil, who enjoyed an uninter-...upted possession until the advent of the Malays ...wards the middle of the twelfth century.

Driven by this invasion from the Island of Singa-...and from the seaboard of the peninsula, they ...led a nomadic life, wandering about from one part ...the territory to another, yet still content and happy ...the enjoyment of the solitary grandeur of the ...forest. From the simplicity of their tastes they ...except those few who have had the use of opium ...tobacco pressed upon them, independent of inter-...with the world at large. In return for the ...exertion, the soil will yield an abundant ...of fruit. Indeed the exertions of the fathers ...provide for the wants of the children; for ...fruit-trees, such as the durian, the jack, and the ...mango, do not mature for ten or twenty years, and

8—2

then continue bearing for, it is supposed, double
treble that period. A right of property in these
is acknowledged to lie in the children of those
had planted them, and such right is respected
punctilious honesty. There are certain parts
forest more suited than others to the growth of
cular trees, and the groves of an entire tribe
together. Great jubilees are held at the various
seasons, and the divisions of the tribe, which
scattered far apart throughout the year, gather
round the district where the trees are planted.
they probably find the huts that served them
same season the year previous, and if their num
have increased, or if any of the huts have
destroyed by the weather, they are not long in
structing new ones. Their stay lasts as long
fruit remains on the trees, and in some cases
fully six weeks.

During these jubilees it is that marriages gene
take place. The ceremony is a simple one,
new-made acquaintance of the morning is
wedded wife of the evening. On the part of the
it is more a matter of arrangement with the
than of courtship with the daughter; but there
form generally observed, which reminds us str
the old tale of Hippomenes and Atalanta.
tribe is on the bank of a lake or stream, the
given a canoe and a double-bladed paddle, and
a start of some distance; the suitor, similarly
starts off in chase. If he succeed in over
her she becomes his wife, if not the match is

Like similar arrangements in our own country, it is but seldom that objection is offered at the last moment, and the chase is generally a short one; the maiden's arms are strong, but her heart is soft and her nature warm, and she soon becomes a willing captive. If the marriage takes place where no stream is near, a round circle of a certain size is formed, the damsel is stripped of all but a waistband, and given half the circle's start in advance, and if she succeed in running three times round before her suitor comes up with her, she is entitled to remain a virgin; if not, she must consent to the bonds of matrimony; as in the other case, but few outstrip their lovers.

When the fruit-trees are all exhausted the tribe retires in a body, either to some new grove, or, if none other is ready, the divisions separate, and betake themselves once more to the thick of the forest, where they can always obtain a plenteous supply of wild hogs, deer, and birds, besides wholesome roots and berries; the streams, too, afford them abundance of fish.   The aborigines do not so much hunt their game as snare it. It is true they have spears which they throw with great precision, but they seem to rely more on the efficiency of their traps.   It is long since elephants, rhinosceros, and the larger denizens of the forest ceased to be the objects of their chase, though as late as the time of Albuquerque we read of these aborigines bringing down ivory and tusks for barter.   It is deer chiefly which they now seek to entrap, and this they do in a very primitive manner.   Across the valleys through which the deer sweep, they construct slight barricades of bamboo and timber, with numerous narrow openings, in each of which a trap is laid by bending down a young sapling, and fixing it by a slight string which must be broken before a way can be forced through the passage ; the sapling let loose springs up, and drives a spear which is attached to it into the entrails of the unwary animal.

Another deadly weapon possessed by these tribes is the sumpitan, or blow-pipe, which is used chiefly against birds and squirrels, and by which deer, too, are not unfrequently killed. It is made of two thin pieces of hollowed-out bamboo, about six feet long, one within the other ; the outer bamboo is highly orna- mented, and intended evidently as a casing for the inner tube, which is very carefully bored. At one extremity of the inner bamboo a mouthpiece is attached ; into this mouthpiece a small poisoned arrow about six inches long is placed, with a bit of wad or fungus behind, and by a strong sudden puff of the breath the arrow is sent with great velocity some fifty or sixty yards. I received one of these instruments from the Jacoon tribe in the Malacca district, and with a little practice became tolerably proficient in its use.

These people do not fish by means of a hook and bait, but use nets stretched upon the four extremities of two pieces of stick, laid one across the other, and tied together at the centre ; this the fisher dips gently into the most likely part of the stream, and then quietly awaits the passage of some fish over it, when he draws it up to the surface and bags his prey. I

...y mention here a rather remarkable feature of fresh-
...er fishing which I have noticed in Singapore. The
...ds there are generally lined by ditches a few feet in
...th, which carry off the rain in wet weather, but are
...ally dry after three days' drought. I have often in
... mornings on my way to town passed by these
...tches when they were as dry as the road over which
...travelled, and on my return in the evening, after a
...y of heavy tropical thunder showers, found two or
...ree feet of water flowing through them, and men
...d women with rods a couple of feet in length sitting
... the banks pulling out good-sized wholesome fish—
...ane of them four or five inches long. I believe that
...ase fish, when the water begins to dry up, burrow
...to the mud, and lie caked there till the next wet day
...news the stream.

The dwelling of the aborigines varies according to
the custom of the tribe; all, however, are well elevated
...m the ground. The greater number are built upon
...sts some seven or eight feet high, and covered with
...ves or bark; but as they are liable to be forsaken at
...y moment, it is seldom that much care is bestowed
...n their construction, or that they contain much
...rniture or many stores. Confident in the resources
...f the forest and its streams, these primitive people
...ver lay by the surplus of to-day to provide for the
...nts of to-morrow, but share it with their dogs.
Many of the Jacoons, who according to some are the
lowest type of the aborigines, build their huts in the
trees, often at an elevation of twenty-five to thirty feet,
and seldom of less than twenty feet. They are reached

by means of ladders, up which their old men and
women, their children, and even their dogs, learn to
climb with ease.   It is difficult for the traveller to
detect the locality of these huts by any indication
which the surrounding forest offers; but on a windy
day he will be apprised of their vicinity by hearing
strange wailing musical notes rising and falling with
the breeze.   These sounds are produced by long thick
pieces of bamboo, split between the knots so as to
resemble the chords of a harp, which they hang on the
tops of the highest trees in the forest in such a manner
that the wind vibrates the chords as it sweeps by.   In
addition to these Eolian harps, they make out of the
smaller bamboos a number of pipes, which they string
together and expose, so as to be sounded by the passing wind.   In stormy weather the soft wailing notes of
these instruments can be heard miles off.

In appearance the aborigines are prepossessing,
though it is evident at a glance that they are a low
type of man.*   They are of exceedingly short stature,
the men seldom over five feet in height, their bodies
and limbs are neatly moulded, but the former appear a
little too heavy for the latter.   Their heads are small
and the foreheads slightly retreating, the mouth is
large and the lips thick and hanging, almost entirely
devoid of nerve—the nose is low in the face and shows
no sign of bridge.   Their eyes are small, but well set

---

* The Jacoons are believed to be the wildest of the tribes; and it
was solemnly asserted by early travellers that they had short tails; and
this is still not an uncommon story imposed upon the credulity of new
arrivals.

not sunken, and have an honest open look; the
is generally woolly. But the various tribes differ
appearance materially, and I cannot do more than
superficially describe them; any minute examina-
though it might be valuable as applied to one
would be useless in a description of the whole

In disposition they are simple and amiable, sen-
of and grateful for the slightest good turn or
word; they are, however, timid to a degree that
their seeking intercourse with Europeans.
and happy among themselves, they are little
to alter or improve their mode of life.
are indifferent even to laziness, and are only
to exertion by the hunger of themselves or
families. They live peaceably one with another, and
is seldom indeed that even an altercation ensues
between them; but if any cause of dispute should
they do not resort to blows, but the party
himself injured withdraws with his family
friends to another hunting ground until a recon-
is sought by the offender. The wandering
of their life, and the little attachment they
have to locality, renders these separations often per-
ones. They are like children—playful and
disposed to all, but acutely sensible of wrong or
unkindness. They are thoroughly truthful, and have
not yet learned to lie—leading simple lives, they have
little to conceal.
That these aborigines believe in a God may be
gathered from the accounts they themselves give of

their origin; and that they believe in the immortality
of the soul may be also conceded, though some of
them seem to doubt as to the preservation of their
individual identity, and look upon life as a simple
element in creation, distinct from substance, which
on death will return to a common source to be redis-
tributed as required.   Others again speak of a heaven
to be the reward of good men, and of a hell as the
punishment of the wicked; but their religion whatever it may be is strongly mixed up with demonology.
They believe that every man is accompanied by a good
and bad angel—one leading him into danger and sick-
ness, and another bringing him happiness and good
health—but it is worthy of remark that they are much
more anxious to appease and conciliate the latter than
to improve acquaintance with the former; in fact, it
would appear that they are rather influenced by fear
than by hope.   It is only when on the point of death
that any of them offer up prayers to God, and these
are little else than the expression of a vague desire
that their souls should be well cared for.   They bury
their dead sometimes in a sitting posture and sometimes erect, and lay beside the bodies a supply of food
and some weapons, which would seem to indicate a
hope of resurrection.

The following account of the end of the world is
related by the Mantra tribe.* " The human race having

* Some interesting details of these people are given by Father Borie,
the Roman Catholic missionary to the Jacoons, stationed near Malacca;
when I visited this gentleman in February, 1863, he gave me some
papers he had written concerning them, a translation of which I afterwards contributed to the Singapore newspapers.

...ed to live, a great wind will rise accompanied by ..., the waters will descend with rapidity, lightning ...fill the space all around, and the mountains will ...down; then a great heat will succeed; there will ...no more night, and the earth will wither like the ... in the field; God will then come down sur-...nded by an immense whirlwind of flame ready to ...ume the universe. But God will first assemble ...souls of the sinners, burn them for the first time ...weigh them, after having collected their ashes by ...this of a fine piece of linen cloth. Those who will ...be thus passed the first time through the furnace ...hout having been purified, will be successively ...ned and weighed for seven times, when all those ...als which have been purified will go to enjoy the ...piness of heaven, and those that cannot be purified, ...at is to say, the souls of great sinners, such as homi-...des and those who have been guilty of rape, will be ...t into hell, where they will suffer the torments of ...es in company with devils—there will be tigers ...serpents in hell to torment the damned. Lastly, ...d having taken a light from hell, will close the ...portals and then set fire to the earth."

No doubt when the Malays first conquered the ...peninsula they must have mingled with these people, ...probably drawing from among them the wives which ...they had neglected to bring with them at their inva-...sion. This is evidenced in the features of some of ...both; but the two peoples being ill-suited to amal-...gamate, the aborigines retired to the solitudes of the interior, and there remained for centuries in the con-

dition I have described. Not many years, however, when the virtues of gutta percha became ...
the Malays pushed into the forests, and induced ...
of the border tribes to collect this valuable ...
exchange for cloth, tobacco, opium, &c. ...
meeting of these two people has proved to the aborigines more unfortunate even than the first ...
wherever the contact has taken place it has induced among many of them, tastes to which they
formerly strangers, but that when once acquired ...
cannot control. To satisfy these, they ...
place themselves under a bondage of debt, which
many cases ends only with life. In their dealings
these childlike people the Malays are most ...
pulous and practise all sorts of imposition ...
aborigines though conscious of their own ...
and alive to the roguery they suffer, are too
honourable to throw off obligations into which
have voluntarily entered, no matter by what ...
they were induced to do so. Their timid nature,
ever,* and the subdued demand for the product ...
forest, will it is to be hoped preserve the ...

---

* The dread some of these tribes entertain of contact ...
Malays was lately illustrated in a peculiar manner. The ...
had to cut a road through the forest, across part of his ...
Johore; the aborigines were the only people who could do it
and an intimation of the Tumongong's desire that they should
take the work, was by some means conveyed to them. They ...
operations at once, without any bargain being made, but fled ...
jungle on every attempt to approach them; they, however, ...
stump of a tree in a peculiar manner, and on this the reward ...
labour was placed from time to time. It was always taken away
night, no complaints being made as to its sufficiency. The whole
was completed in this way.

the aborigines for a long time to come from this
contact; and the benignity of the British Government at Malacca will at least secure to the tribes
who wander there, protection from oppression and
spoliation. But it would be unjust to the Malay to
allow him to be judged by the influence which his
contact has had and is likely to have upon the aboriginal tribes. The Malays, who have pushed their
way into the recesses of the jungle to force a trade
on its primitive people, are not a fair representation
of the race. They are those who have themselves
been sadly corrupted by intercourse with the hetero-
geneous trading communities of European ports, and
who have had their avarice and cupidity excited to the
exclusion of many good and amiable qualities. Both
in Singapore and the other English settlements the
bulk of the Malay population mix but little in commercial pursuits, and retain most of the good qualities
and many of the original habits of their race.

The Malays are entitled to be looked upon as the
first rulers and the present people of Singapore and
the Malay peninsula; for the aborigines were never
numerous, nor do they appear at any time to have
raised up a system of government, but only to have
wandered about in scattered tribes; and though their
traditions point to a time when they checked the
Malayan invasion, it seems to me that this was in
all likelihood only the driving back of a few stranger
prahus, and not the repelling of an invasion. It will
be seen from the short sketch which I have given
of the early history of Singapore, that there at all

events the Malays were met by no ....
as they had greatly increased in numbers .....
were driven from that island by the Jav......
a new settlement on the mainland of the ....
near Malacca, it is highly improbable that th....
there could have been seriously opposed .....
rudely armed tribes possessing no organisa....

For the origin of the Malays we must ....
way beyond either Singapore or the pen....
though we know it was from Sumatra that .....
there, still it is believed by some that Sum....
had been invaded by them not many cent....
But the search has proved a fruitless .....
painstaking inquirers. We find the entire ....
as far east as New Guinea, and from .....
north of the line to the borders of Austra....
by Malay races more or less resembling th....
Straits, and using many words in common ....
impossible to say for certain where they are ....
and where they have merely planted th....
migration, or, perhaps, by conquest. In all ....
the Javanese, the Dayaks of Borneo, and ....
of Celebes, are the aborigines of the isl....
inhabit, but whether they alone have peopl....
of the Archipelago, must remain a matter of ....
The maritime habits of all these peoples, th....
tempestless waters of the seas that surro....
and the regular and reliable changes of the ....
point to an easy and rapid colonization. M.. ....
inclines to the belief that each tribe came ....
in the country in which it is found, like the ....

...ts and animals that surround it, and that the
...larity of languages is owing to those circumstances
...ich I have set down as favourable to the idea of
...tification; but it appears to me that the bulk of
...dence is in favour of the whole of the inhabitants
...the Archipelago and of the Malayan peninsula being
...one family of the human race.

...Long separation, however, the seclusion of the
...habitants of some countries and the exposure of those
...others, first to the converting zeal of the Mahom-
...dan missionaries, and afterwards to the contact and
...fluence of western nations, has gradually given birth
...distinctions of greater or lesser breadth; and the
...Malays that we find in Singapore and the British
...possessions in the Straits are but in part the repre-
...sentatives of the entire race. It is to them, however,
...that I must here confine my observations. They
...number, as will be seen from the table given near
...the beginning of the present chapter, nearly 140,000
...in the three possessions; in Singapore, 13,500; in
...Penang and Province Wellesley, 72,000; in Malacca,
...55,000. The independent native states of the penin-
...sula are entirely peopled by them, and from these
...and from Sumatra, constant additions are being made
...to the Malay population of the British possessions.

...Unlike the nomadic tribes of the aborigines, the
...Malays of the peninsula have always been lovers of
...good order and an established government. In their
...independent states they have first a sultan, who is
...all-powerful; under him there are datuhs, or governors,
...selected from among the men of rank, and under these

again there are pangulus, or magistrates, all standing very much in their relation to the people as our own nobility stood in feudal times to the people of England. They are, therefore, easily governed, and sensible of the benignity of English law, they form the most peaceable and probably the most loyal portion of our native population.

The Malays in the Straits of Malacca were converted to the faith of Mahommed in the thirteenth century; but whether it be that their conversion was not at first complete, and that many of the early superstitions were left behind, or that it is simply the result of degeneracy, certainly the duties of their religion seem to sit very lightly upon the great bulk of them. It is true that when they accumulate a fortune, which very few of those in the Straits ever do, they expend a portion of it in a trip to the shrine of the prophet at Mecca; but this is scarcely an indication of great piety; it is rather a desire, by one considerable temporal sacrifice, to make up for a good many spiritual shortcomings, both past and future. But their sins, or at least the sins of those who are uncorrupted by the vices of the other populations who have crowded in upon them, are not heinous, and, as concerns their own religion, are chiefly those of omission. I should perhaps here except the ancient practice of piracy, which is not yet quite eradicated; but this sin has to be laid to the doors of a seafaring population, for whose shortcomings even in our own country, we are accustomed to make considerable allowances. Malays as a rule seldom

in common to
and occupied by
The people of a hamlet
by birth or by marriage and
and sorrow. A marriage in
and a death a day of mourning
Under the shade of the same
seats the village repose.
cattle and wooden plow
have noted above they still

appear in our criminal courts; when they do, it is generally for some act committed in a sudden outburst of passion; they are rarely charged with theft or fraud.

In their domestic relationship they are frank, amiable, and often generous. Deceit forms but a small part of their nature. They are strongly attached to their homes and to their families, and there is probably no more pleasing picture of social happiness than is presented by many of the Malay hamlets, even in British territory. And it is, indeed, rather to these than to the crowded streets of our towns that we must go for a glimpse into the life of this people. Their hamlets are composed of twenty or thirty neat little houses or huts, built of the leaves of a species of palm-tree, usually raised on posts some four or five feet from the ground, with little ladders reaching up to the doorways. The houses are uniform in appearance, but not planted with much regard to order; and the entire hamlet generally reposes under the shadow of a cluster of cocoanut and other fruit-trees, which though unfenced are not held in common, but are allotted so many to each family, and scrupulously respected as private property. The people of a hamlet are generally connected by birth or by marriage, and share each other's joys and sorrows. A marriage is a feast and a holiday, and a death a day of mourning for the entire hamlet. Under the shade of the same trees as shelter these houses, rests the village cemetery; and round the grassy mounds and wooden posts that mark the graves, I have noticed their little naked

9

children playing fearlessly. I have often seen, too
gently laid on an old grave from which the head
post had nearly rotted away, garlands of fresh, sweet
smelling flowers—a fair token that their dead are no
soon forgotten.

Though their religion permits it the Malays have
seldom a multiplicity of wives. The poverty of the
bulk of the people, and the proportion of the sexes
probably combine to prevent it. I once asked a
sensible Malay how it came that so few of his country
men had more than one wife, when the prophet
authorized polygamy both by precept and example
" The women in the prophet's time," he replied
" must have been different from what they are now
" for I never knew a man yet who kept two wives in
" one house here, and led a happy life." Whateve
may be the cause of these single marriages, they hav
had a very happy effect on the life of the Malay
for between husband and wife, though the matrimonia
contract is easily completed and as easily annulled
there subsists a sincere and generally lasting attach
ment. The men are far more gallant than the native
of other parts of the East, and those they love, they
also respect. But as a consequence of the sligh
nature of the legal bonds that bind man and wif
together, and of the ease with which divorce can b
obtained by either party, they are jealous in proportion
to the intensity of their love. The Malay who know
that a few dollars to the katib, or priest, will obtain
for his wife a divorce which is valid both in the eye
of his own society and in English law, watches with

natural uneasiness the attentions paid to her by another man; and very many of the amoks which have taken place in Singapore have had their origin in jealousy.

As a rule, however, the women are constant and faithful, and after marriage esteem their virtue their chief ornament.   Before marriage I am not quite clear but that gallantry is carried to somewhat extreme lengths, and that small attentions to the gentler sex are rewarded by favours altogether fatal to maiden chastity; but as betrothal frequently takes place before puberty in the female, and very seldom long after it, but few are ever exposed to these dangerous attentions, and those who are so, suffer but for a short period.   When women become mothers they throw aside, apparently without regret, their pleasures, and the finery of their own persons, to give their whole heart to the nursing of their offspring; and, indeed, before they are many years married, they have time for little else, for they are fruitful to a degree unknown in colder latitudes. It is a common sight to see one of these dusky matrons, still young and comely, with a baby at her breast, another too young to toddle—slung behind her, and a troop of four or five naked urchins gambolling at her heels.   Both parents are kind to their children, and govern rather through affection than by force, the result being that old age is with them an honoured estate.

The physique of the Malay is of a high order. The men are short, being on an average about five feet three inches in height; but they are well pro-

portioned, round, full limbed, and generally possessing
a good, honest, open countenance. Their feet and
hands are small, and their fingers long and tapering
with well-shaped nails. In fact, they show most of
those points which we ourselves set down as the
indices of good breeding. Their eyes are dark brown,
or black, with a bold, yet not impudent expression;
and their hair—which only grows upon the head—is
jet black and usually cut short. In hue they are a copper
colour, varying a good deal in intensity, and when
young have soft, smooth skin. The women are generally fairer than the men, equally well made, and with
all the more liberal development of the sex; in one
respect, at least, they have in form the advantage over
the women of Europe. Their eyes are soft and
lustrous, with long drooping lashes, their lips are full,
but not thick, and when they part, discover well-set
pearly teeth, except in those, by far too numerous,
who are given to siri chewing. The women wear
their hair long, combed back from the forehead, and
gathered into a thick knot behind. The expression of
the face is one of modesty, kindness, and good-nature.
I would describe the majority, when young at all
events, as good-looking, and very many are more than
that. Nor is their comeliness of a kind attractive
only to their own countrymen; they are eagerly sought
for in marriage by the Chinese, the Arabs, and other
native races; and it is well known that they have not
unfrequently charmed the taste, and won the love of
Europeans, who if they do not take them to wife, at
least ought to do so, according to strict justice.

Both men and women dress neatly and tastefully, and however meagre and worn out the garments they may use while at work, still the very poorest never fail to appear to advantage on holidays. The uniform dress of the men consists of a *baju*, or jacket, generally white; of the *sluar*, or a short pair of pants, with a *sarong*, a sort of petticoat, as wide at the top as at the bottom, gathered round the waist, and reaching as low as the knees, and a coloured handkerchief, or *saputangan*, tied round the head. The garb of the women is even more simple: a *sarong* is fastened under the arms and over the breast of the young, and round the waist of the full grown, reaching a little above the ankle; and over the shoulders is worn a *kabia*, a loose flowing robe open in front, and reaching to within one or two inches of the ground. A few wear the same handkerchief over the head as the men, but tied in another way; the majority, however, wear no covering, but have the hair adorned with gold or copper ornaments. With many virtues, the Malays of the present day are not industrious. It has been claimed for the Dyaks of Borneo, that they are all gentlemen, because they never accumulate the fruits of their labour; they will work, it is said, for the day's, or it may be the week's support; but, when they have attained the required means and laid toil aside, the payment of no consideration will induce them to break in upon their leisure or enjoyment—they are above everything but the immediate pressure of want. According to this theory, which I do not dispute, the Malays are essentially gentlemen too; they have no acquisitiveness, and if they

can satisfy the wants of the moment they are happy—
they lay great store by the proverb that sufficient for
the day is the evil thereof. In a less genial clime,
and with a more selfish people, the philosophy would
be a poor one ; but here, where nature is so kind, and
where generosity is a native characteristic, it is sound
enough. Long usage gives the Malay almost a right
to partake of the hospitality of his neighbour, whom it
might be his turn to relieve next day, and should the
worst befall, he knows that with the jungle before him
he need never starve. Under these circumstances, it
is no wonder he is a more independent man than the
English labourer at home, who sees nothing before
him but daily work or starvation.

Those who live in the country districts of the settlements, and are not labourers in plantations, direct their
attention altogether to the cultivation, generally of fruit
and paddy ; * seldom or never to that of gambier or
tapioca, probably because both these require a laborious
preparation before they are fit for market. They also
hunt and fish when the seasons and circumstances are
favourable. The occupations of the Malays in the
town are much more diversified, a very considerable
number become sailors, and form the crews of most of
the vessels employed in the country trade of the
Straits ; that is, with China, Siam, Java, the Archipelago, Burmah and India, and very good sailors they
make as long as they are kept in warm latitudes.
They divide with the Chinese the supply of the town

* The rice plant.

with fish; but while the Chinese adopt the more laborious and more profitable method of casting and hauling their nets, the Malays in most cases simply erect permanent stakes on the fishing banks, and content themselves with the few chance fish which each ebb tide leaves them. Nearly all the private coachmen and syces, or grooms, in the employment of Europeans are Malays; they appear to be fond of horses, and manage them well. It is remarkable that though Chinamen are to be found in almost every calling here, there is not I believe in the three settlements, certainly not in Singapore, a single Chinese groom or coachman; nor on the other hand have I seen or heard of a Malay tailor. Most of the gardeners attached to the residences are Malays, and a few are employed as private house-servants. Besides these regular employments, a very large number of Malays find a living by hawking poultry, fruit, and other products about town.

Though there are numerous Malay traders arriving throughout the year from all parts of the Archipelago, it is somewhat remarkable that as yet in none of the three settlements are any Malay merchants to be found. Parsees, Chinese, Klings, and Bengalese have mercantile establishments that closely vie with those of Europeans, but the Malay never rises to be more than a hawker; and this is the result, no doubt, of that want of ambition to be rich which I have noticed before. It cannot be from want of education, for the larger proportion of them here can both read and write their own language. When the Malays were converted to Mahommedanism, 600 years ago, they were also taught by the priests the use of the Sanscrit character, and this has been preserved to the present time with singularly few alterations, so that an Arabic scholar would find no difficulty in reading Malay writings.*

The head of the Malays in Singapore is the Tumongong, whose grandfather, with the then Sultan of Johore, signed the treaty by which the island was ceded to the British. By a subsequent arrangement

---

* I have not alluded to the manner or to the implements either of husbandry, of the chase, or of other pursuits, though some of these might be worthy of notice in a work of more extended limits. There is one peculiarity, however, which I will mention, as it might, I think, be capable of improved application at home; it is the method adopted by some of obtaining fire. It is true that this is not the usual method, nor do I remember to have seen it alluded to by any other writer; I have witnessed it, nevertheless, repeatedly availed of by the Malays of the Straits; and in some of the islands to the eastward of Java where I first saw it, it is in constant use. A small piece of round horn or hard wood about three or four inches long and three-quarters of an inch in diameter is carefully bored through the centre for three-fourths of its length, with a hole about a quarter of an inch in diameter. To fit this, a sort of ramrod or piston of hard wood is made, loose all along, but padded with thread and cotton at the point, so as to be as nearly air-tight as possible, when placed into the hole of the little cylinder. In fact, the apparatus exactly resembles the small tow or pop-gun used by boys at home, except that the hole is not all the way through, but only three-quarters. When used, the cylinder is held firmly in the fist of the left hand; a small piece of tinder, generally dried fungus, is placed in a cavity on the point of the piston, which is then just entered into the mouth of the bore: with a sudden stroke of the right hand the piston is forced up the bore, from which it rebounds slightly back with the elasticity of the compressed air, and on being plucked out, which it must be instantly, the tinder is found to be lighted. The light thus produced has certainly nothing to do with friction, for it is the stuffing of the piston only that comes in contact with the cylinder, the tinder being placed in a cavity on the point of the piston, clear of the sides of the cylinder. I can only attribute the light produced to the sudden and powerful compression of the air in the bore of the cylinder.

between themselves, but with the approval of the British authorities, and to which I have already referred, the present Sultan not long ago sold his birthright of the sovereignty to Johore to the present Tumongong's father, who was his hereditary vassal; but, strange to say, retained as he still does the title of Sultan. It has been a badly managed piece of business, and has given rise to great dissatisfaction among the rajahs of the peninsula, who refuse to acknowledge the Tumongong—because, in point of hereditary rank, he is beneath many of them. With respect to the island of Singapore it is beyond doubt that the Tumongong's family had great claims, both because they so cordially assisted our settlement, and because, though subject to the seignory of the Sultan, the soil appears to have been their property. In point of ability and education, too, the Tumongongs have been far in advance of the Sultans; and, in the affairs of the island, have been the men with whom our Government has invariably had to deal. But, on the other hand, we have done a great deal for the Tumongong's family, which by our occupation has been raised to a wealth and importance it would never otherwise have attained; and it appears to me that the English Government will do wisely to abstain from much interference in the native politics of the peninsula, and should disturbances arise there, our course should be to let the popular will have its way. We had a lesson taught us in the Tringano business, which it will be well to bear in mind. Our moral influence, added to a few days' vigorous bombardment, was used in favour of one claimant to the Bandahara-ship of Pahang, whose family has after all been set aside, and the man whom we opposed now reigns peaceably and quietly by the people's choice. The present Tumongong is an amiable and high-minded native gentleman, more desirous, I think, of peace and quiet than of great power; and if difficulties should afterwards arise in our relation with him, it will be very much the blame of those who inconsiderately forced ambition upon him. In illustration of the false position which some people in their zeal assign to him, I may mention, that not many months ago—in a civil action brought against him in Singapore—the jurisdiction of our court was disputed, because it was argued that the Tumongong was an independent sovereign, and the evidence of the resident councillor was decidedly in favour of the inability of our court on that account to try the case. The point has not yet been determined, but it is to be hoped the court may be able to rule otherwise, and so avoid a precedent which would be most calamitous in its consequences.

I now pass on to the Chinese population, which, though entirely the result of immigration since the British settlement in the Straits,* stands next to the Malays in the census of the colony—numbering over 120,000—at the three stations. They are by far the most industrious, and, consequently, the most valuable people we have in these possessions—the development

* Except at Malacca.

— of the internal resources of which is almost entirely due to them. In Singapore all the gambier and pepper produced is of their growth, and the sago is of their manufacture; in Penang and Province Wellesley also, the chief plantations are in their hands or worked by them; and in Malacca all the tin, all the sago, and all the tapioca is of their production. Unlike the Malays, they are ambitious and become rich; and though this ambition has generally its origin in the desire to return to China in affluent circumstances, yet our possessions not the less benefit by their labour, and while many never attain the full realisation of their aspirations, others as they grow rich become attached to the country and its laws, seek wives from among the comely daughters of the soil, and abandon all idea of returning to their native land.*

The proportion, however, of those who may be said to have permanently settled down is small, and the yearly addition to the Chinese population from birth altogether insignificant. The number is kept up entirely by immigration. During the months of December, January, February, March, and April, fleets of junks crammed with Chinese coolies arrive at all the ports in the Straits from the different provinces of China. In Singapore the arrivals for the first four

---

* A Chinaman who had come to Singapore a poor man about thirty years ago, died in March this year (1864) worth close upon two millions of dollars. He had gradually grown up to be an extensive merchant, planter, and tin-miner; had adopted the settlement as his home, and has left behind him many memorials of his public spirit and charity. Another Chinaman, I ought to mention, failed this year for about 750,000 dollars.

months of the present year (1864) were 8,560 males
and 109 females—and for the whole year about
14,000, which is not much above the average of
other years. Were this immigration in no way counterbalanced, the Chinese population of the Straits would
soon become enormous, but it may be estimated that
those who yearly return to China number quite two-
thirds of the arrivals. The manner in which this
Chinese immigration is carried on, and the contracts
by which the men are bound down, I have already
mentioned; they are often unsatisfactory enough, but
those upon which the females are brought into the
country are, according to all accounts, still more
deplorable: young girls from twelve years old and
upwards being retained in forced courtezanship to a
population where the males are as fifteen to one
of the females. Thanks, however, to the demand for
labour and its high reward on the one hand, and to
the demand for wives on the other, neither condition
of bondage endures long.

    The character of the Chinese has frequently been
described, and no change of scene or circumstance
seems materially to affect it. They have attained a
high civilization of their own sort, and this keeps, and
I think always will keep, them distinct from the other
peoples with whom they mingle. I have met them in
the most out-of-the-way islands in the Archipelago,
where, perhaps, a dozen of them had formed a settlement, and had gradually monopolized the trade of a
people numbering many thousands, without any con-
cession in dress, in religion, or in manners; they were

same in every respect as are to be found in Java,
the Straits, and in the sea-ports of their own
country. There are good and bad among them; the
best have bad points, and the worst a few redeeming
ones; it is only as their character and manners affect
them as an element in the population of the Straits
that I have anything to say.

One of the characteristics they seem to carry with
them into whatever country they may adventure, is a
strong love of home, not a patriotic attachment to
China generally, but a love for the province, the town,
and the very homestead from which they come. This
involves many good and amiable qualities—a kindly
regard for all who may belong to the same province
or district, and a constant industry and a careful
economy, that they may by a yearly remittance testify
to their relations they have left behind at home that
they do not forget them. But from this very love of
home and country springs the great evil which marks
the Chinese population of the Straits. China is
divided into many large provinces, with nationalities
as distinct as the different States of Europe, and this
is no exaggeration, for the inhabitants of each speak a
different language. Between these, from time out of
mind, have jealousies existed and feuds been carried
on; the people of the one are born and reared up in
hatred of the other, and these jealousies are not
obliterated by emigration. The Chinese who arrive
in the Straits come from several of these distinct
provinces; and the people of each find themselves, for
the first time in their lives, thrown together in a town

or in a district where they must lay aside at least all
outward display of enmity.

Instead of forgetting their national prejudices, or
postponing their indulgence of them till their return to
China, the people of each province clan together and
form a hoey or secret society. The avowed object of
these hoeys is to afford mutual protection, but they are
often used for the infliction of wrong, and have been
found a great stumbling-block to the perfect administration of justice in the law courts of the Straits.
The form of admittance to these societies is sufficiently
solemn in the eyes of the Chinese, and the oaths
administered, sufficiently binding, to afford security
against the disclosure of their organization, and always
to obtain implicit obedience to their mandates. Every
candidate for admission is led blindfold to the hall
where sit the officers of the society; all the doors
are guarded by men dressed in rich silk robes, and
armed with swords. A few preliminary questions are
put to the candidate, when he is led into the centre of
the hall, and the bandage removed from his eyes. He
is then forced to worship in silence for half an hour
before any oaths are administered to him. After this
a priest comes up, and opening a large book swears in
the candidate : " You have come here uninfluenced by
fear, by persuasion, or by love of gain, to become a
brother; will you swear before God to reveal nothing
that you see and hear this night, and to obey all orders
you receive from the society, and to observe its laws ?"
On the candidate solemnly affirming to this, the laws
of the society are read out, each being separately

sworn to. Some of the chief of these, for they are very numerous, are—

" You shall not reveal the proceedings of the society to any but a brother."

" You shall not cheat or steal from a brother, nor seduce his wife, his daughter, or his sister."

" If you do wrong or break these laws, you shall come to the society to be punished, and not go to the authorities of this country."

" If you commit murder or robbery you shall be dismissed for ever from the society, and no brother will receive you."

" If a brother commits murder or robbery you shall not inform against him; but you shall not assist him to escape, nor prevent the officers of justice from arresting him."

" If a brother is arrested and condemned, and is innocent, you shall do all you can to effect his escape."

A number of signs by which the members may recognize one another are also communicated. The whole ceremony has a strongly religious aspect, and the hall of meeting is furnished very much as their temples are. Nor would there be much cause to complain of the influence of these societies were their rules conscientiously adhered to, and the exercise of power by their head men confined to the settlement of disputes between the members, or to the punishment of petty crimes. Or, could there be but one society for the whole Chinese population, its influence might be equally harmless. But each nationality has one or more societies of its own, and they keep alive all that rancour and clan jealousy which is imported from China. The Chinese riots of 1854 were originated and maintained by the power of these societies, and almost all the fights which so frequently take place in the streets of Singapore are due to the party spirit which they foster.

The manner in which they interfere with our administration of justice is very deplorable, as it renders Chinese evidence on oath a most unreliable test, in any case where members of rival hoeys are concerned, or where the heads of a society have prejudged the matter for or against a culprit; in these cases, every means is deemed legitimate to bring about the purposes of the hoey. A case strongly illustrative of this occurred in Singapore many years ago. A murder had been perpetrated, and three men were charged with the crime before the police magistrate, on the evidence of an eye-witness. The prisoners were committed, and on the day of trial at the Supreme Court the principal witness stepped into the box, declared to having seen the murder committed, and gave all the details which had been taken down by the magistrates. The man was about finishing his evidence, when the magistrate himself happened to come into court, and looking narrowly at the features of the witness declared to the recorder that he did not believe he was the same man who had appeared before him at the police court. A strict inquiry was made, and at last the witness confessed that the man who had seen the murder, and given evidence before the police, had run away.

and that he was told to take his place, and say what he had said. The recorder ordered him to be taken at once to the bridge across the river, and there receive six dozen. No doubt, one hoey, on behalf of the prisoners, had procured the deportation of the original witness, and another, determined that justice should not be defeated, had obtained this substitute.

Were it not for the evil influence of these societies, the Chinese would be unexceptionable, as they certainly are very valuable citizens ; but as it seems that these institutions are ineradicably planted among them, I think they might be taken advantage of to introduce a system of registration so much required among this section of the population of the Straits.

When I say that the Chinese would be unexceptionable citizens were it not for these secret societies, I mean as regards the commonwealth, for individually considered they have many vices. They smoke opium, and they gamble ; the former is a vice which extends in a greater or less degree to probably one-third of the Chinese population. I have explained in a previous chapter the method of opium smoking; its consequences when indulged in to excess are too well known to require that I should describe them; it is enough to say that continued and heavy indulgence utterly destroys the strongest and most robust constitution, leaving the miserable sensualist for ever unfit to enjoy life if he be rich, and unable to continue labour, if poor. I am not aware, however, that its moderate use is attended with any particularly distressing consequences, nor do I think that this mode-

10

rate use of opium is half so likely to lead on to an abandoned and unlimited indulgence as a moderate use of alcohol is likely to lead to excess and drunkenness.

Gambling is a vice which may be said to be national among the Chinese, and all more or less indulge in it ; it is also shared, but in a much smaller degree, by the Malays. They elect various games upon which to hazard their money, but the favourite one is Poh, played with a single die, which is remarkable in so far that, though a bank game, it gives no advantage to the banker, who is paid by a percentage on the winnings. It has this in its favour, too, that it leaves no room for cheating. A heavy fine is now exacted from all found gambling, but the vice does not appear to yield to this treatment, and there is too much cause to fear that compromises for these fines are paid in advance to the police, who are thus corrupted while the vice is unrestrained. Some disclosures which took place four years ago will bear out my remarks respecting the police.

The morality of no people that I know of varies so much with their circumstances as that of the Chinese. From among the poorer and lower orders our criminal calendars are chiefly filled ; they supply all sorts of offenders, thieves and housebreakers in the greatest number ; nor do they appear to be very straightforward in their dealings with one another. The upper classes—those that have grown rich—on the other hand, leave behind them nearly all their vices, and lead a life distinguished by outward probity.

It is the old story: the pressure of want and the influence of temptation removed, the same people which subject to them would be vicious and debased, become moral and virtuous. But when we remember that nearly all the industry and much of the enterprise of the Straits is due to it; that it furnishes good hard-working coolies and persevering, adventurous traders, the Chinese element in the population of these settlements is entitled to be esteemed among the most valuable.

Next in the population tables of the Straits come the natives of India, chiefly Klings from Madras and the Coromandel coast, and Bengalese from Calcutta. The Klings are by far the most numerous, and are a conspicuous element in the population. They immigrate much as the Chinese do, but, leaving one British territory to come to another, the terms of their engagements are usually reasonable and just; latterly the arrivals of this class under the coolie system have very much decreased in number. The occupations sought by these people are numerous, and some of them distinct. They are traders, shop-keepers, cooks, boatmen, common labourers, hack-carriage runners, and washermen; the two latter occupations are almost entirely monopolized by them. They are industrious and persevering, and consequently valuable to the Settlement; but they have failed to obtain any measure of good-will either from the Europeans or the other native races in the Straits. The dislike of the European is due to an insolence of manner, which is either natural to them or acquired

10—2

in the pursuits they adopt. As hack-carriage runners,
the bargainings and bickerings they have about their
fares are not well-calculated to encourage a respectful-
ness of manner. Neither is their appearance prepossessing; they are very black, often ugly, and go about
nearly naked.

The Bengalese are not numerous, nor do they
appear to have selected any distinctive occupation as
the Klings have; but may be found sharing various
employments.

Under the term "other Asiatics," are included
Burmese, Siamese, Javanese, Bugis from the Celebes,
Boyans from the Island of Bawian off the coast of
Java, Parsees, and Arabs. I have also allowed to be
added to the numbers under this head all such as
are of mixed blood, and whom it has been usual to
class as the "descendants of Europeans." I have
done this with no view to disparage the immense
superiority which an admixture of European blood
undoubtedly gives, but because I am anxious to keep
the Europeans themselves distinct, as I believe a
better conception of the condition of the Settlement
will be thereby secured to the reader. The number
of those who are not of pure European blood may
be set down at 6,500 ;* but the degrees of remoteness
are exceedingly varied, which is another cogent reason
for the course I have adopted.

The populations of all the three stations have

---

* Inclusive of the Portuguese of Malacca, who number about 2,500,
but who almost appear to have lost every trace of the blood as well as
of the spirit of their ancestors

steadily increased during the past forty years, as will
be seen from the following table : —

—	Singapore.	Penang and Province Wellesley.	Malacca.
1824	11,500	48,500	—
1834	20,000	82,000	29,000
1844	40,500	94,000	49,000
1854	65,000	113,000	63,000
1864	91,000	127,000	71,000

And it would be difficult to show any good reason
why this increase should not go on by similarly rapid
strides. I am, however, of opinion that at Singapore,
at least, it will not. Province Wellesley (the population
of which has, since 1827, always considerably exceeded
that of Penang, with which it is incorporated,) and
Malacca may continue to be largely increased by an
easy immigration from the native states of the peninsula around them; and both containing an extensive
territory of rich agricultural soil besides mineral wealth,
may turn the increase to the best account. But with
Singapore, I think it must be otherwise; it has no
internal resources to develope beyond the cultivation
of its soil, and the success of the few gambier and
pepper planters at present on it has apparently not
been such as to lead of late to an increase of their
numbers. Any additions, therefore, that are now
made to its population will, in all probability, do
little more than swarm the town; they cannot very
well, at any rate in proportion to their numbers,
increase its trade.

CHAPTER VI.

CULTIVATION: CLIMATE — FRUIT — PRODUCTS.

Temperature — Rain — Freedom from Disease — Fruits: the Mangosteen; the Durian — No fixed Seasons — Products — Gutta Percha: Manner of Collection — Gambier: Method of Preparation — Pepper: Preparation of White and Black — The Nutmeg: early Plantations at Bencoolen and Penang — Begun at Singapore — Planting Munia — Appearance of Disease or Blight — Its rapid Progress — Death of all the Plantations — Cultivation Extinct — Cocoanuts.

WITHIN seventy-seven miles of the equator, it might be expected that the climate of Singapore would be ill suited to Europeans. Such, however, is not the case. Neither is the high temperature nor the extreme humidity of the atmosphere found to interfere seriously with their health or even with their comfort. So green and beautiful is all around, that heat which would be intolerable in an arid plain or sandy desert is there scarcely appreciated, and is borne without difficulty. In Singapore time ceases to be reckoned by summer and winter; there are no seasons, not even a wet and a dry season—all is constant midsummer; and this extreme equableness, while its most remarkable feature, is after all, perhaps, the greatest objection to the climate. It has the effect of slowly enervating the system, and unfitting it to withstand any acute disease that should overtake it. No bad effects, however, should be felt from a residence of six or seven years, and it has been maintained by all the best medical authorities in the Straits that, after such a residence, one year in a cold bracing climate is sufficient to completely restore whatever vigour may have been lost, and fit the European for another term of residence of similar duration.

The extreme range of temperature, as shown by the thermometer for the last three years, has been—

	Deg.		Deg.		Deg.
1861	71	to	92	or	21
1862	71½	„	92	„	20½
1863	70	„	92½	„	22½

In the last year, which may be fairly taken as an illustration of all others, the average range of the temperature of each month was—

	Deg.		Deg.
January	70	to	91½
February	71	„	90
March	71½	„	91½
April	72½	„	92½
May	72½	„	91½
June	73	„	91
July	73	„	90½
August	72	„	91½
September	73	„	91
October	72	„	91
November	72	„	89½
December	71	„	88½

It will be seen from this how very slight is the difference between the temperature at one time of the year and another. But though this uniformity is, as I have

remarked, the most unfavourable characteristic of the
climate, still it is not accompanied by a never changing
aspect of the elements—in fact, there is not an everlasting sunshine, as untravelled folks are so apt to
associate with the extreme heat of tropical zones. On
the contrary, there is throughout the entire year—it
might be said, throughout every day in that year—an
agreeable alternation of sunshine and shower. Latterly,
as the jungle has been cleared away from the vicinity
of the town, rain is not quite so frequent or so copious
as formerly, when it used to be said of Singapore,
and apparently with much more justice than a similar
proverb is related concerning the Scotch town of
Greenock, that it rained every day. Even to the present time the longest drought that is remembered did
not last quite a month, and this was broken by one or
two light showers. From the observations made by a
friend, and which he has kindly placed at my disposal,
I find that in the last year (1863), rain fell on 184
days, and that the quantity as indicated by his
pluviometer for the whole year was 86¼ inches—a
quantity, I believe, considerably in excess of that of
temperate countries generally.

It seldom rains a whole day through ; the greater
part is discharged in short but heavy showers, and in
big drops like those from thunder-clouds at home.
The effect of these is very refreshing ; they generally
come when the air is unusually close and warm, and
though not lasting perhaps more than half an hour
or an hour, they leave it both cool and purified.
Another good point in the climate is the rare absence

of a good stiff breeze from one quarter or another during the day, and of the soft land airs breathing out from the jungle at night when all more boisterous winds are hushed to rest. To these land winds is due in a great measure the coolness of the nights, which will generally admit of good sound slumber—a *sine quâ non* to health here as elsewhere.

By resorting to the neighbourhood of the jungle a degree at least of reduction in the temperature may be secured. In such places as Selita, mentioned in the fourth chapter, lying well in the interior, and with the primeval forest all around them, the additional coolness is palpable, and cannot be less than two or three degrees. Sea bathing is also a relief within easy reach, and is often availed of; but the neighbourhood of coral banks which are exposed at low water is avoided, as the exhalations produced by the heat of the sun have been found to be very unwholesome.

The climate is also one in which more out-door amusement can be enjoyed than in that of most other tropical countries. From sunrise till eight o'clock in the morning, and from half-past four in the afternoon till sunset, the sun is comparatively harmless, and even in midday Europeans walk about the square in town with apparent impunity. To be safe, however, the head should always be kept well covered, and with this precaution, the more out-door exercise indulged in the better.

Free of nearly all the diseases experienced in colder latitudes, neither Singapore, nor, indeed, either of the other stations in the Straits, is subject to any peculiar epidemic among the natives or among the Europeans. Small-pox breaks out from time to time in the native hamlets and districts, but it is not peculiarly fatal; and latterly, as the benefits of vaccination have become more generally understood, its ravages are confined within much narrower bounds. Cholera at intervals of one or two years makes its appearance, but has never yet extended to an alarming degree, nor attacked Europeans. The last time it showed itself was in the early part of 1862, after some more than ordinarily heavy rains, but the number of victims did not exceed 100. What the European has to fear is the same as in all other hot countries, namely, a disordered liver. But this is due, perhaps, as much to the over-luxurious style of living as to the climate; and all the doctors agree that, keeping the head well protected, living temperately and regularly, and taking plenty of exercise, Europeans should, with the periodical changes indicated, enjoy nearly as good health in Singapore as at home.

Such is the climate of Singapore as it affects the residence of Europeans; and to its influence, much more than to that of the soil, is due the luxuriance and variety of the island's natural products. The soil is not particularly rich, consisting chiefly of decomposed granite, overlaid in the low-lying lands with a thin alluvial deposit, erst time carried down by the hill streams, and in the jungle by a few inches of decaying vegetation. It is to the extreme moisture—to the almost daily occurrence of refreshing showers, and to y night dews—that the green grass, the rich foliage, and rare fruits of Singapore owe their excellence. Every intertropical plant known will grow, and most will flourish, in the Straits. Possessing comparatively few indigenous fruits of excellence or plants of commercial value, the best have, by constant importation and acclimatisation from the countries around, begun even as far back as 300 years ago, been so increased as to preclude their being enumerated in the text. Among the appendices to this volume will be found a list of the chief fruits to be obtained in the market places of the three stations.

Entitled, however, to some prominence as being fruits which are indigenous, and in a great measure peculiar to the island, are the mangosteen and durian. The first is the seductive apple of the east, far more delicious and delicate in flavour than its English prototype; by many it is declared, par excellence, the finest fruit in the east, if not in the world. The durian differs essentially in nature as in appearance from the mangosteen; it grows on a very tall, wide-spreading tree, and does not ripen on the extremity of the branches, but like the jack and some other fruits, drops by a short stalk from the trunk, and the thickest of the branches. It is somewhat less than a man's head in size; outside is a thick, prickly husk, in the inside chambers of which lie the sections of the fruit, consisting of a number of seeds of about the size of a walnut, surrounded by a soft, pulpy substance, like custard in appearance, which is the edible part. The taste of the fruit it is impossible to describe, but the smell of it, from which the flavour may be judged, is such that no gentleman in England would care about having one in his house ; even in the Straits it is never set upon the table. The Malays and natives generally are passionately fond of it, and will go through any amount of hardship to procure it. A former King of Ava is said to have spent enormous sums to obtain constant supplies ; and the present king keeps a steamer in Rangoon awaiting the arrival of supplies there. The fruit as soon as received is sent up the river as speedily as possible, to the capital 500 miles distant. With Europeans the liking for it is, I think, in all cases acquired ; the first venture is generally made in bravado, and so singular is the fascination it possesses, that if the new arrival can overcome his repugnance sufficiently to swallow the coating of one or two seeds, he will in all probability become strongly attached to it.

I do not think, however, that the most passionate lovers of durian are disposed to acknowledge their taste. There is something decidedly unclean about the fruit ; a tacit acknowledgment of this is, I think, to be gathered from the fact that it never appears on any gentleman's table, but is devoured in silence and solitude in some out-of-the-way part of the house, and a good bath indulged in afterwards. I cannot forget the exclamation of an old Scotch lady in Batavia, well known there, when she saw a newly-arrived countryman of her own being sorely tempted to try the strength of his stomach on a full-grown durian.

" Maister Thampson ! Maister Thampson ! ye

ma'na eat that, it'll no' agree wi' ye ; and, besides, it's a maist unchaste fruit." The old lady was right and hit the proper expression.

Though I have particularly noticed the mangosteen and the durian, it is not because the supply of them is particularly great, but because they are peculiar to the Straits. The most abundant fruits are the plantain, or banana—of which there are about thirty different varieties, the pineapple, the jack fruit, the mango, the rambutan, the docoo, the orange, and the custard apple. The mangosteen is most plentiful in December, January, and February ; the durian, of which there are two crops a year from the same tree, in June and July, and in December and January ; and the docoo in November, December, and January. The other fruits are, I think, not more abundant at one time than at another, and even those I have mentioned can be obtained in any month of the year. So great is the uniformity of the temperature and the climate, that even nature thus neglects to mark the passing year by her usual order in the distribution of her gifts.

But the fruits which are consumed on the island possess less interest in many points of view than the products that are prepared for export. These latter are not numerous, and as very little is known of their origin, however prominent a place they may occupy among the East Indian produce sold in the English markets, I propose to allude to them at greater length.

Gutta-percha, though not now obtained in any

appreciable quantity from the forests of Singapore, continues to pour in from the various native states in the peninsula, and forms an extensive item of export. The tree from which it is procured is termed by the Malays the tuban; it is of large size, with wide, spreading branches, and a trunk varying from seven to ten feet in circumference. It bears a fruit at very long intervals, it is believed, but which it is very difficult to obtain. It flourishes luxuriantly in the alluvial tracts which lie between the hill ranges, and forms in many localities the chief foliage of the jungle. Unlike the means adopted by the Burmese to obtain the caoutchouc, the gutta-percha, or tuban tree, is not tapped merely, but cut down and absolutely destroyed to obtain its juice. It is stated that the quantity of juice obtained by tapping the live tree is so small that it would never remunerate the search for it. This is much to be regretted; the tree is of very slow growth, and under the present system, which requires the destruction of ten trees to produce one cwt., the supply must sooner or later fall short from the forests of the peninsula, as it has already done from those in the Island of Singapore.

The Malays obtain the gutta-percha in the following manner :—A full-grown tree, which must be twenty or thirty years of age at least, is cut down and the smaller branches cleared away; round the bark of the trunk and the larger branches, circular incisions are made at a distance from one another of a foot or a foot and a half. Under each of these rings a cocoanut-shell or some other vessel is placed to receive the juice, which, exuding from round the cut, trickles down and drops from the under part of the tree. In a few days the tree has given forth its life-blood. The juice in the vessels is then collected into pitchers made of the joints of the larger bamboo, and conveyed to the huts of the collectors, where it is placed in a large cauldron and boiled so as to steam off the water which mixes with the juice, and to clear it of impurities. After boiling, it assumes its marketable consistency and is brought in for sale.

The introduction of the article to the world as a merchantable commodity is due to Singapore. About twenty-one years ago attention was directed to the coach-whips and to the various other articles which were hawked about town by the Malays, made of a peculiar elastic gum differing essentially from caoutchouc. Specimens of the gum were sent home, and when its valuable qualities were acknowledged, a search for the tree from which the gum was obtained commenced. At that time the jungles of Singapore were well stocked with them, but they rapidly disappeared before the increased demand for the article, and now very few remain. One of the uses to which it was put by the Malays before it obtained European notice, was in the composition of a sort of bird-lime with which animals as well as birds were captured. The tenacity of this composition is described as something extraordinary, and a story is told of its being used successfully in the capture of a tiger. " A man having been killed by one of these animals, the body was left upon the spot, and a large quantity of this gutta bird-lime disposed on and about it; all around at a few paces distant the chaff of paddy was thickly strewed, and more bird-lime applied. The animal returned to finish his repast, and his mouth and claws were soon clogged by the bird-lime, while quantities stuck to his body. To get rid of this annoyance he rolled himself in his rage on the chaff, which soon swelled his body to a most portentous bulk; and after having exhausted himself in fruitless exertions, he was easily killed." *

Another commodity which still continues to be produced in considerable quantities in the jungle dis-tricts of Singapore, and of the growth of which probably less is known at home than of any other eastern import, is gambier, or terra japonica. As it is brought to the market there, edible gambier resembles in appearance and consistency little square rich blocks of yellow mud, in a half-dry condition, and is as little suggestive of its origin as can possibly be conceived. I have already alluded to the gambier plantations in the interior of the island. They are selected far from town, in the midst of the jungle, and very picturesque little clearings they are. The plants, which are small and bushy, seldom over seven or eight feet high, are planted six feet asunder; the leaves are small, smooth, and of a dark green colour, having an astringent bitter taste. In about fourteen months from the time they are planted the first crop of leaves may be cut, but in about two years' time the plant has attained full

* Related by Colonel Low.

strength, and may be cropped once in two months.
The croppings, which consist of leaves and young
branches, are gathered together, and thrown into a
large cauldron of hot water, and boiled till all the
strength has been extracted; after this, what remains
of the twigs and the leaves is withdrawn, and the
liquid, which contains a strong decoction, is kept
boiling for six or seven hours, till a great part of the
water has evaporated, and nothing but a thick, pasty
fluid is left behind. This is now poured into shallow
troughs, a little more than an inch deep, and allowed
to cool and then dry, when it is cut up into little
inch blocks, and is then ready for market.

The reason of its being cut up in this manner is
twofold—first, to enable it to dry and harden more
quickly, and secondly, because in this shape it is better
suited to the markets in Siam, Cochin China, and the
Archipelago, where it was originally, and still is largely
consumed as a masticatory, wrapped with betel-nut in
leaves of Siri.

Pepper, that has all along formed such an extensive
article of export from the Straits, is still grown in large
quantities both at Singapore and Penang; but it does
not appear extensively among the products of Malacca.
In Singapore it is grown in the same jungle districts
as gambier; indeed the cultivation of the two plants
generally goes on together, and it is advantageous that
it should do so, both because the refuse of the gambier
affords an excellent manure for the pepper, and because,
the gambier plant not requiring much attendance
between the croppings, the labourers of the plantation,

11

when that work is over, can devote their time to
pepper. The plant, or rather shrub of the pepper
planted more frequently from slips than seed.
These are set out at distances of ten or twelve feet
regular rows, with props to each slip, up which the
young tendrils may creep. These props are of the
thorny tree strongly tenacious of life, and soon
take root, and thus afford not only a support but
a welcome shade to the young vines. When these
have been some months planted, and have attained
three or four feet in height, their tendrils are detached
from the props, and the whole plant bent down and
buried a few inches below the surface of the ground.
In a short time the buried vine sends up a number of
shoots, and the strongest of these are selected and
carefully trained up the props.

In appearance of leaf and manner of growth the
pepper is a compromise between the common grape
vine and the currant plant at home, though the leaves
are perhaps a little darker. At the end of each of the first
three years a small quantity of pepper is obtained, and
in four years the plant may be said to have matured,
and yields its full return—probably three or four
pounds weight. The berries, which are about the size
of a pea, grow in clusters exactly like currants. To
produce black pepper, the berries are gathered while
green, about a month before they would ripen, and
are first exposed to the sun, which causes the soft
outer skin to dry up round the little seeds inside,
giving the rough, shrivelled-up appearance which the
marketable article possesses. They are next con-

veyed to a shed, and placed in a series of sieves over a slow wood fire; this last process appears to give the pepper its black tint.

If white pepper be desired, the berries are allowed to ripen, and become of a beautiful bright red colour; the outer, or fruity skin becomes tender and soft, and is of a sweetish taste. When plucked, the berries are collected in loosely-woven bags, and steeped for a day or two in water, either cold or hot. This serves to loosen and detach the pulpy red skin that covers the seed, and when taken out and dried in the sun, a little hand friction is all that is required to clear the seeds. They are then winnowed, and thus made ready for market. There are some slight differences in the manner of preparing both the dark and white pepper on some plantations; but in the main they resemble that which I have described, which is certainly the most general.

The owners and labourers of both the gambier and pepper plantations in the Island of Singapore are invariably Chinese, and such is generally the case at Penang too. It seems that this section of the population is the only one gifted with that reliant and steady perseverance which will toil on with only a distant reward in view. The Malays encroach upon neither of these occupations; they appear to have a rooted aversion to the culture of any product which requires the least manufacture or manipulation to prepare it for market. To this they add a complete want of enterprise, and seldom attempt culture of any sort on a large or combined plan; indeed, I never heard of a Malay on the island who, on his own

11—2

account, regularly hired and paid wages to other
labourers.   What products they bring to market are
the growth of the numerous little homestead gardens
in the country districts, where each man with his
family labours separately.

The nutmeg still continues to be exported from
Singapore, but in very small quantities, and before
long its production there will have ceased altogether.
It has proved a most disastrous deception to all who
have engaged in its culture.   Though a wild species is
indigenous to many of the islands of the Archipelago,
and, it is said, to the forests of the Malay peninsula
itself, the nutmeg of commerce was first cultivated
and brought to perfection in the Moluccas, by the
Portuguese, nearly 300 years ago.   The spice riches
of those distant islands, held in such a rigid monopoly
by the Dutch, into whose hands they fell by conquest
in 1605, were long regarded by the English East India
Company with the most covetous eye.   Despairing of
any pretext which might enable them to take forcible
possession of the rare gardens of Amboyna and Banda,
they determined to rear up rival ones for themselves
in their possessions near the Straits of Malacca.
Bencoolen was the first station at which the culture of
spices was tried.   By some means a supply of seeds
and young plants both of the nutmeg and clove had
been procured from the Moluccas, and they were
guarded with great care.

During the first year, the progress of the plants
was so promising that it was determined to extend
the cultivation to Penang also, and we read that, in

1800, five thousand nutmeg and fifteen thousand clove plants were imported from the Dutch spice islands. In 1802, twenty-five thousand nutmeg seedlings were obtained from the same quarter, and in the latter part of that year, the company's botanist reports that, "up to that time, he had imported in all seventy-one thousand nutmeg and fifty-five thousand clove plants." By what means these large quantities were obtained does not appear, but something more, I think, than diplomacy must have been resorted to. The Dutch authorities, it is true, when an expedition was despatched to the Moluccas about twenty years ago from Singapore, to endeavour to obtain a supply of fresh nutmeg seeds, showed every desire to oblige, and granted much larger supplies than were demanded; but forty years had worked a wonderful change in Dutch policy, and it is well known that at the time these spices were first introduced into Bencoolen and Penang, the Netherlands East India Government would rather have parted with pure gold at once than knowingly have furnished to English rival possessions the germ of a source which to them had proved equal to many a golden mine.

The nutmeg is a very beautiful tree; when of full size, it is about twenty-five or thirty feet high, and, if well formed, should have a diameter from the extremes of its lower branches of little less. It is thickly covered with polished dark green leaves (like those of the bay tree at home), which continue thick and fresh all the year round, one leaf being ready to take the place of the other as it drops. The blossoms are small, thick, waxy bells, closely resembling in size and form those of the common hyacinth, or lily of the valley. The fruit grows slowly up, and to within a few days of ripening, might be readily mistaken for the peach; it is of the same size, and has the same downy texture of the skin—all it wants to complete the resemblance is the pink cheek. When the nut inside is ripe, the fruit splits down the centre, and remains half open, discovering the bright crimson mace that enshrouds the nut. In a few days, if not gathered in, the fruit opens wider, and the nut, with the mace around it, drops to the ground, leaving the fruity husk still hanging to the tree, till it withers away and falls off. When the nuts are collected, the mace is first carefully removed and placed in the sun to dry. Under the mace is a thin hard shell containing the nutmeg, and this is not broken till the nutmegs are prepared for shipment. A good tree yields 600 nuts per annum, or about 8 lbs. weight. There is no particular season for the nutmeg crop, and the blossoms and the ripe fruit may often be seen hanging together on the same branch. Altogether there are few prettier trees—prettier in form, in foliage, in blossom, and in bearing, than the healthy nutmeg.

The spice gardens both of Bencoolen and Penang remained for the first few years entirely in the hands of the company, though it does not appear that private residents were forbidden to venture upon the cultivation, and long reports used to go home regularly to

Leadenhall-street concerning the number, progress, and prospects of the trees. At Penang the plants were less fortunate than at Bencoolen; many of them died in the second or third year, and half the survivors proved to be male trees, which do not bear. Large sums had been spent, and an expensive botanical staff was still to be maintained; so the directors, tired of an experiment so expensive and so problematical in its results, sent out instructions to sell both the gardens and the plants.

This gave an impetus to private enterprise, and the number of plants and plantations rapidly increased. When Singapore was settled, the fruits of many years' labour and outlay were just beginning to be reaped at Penang. But the outlay had been so great, and the fruits so long delayed, that it was some years before any were found bold enough to adventure upon spice planting in the new settlement. A report, however, which spoke of the soil and the climate as much better suited to the growth of spices than that of Penang, induced a commencement to be made with nutmegs; but it does not appear that cloves were introduced with the view of extensive cultivation. A great many of the disappointments that had been experienced at Penang and Bencoolen were also met with at Singapore, and it was long before the planters obtained any return for their labour and outlay.

When this return did come, however, in Singapore, it was a good one, and promised to be a steady one. The trees grew strong and vigorous, and were fruitful to an extent unknown even in the Moluccas. These were powerful inducements to hold out in a settlement whose residents had not only grown rich beyond measure, but who had grown attached to the land itself, and were ready and willing to embark in any enterprise that, while likely to be remunerative for the capital invested, tended further to develope its resources. Planting in Singapore now went on with a vengeance. A nutmeg mania seized upon all the landed proprietors. What had been flower gardens and ornamental grounds of private residences were turned over, and nutmegs planted to within a stone's throw of the house walls. Besides this, large tracts of jungle, at a distance of four or five miles from town, were bought up from Government, cleared at great expense, and turned into plantations. Some of these newly reclaimed properties, upon which the young plants looked strong and healthy, changed hands at exorbitant prices.

But all this planting was destined to end in bitter disappointment, and many of those who had adventured on it most boldly were brought near to ruin's doors. Never, perhaps, was there a clearer example of those curses which at times overtake man's industry, apparently unprovoked by his own default. Ere the first trees of the new planting were in fair bearing, a disease showed itself, the nature or origin of which has, as far as I know, defied all conjecture. Beginning at the top of the tree, the leaves would slowly wither off, the twigs and branches whiten and die, and this while the lower part was in apparently vigorous health. The descent from top to bottom was very slow, but

was very sure; and probably in a year from the
first appearance of the blight, nothing remained of
the once green, bushy tree but a bleached skeleton.
The progress made by this disease upon a plantation
was alike strange and unaccountable. It did not
commence at one spot, and then extend itself by a
gradually widening circle, but generally broke out in
several places simultaneously, and this without regard
to situation or soil. The trees on the hill-tops and
those in the valleys suffered alike. Some plantations
decayed more rapidly than others, but in most cases
the destruction has been slow, especially with trees
that had matured before the disease broke out.

Great efforts were at first made to check it. Trees
were rooted out as soon as they showed the first
symptoms of decay, and those that remained sound
were carefully manured and tended. Sums as great
as the original cost of the plantations were expended
by many planters in their attempts to overcome the
disease. But all was in vain. Slowly but surely
tree after tree died away; hope and perseverance
were worn out, and disgust and recklessness took
their places. Whole plantations were abandoned before half the trees were dead, and the fruit of the
good trees left to rot or be picked by any one who
took the trouble to look for them. To the present
day, so slow has been the decay in plantations that
have long since been abandoned and become choked
with jungle undergrowth, that the rich green foliage
of many a sound, healthy tree may be seen standing
out in welcome relief from among the whitened

branches of its dead neighbours. The few nutmegs that are now brought into town and sold, are for the most part the collections made by Malays and Chinese from these half-dead plantations. I only know of one plantation on the island which is still cultivated ; it is well inland, but it has lately suffered severely from the blight, and will in all probability soon cease to form an exception to the statement that the cultivation of the nutmeg in Singapore is extinct.

Another extensive product of Singapore, and one which, unlike the nutmeg, is rapidly on the increase, is the cocoanut. It is an article of extensive local consumption, but, as yet, of export only to the neighbouring native states and to Burmah. It is quite possible, however, that before very long oil may be produced in such quantities as to figure in the list of exports to Europe. The tree does not appear to have been indigenous, for none are ever found in the jungle ; but, together with the common plantain, must have been introduced by the Malays many centuries ago—probably when they first colonized the island. The natives had never cultivated it to any extent, and for many years after the settlement of the English it was considered too insignificant or too remote a means of acquiring wealth to be embarked in largely. Twenty years ago attention was for the first time directed to its cultivation on an extended scale, and several Europeans bought up large tracts of land along the sea-shore, and systematically commenced to lay them out as cocoanut planta-

tions. These have now been long grown up, and in
full bearing, and the richness of the first crops they
yielded soon led others to follow in the footsteps
of the earlier adventurers. Low-lying lands, formerly
considered of no value, have within the last seven
or eight years been greedily bought up and covered
with young cocoanut plants, which before very long
will commence to yield a crop profitable to the planters
and valuable to the island.

A cocoanut plantation has altogether a singular
appearance. The trees being of one age are of a
uniform height, thickness of trunk, and spread of
top; they are planted in horizontal lines at equal
distances, and growing up straight and perpendicular,
present a series of long tall thin grey columns roofed
over by green feathery foliage. The trees at maturity
attain a height of forty feet, unbroken by a leaf or
branch, and rarely inclining more than two or three
degrees from the perpendicular; the tops have a spread
of about twenty-five feet in diameter, and, as the trees
are seldom planted further apart than thirty feet, their
foliage forms nearly an unbroken canopy, shading the
ground below. The nuts grow in clusters between
the roots of the leaves or branches at the top, in all
conditions of ripeness. If not picked when ripe they
drop, and even with careful picking many nuts are
lost by dropping and being broken on the ground.
Indeed, in a large plantation the noise of the falling
nuts and the dead old branches strangely breaks the
silence that reigns around. The force with which
they fall is considerable,—sufficient, if they alight on

CHAPTER VII.

COMMERCE: SINGAPORE — PENANG — MALACCA.

Nature of the Trade of Singapore—Its rapid Progress—Comparativ
Progress of the three Stations—Imports at Singapore from differer
Countries—Their Character—Singapore Exports—Of what the
consist—Number and Nationalities of Vessels arrived during tl
Year at the Port of Singapore—Future Commercial Policy-
Imports at Penang—Sumatra Produce—Exports from Penang-
They exceed the Imports—Number and Nationality of Shi
arrived at Penang during the Year—Imports and Exports
Malacca—Tin, the chief Export—Royalty reserved by Gover
ment—Concluding Remarks on the Commerce of the Straits
Malacca.

THE commercial prosperity of Singapore has bee
steadily progressive from the first year of the settl
ment, and there seems no good reason to belie
that it has yet reached its extreme limit. But
may be well, at the very outset, to put prominent
forward the fact, that, comparatively speaking, tl
island neither produces nor manufactures. It neith
grows to any extent the products it exports, n
much improves or renders marketable those whi
pass through it; and it is in the measure of caref
regard to be paid by our legislators to these circun
stances and their consequences that we must look f

the future advance or retrogression of the trade of Singapore. So evenly balanced are the causes which at present affect favourably or otherwise the commerce of this entrepôt, that the slightest burden thrown in the scales against it, would sink it, it might be irrevocably, below the reach of the current of prosperity. The two great advantages that at the beginning drew the trade of the East towards Singapore, were—first, the central and convenient position of the station; and, second, the entire exemption from commercial imposts or taxes on trade, at a time when the Dutch in the neighbourhood drew their chief revenue from import and export duties, and when even the Company themselves had no other free port. The first of these advantages still remains, and must continue to remain, in its favour; the second exists, too, but in a qualified degree. The port is still as exempt of trade restrictions* as it was at its foundation, but it does not now possess this exemption singly; our policy has been, at length, widely copied by our Dutch neighbours, who have scattered half-a-dozen free ports over the Archipelago, one of which is only sixty-three miles distant from Singapore. These Dutch ports, it is true, have not robbed the Straits of much of its old trade, but they have certainly deflected a good deal of that which, in their absence, would doubtless have reached it, especially towards the south-east of the Archipelago; and they remain ready at any moment to

---

* The stamp tax imposed nearly two years ago can, I think, scarcely be said to be a trade restriction, at least of the port; and the ease with which it has worked, proves that it is not severely felt.

engulph all that may be driven from it by restrictive legislation.

The gradual increase of the imports and exports of Singapore from 1,200,000l. of the former, and 950,000l. of the latter, in 1823, to 6,500,000l. and 5,500,000l. respectively, forty years afterwards, in 1863, is owing in a large measure to the development of the native states around it, to the extension of their knowledge of and taste for British manufactures on the one hand; and, on the other, to their anxiety to derive from the cultivation of their soil, and from the free products of their forests, the means to obtain them. Undoubtedly this development may, and indeed must, reach a limit when it will cease to benefit Singapore. Native ports, whose earlier trade was conducted in junks, will, under the impulse given by the new-felt wants of the people and their newly-devised means to satisfy them, grow in importance till they become the resorts of large shipping and have direct intercourse with Europe. We have already had this illustrated in the case of Borneo and Siam. But so vast is the population of the Archipelago and of the native states on the eastern continent, that, as one port is withdrawn from the supply of Singapore, another will be ready to take its place; and this must go on for the next century at least, provided always we keep its port completely open and trade unfettered.

Singapore, however, has a large trade quite independent of the native states that through it may draw their supplies and transmit their produce. It arises

from the central position of the island, and is carried
on between Calcutta, Burmah, Java, and China; consisting chiefly of imports from the two first, and of
exports to the two latter. It is not at all unusual in
England to send goods to Singapore which are ultimately intended either for China or Java, because
doing so gives the choice of two or three markets.
If on arrival there, the goods are low in China but
high in Java, they are of course sent on to the latter
port, and *vice versá*; or, if both in China and Java
they are unsaleable, there is still the chance of Siam,
Saigon, and Borneo.

The same course is adopted with the opium and
rice of India. Fully one-half of the opium, and more
than three-fourths of the grain that comes down to
Singapore from India is consumed in China; and a
large portion besides goes to Java. There is, undoubtedly, as little difficulty in procuring freight from
India to China, as there is from India to the Straits,
and the cost of direct shipment is always considerably
less; still, to take the chances of the several markets,
obtained through Singapore, is found the most profitable course.

This trade, as I have said, has not had its origin
in the insignificance of the ports with which it is
carried on, nor can it be adversely affected by their
future growth and prosperity. It appears to me, too,
that, as the native markets around grow into an
importance deserving direct intercourse with Europe,
they will come to rank in the trade of Singapore as

12

the ports of China, Java, and Siam do now. The
only peril to this part of our commerce is too clear
to be mistaken. As long as the port of Singapore
remains free of tonnage dues, or of harbour dues, as
long as bonded warehouses are unnecessary because of
its freedom from import or export duties,—in point
of fact, as long as ships can enter and leave its
harbour at will, and goods can be landed and shipped
at no cost beyond the cooly and boat hire—so long
need we fear no diminution of what might be termed
its inter-colonial trade. Singapore has grown too
great to fear any rivalry on equal terms. It has paled
the ineffectual fires of the Dutch, while it keeps down
and makes subservient to itself the commercial ardour
of the French at Saigon. But as surely as any attempt
is made to tax its imports or its exports, or to burden
its port with any tonnage or harbour due, that moment
the ebb of its commercial greatness begins.

Though I have directed these observations to Singapore only, they have also, in a smaller degree,
application to Penang. To Malacca as yet they have
none; nor does it seem likely that they ever will have.
But, as the three settlements form one colony, it is
desirable that a comprehensive view of the whole
should be given, and I propose first to estimate
the commercial condition of them together, before
passing on to the separate consideration of each.
In order to shew, without entering at present into
details, that, however varied the degree, the trade of each
of the settlements has been progressive, I may refer

to the following table, which I have accurately prepared, of the imports and exports during the years
1833–43–53 and 63 :—

Date.	—	Singapore.	Penang and P.W.	Malacca.
		£	£	£
1833	Imports	2,043,000	427,000	104,000
	Exports	1,705,000	440,000	58,000
	Total.............	3,748,000	867,000	162,000
1843	Imports	2,953,000	473,000	95,000
	Exports	2,505,000	549,000	62,000
	Total.............	5,548,000	1,022,000	157,000
1853	Imports	3,488,000	725,000	299,000
	Exports	3,027,000	962,000	218,000
	Total.............	6,515,000	1,687,000	517,000
1863	Imports	6,462,000	1,684,000	453,000
	Exports	5,555,000	2,392,000	360,000
	Total.............	12,017,000	4,076,000	813,000

		£
Gross total for 1833	....	4,777,000
„ „ 1843	....	6,727,000
„ „ 1853	....	8,719,000
„ „ 1863	....	16,906,000

or, summed up, a business for the joint settlements of
four millions and three quarters in 1833, of six millions and three quarters in 1843, of eight millions
and three quarters in 1853, and of no less than
seventeen millions in the year that has just closed. It

will be found on examination, that the trade of both Penang and Malacca as shown in these four periods has progressed proportionately by even a greater ratio than that of Singapore—for whereas the latter has been a little more than trebled, the two former have been multiplied, the one four and a half, and the other five-fold.

The magnitude of the amount in the one case, however, is now such as to involve a tremendous body of trade in any proportional alteration of the figures. And if we go ten years further back, say to 1823, with Singapore and Penang, and to 1825 (the date of our final occupation) with Malacca, and estimate the progress of the respective stations since then, we shall find the retrospect considerably less favourable to the two latter. It will be found that from 1823 to the present time, the trade of Penang has barely multiplied itself three and a half times, and that of Malacca, since 1825, has progressed in no better proportion, while that of Singapore has increased seven-fold.

But it is satisfactory to gather, at the same time, that however rapid and gigantic the progress made by Singapore, it has not involved, as has frequently been asserted, a retrograde movement on the part of the other stations; on the contrary, I believe that the continued prosperity of the younger settlement has been, and will be the strongest stimulus to the trade of the other two.

So much for the commercial progress of the three

stations of the new colony. It will now be necessary
to consider the present condition of each apart. The
imports of Singapore for the year ending 30th April,
1868, have been from the following countries, and of
the values placed opposite each :—

IMPORTS.

	£
Great Britain	1,500,758
North America	80,222
Europe	388,099
Australia	52,006
Calcutta	699,832
Madras	32,256
Bombay	85,590
China	902,922
Cochin China	168,722
Siam	242,093
Manila	26,599
Java, Rhio, &c.	959,174
Borneo	138,096
Celebes	112,616
Sumatra	109,933
Malayan Peninsula	170,503
Miscellaneous, including Malacca, Penang, and British Burmah	942,209
Total	6,461,720

To give a complete and exact analysis of these
extensive imports would occupy too great a space, and
prove of comparatively small value. I shall, however,
briefly enumerate the chief articles which make up
the sums respectively standing opposite each country;
and with regard to Great Britain, British India, China
and Java, where the amounts are so considerable, I
shall be more particular.

1.—The principal imports from Great Britain for
the period embraced in the table above I have carefully

gone over, and for the sake of brevity have tabulated
the principal items as under :—

	£
Treasure	800,718
Cotton Manufactures	717,820
Woollens	47,160
Beer	14,448
Wines	10,827
Arms and Ammunition	57,875
Iron and Ironwork	78,496
Copper and Yellow Metal	98,998
Lead	22,571
Earthenware	18,589
Canvas, &c	16,882

Besides these, there is a long list of miscellaneous
articles which, though amounting together to a considerable value, are individually considered of small
importance. Of the cotton manufactures, arms and
gunpowder imported, only a very small proportion is
for the use of the Straits, the former find their way
all over the Archipelago—the two latter both to the
Archipelago, and, until very lately, in great quantities
to China. The other articles particularized are consumed in greater degree in the Straits, but still the
bulk of these, too, is re-exported.

2, 3.—From North America and Europe the imports partake very much of the nature of those from
Great Britain, with the exception of ice, which is
supplied from the former, and need not therefore be
more than stated at their gross values in the general
table.

4.—Australia furnishes chiefly horses, bread-stuffs,
coals from the mines at New South Wales, and sandal-
wood from Western Australia.

5, 6, 7.—From Calcutta, Madras, and Bombay the
imports have aggregated very nearly a million sterling.
I tabulate together the principal items from the three
presidencies, simply remarking that the opium and
grain are chiefly supplied from Calcutta.

	£
Opium	590,343
Grain	46,252
Saltpetre	7,368
Gunnie Bags	24,782

Cotton in former years also formed a considerable
article of import from India, but since the American
war this importation has altogether ceased.   The
opium that is landed here finds its way to Java and the
Archipelago, Siam, and Cochin China, about thirty-
five or forty chests a month, or 60,000l. worth annually,
being the consumption of Singapore itself.   Saltpetre
is sent on to China and Java.   The other articles are
to a considerable extent consumed in the Straits.

8.—The imports from China more than equal those
from British India, amounting to 902,921l.   They
chiefly consisted of,—

	£
Gold Bars and Dust	205,515
Sycee Silver and Dollars	68,506
China Cash	18,450
Sugar	15,167
Tea	41,233
Camphor	43,405
Cassia	12,371
Alum	3,262
Raw Thread Silk	85,574
Tobacco	60,444

Many of these articles are sent on to Europe or
America.   China cash, 1,200 pieces of which go to

the dollar, is sent down to the islands of the Archipelago to purchase rice and other native products. It is the only coin below the dollar which is current throughout the Archipelago, and being suitable to the payment of very small sums is never likely to be superseded. I believe it has been frequently tried in Birmingham to produce an imitation of these, but it was found impossible to obtain a similar metal at anything like the price.

9.—From Cochin China the imports have chiefly consisted of rice; but of late years, since the French occupation, the quantity has fallen very much below the old standard. Sticlac and bee's-wax are also articles of import from Cochin China.

10.—Siam imports, like those of Cochin China, chiefly consist of rice, but instead of being on the decline, the trade in this staple is progressing steadily. Sticlac, horns, and hides, are the other principal items.

11.—From Manila the largest imports are of tobaccos and sugars; partly for consumption in the Straits, and partly for re-exportation home, and to British India.

12.—The imports from the Dutch ports in Java, Rhio, &c., are very considerable, amounting to close upon a million sterling. The chief items were to the following values :—

	£
Treasure	588,905
Tobacco	64,074
Rice	45,861
Pepper	38,861
Gambier	24,443
Coffee	20,382
Cottons	30,858
Birds'-Nests	11,349

Beside these, there are cloves, cassia, cinnamon, other spices. Nearly all of the pepper, gambier, coffee finds its way to Europe. The rice and birds'-nests are partly consumed in the Straits, and partly sent on to China.

13.—From Borneo, the principal imports were prepared sago, antimony ore, rattans, gutta-percha, from Sarawak, and coals from Labuan. The sago, as it is landed from Borneo, is simply the pith of the sago palm, scraped out and packed in small baskets; it is washed out, dressed, and prepared for the European market by the Chinese manufacturers in Singapore, who were the first to introduce the method of pearling, which has done so much to render it an article of consumption. In the notice of Malacca is an account of a tapioca manufactory. The processes are nearly similar. All the imports from Borneo, except coals, find their way to Europe; the coals are now being consumed by many of the steamers in the trade between India and China; but I believe they are too bituminous, and would be better suited for gas.

14.—The imports from the island of Celebes, which is the fifth in magnitude of the Archipelago, consist chiefly of sandal-wood, sapan-wood, coffee, and gutta-percha, the products of the island, and of mother-of-pearl, bartered for with the natives of New Guinea and other islands to the south-east of the Archipelago. Birds'-nests and a small quantity of bee's-wax also form items of importation from Celebes. The former are obtained at great risk of life from the caves along the rocky coasts of the surrounding islands; the latter is gathered from the forests of the interior without much difficulty, as the wild bees of the Archipelago build their hives like wasps at home, dropping from the branches of the large trees.

15.—From Sumatra, which is just on the other side of the Straits, opposite our own possessions, the more extensive articles of import are pepper, sago (raw), coffee, gutta-percha, gum benjamin, gum mastic, and ivory. Of pepper only a comparatively small quantity comes to Singapore, Penang being a much more convenient market to most of the native ports. Ivory comes also in small supplies, but it is said that the number of elephants on the island is decreasing.

16.—The imports stated as from the Malayan peninsula, do not include those from our own possessions in the Straits. They consist chiefly of rice, gutta-percha, and tin; but also include small supplies of ivory horns, hides, and birds'-nests.

17.—Under the head miscellaneous, in the general table, are included the imports from Penang, Malacca, and British Burmah. From Penang the imports are greatly speculative, and fluctuate according as prices may rise or fall at either port. From Malacca the chief imports are tin and tapioca, the former to the value of 388,357l. From British Burmah the imports are almost altogether made up of rice.

I now come to the exports for the same period as I have given the imports, that is, from the 1st of May, 1862, to the 30th of April, 1863; and as I began in the one case by giving a general table of the gross

lues of the imports from the various countries, I
l pursue the same course with the exports. These
ve been—

	£
Great Britain	652,217
North America	48,448
Europe	79,006
Australia	21,138
Calcutta	810,103
Madras	43,395
Bombay	137,085
China	1,249,137
Cochin China	323,992
Siam	325,254
Manila	19,620
Java, Rhio, &c.	557,490
Borneo	137,521
Celebes	90,317
Sumatra	72,489
Malayan Peninsula	197,858
Miscellaneous, including Malacca, Penang and British Burmah	790,503
Total	5,555,573

What they have consisted of may be gathered in a
eat measure from the table of imports. But a more
rticular inquiry may be useful.

1.—To Great Britain the chief articles of expor-
tion during the year have been,—

	£
Gambier	133,740
Tin	29,846
Sago	68,101
Tapioca	5,200
Black Pepper	109,549
Tortoise Shell	2,825
Mother-o'-Pearl	7,583
Gutta-Percha	103,606
Nutmegs and Mace	3,358
Camphor	17,170
White Pepper	18,318

Gum Elastic	$74,139
Coffee	47,955
Sapan-Wood	4,300
Sticlac	10,060
Rattans	4,278

Of these, gambier, black and white pepper, and nutmegs are the only articles of production on the island, and then only to about one-half of the value exported—gambier being also received in considerable quantities from Java, pepper from Sumatra, and nutmegs and mace from the Moluccas. Sago is imported in the raw state from Borneo and Sumatra, and manufactured here before exportation. Tin comes chiefly from Malacca, and the Native States of the Peninsula. Tortoiseshell and mother-o'-pearl from the far east of the Archipelago; gutta-percha from all over the Archipelago and Peninsula; camphor from China; coffee chiefly from Java and Sumatra; sapan-wood from Celebes, and sticlac from Siam and Cochin China.

2.—The exports to North America have been chiefly of gambier, pepper, gutta-percha, and rattans.

3.—To the continent of Europe the exports have been very nearly of the same character as those sent to Great Britain; but of course in considerably smaller quantities.

4.—The exports to Australia have consisted chiefly of tea, coffee, and sugar—the products probably of China and Java—and of pepper grown here.

5.—To Calcutta the exports exceed in value those to Great Britain, Europe and America put together; but this is owing almost entirely to the large amount of treasure which they include, as will be seen from the following table of the chief items :—

	£
Treasure	587,704
Sapan-Wood	3,544
Pepper	16,402
Cotton Goods	142,466
Camphor	10,971

Next to treasure, in this table, comes the exportation of piece-goods, which has been owing greatly to speculative ventures induced by the American war. The camphor exported comes from China. Besides these, are many other articles in smaller quantities, among which is Japan copper.

6, 7.—To Bombay and Madras the exports have chiefly been of treasure, cotton goods (speculative ventures), sugar, Japan copper, sapan-wood, articles of import from other countries—and nutmegs, pepper, and tin the products of the Straits.

8. The export trade to China has exceeded that to any other country, reaching nearly to a million and a quarter sterling. The chief items are,—

	£
Arms and Ammunition	35,731
Cotton Goods	135,872
Treasure	58,091
Rice	170,333
Rattans	35,183
Beech de mer	16,817
Birds'-Nests	33,977
Sapan and other Woods	33,472
Pepper	52,767
Betel-nut	12,837
Tin	299,455
Opium	144,656

The arms, ammunition and cotton goods are those which have first been imported from Europe. The

opium is, with the exception of a small quantity of
Turkey, the product of India. The rice is that of
Burmah, Java and Siam. Rattans, beech, &c.,
sapan-wood, and birds'-nests are from the islands of
the Archipelago. Pepper, betel-nut, and a great
portion of the tin, are, on the other hand, the products of the Straits.

9, 10.—To Cochin China and Siam, the exports
are similar in kind as they also are in amount.
The manufactured cotton of Europe, the opium of
India, and treasure for the purchase of produce are the
principal items.

11.—The exports to Manila are insignificant, and
are made up of sundry small articles of European
manufacture, and of opium.

12. To Java, Rhio, &c., the exports are considerable, consisting chiefly of the following :—

	£
Treasure	165,145
Opium	120,740
Cotton Goods	56,657
Silks	39,129
Rice	55,665

By reference to the imports previously stated, it
will be found that both treasure and rice are received
at Singapore in large quantities from Java; and it
certainly seems strange that they should here form
such a considerable proportion of the exports to that
country. Treasure, however, is subject to such fluc-
tuation, and is so easily affected in value by the
arbitrary rates of exchange which are from time to
time imposed, that its shipment to and fro is almost

a natural consequence. Rice is more generally an article of import from, than export to, Java; but the severe floods that from time to time desolate that country, create temporary scarcities which have to be supplied from abroad. The opium is from India, the cotton goods from Great Britain, and the silks from China.

13.—To Borneo, the exports which amounted to 167,521l., consisted chiefly of cotton goods, treasure, opium, rice and tobacco.

14.—To Celebes they have consisted principally of cotton goods, opium and gambier, which is eaten with the siri plant.

15.—The exports to Sumatra have been cotton manufactures, treasure, opium, and rice in small quantities.

16.—To the Malayan Peninsula, the exports have been very varied; but the following are the largest items :—

	£
Cotton Goods	40,861
Opium	58,759
Treasure	62,830
Silks	10,059
Rice	3,628

17.—Under the head of miscellaneous are included the exports to Penang, Malacca, British Burmah, and some other parts. The bulk of this part of our trade consists of transhipment and speculative exports to Penang, and the entire supply of Malacca which, with very trifling exceptions, comes through Sin-

These are the chief exports of Singapore. The
imports I have already considered; but as it may
assist materially in arriving at a distinct understanding of the trade of the port, I propose to give the
number of vessels which have arrived throughout the
year, with their tonnage and the places from which
they come. Of the junks and trading prahus which
frequent the port, no very reliable records are kept;
but about 200 arrive annually, and it is estimated that
they carry about an eighth part, in value, of the yearly
trade. The square-rigged vessels which arrived at
Singapore from the 1st May, 1862, to the 30th, 1863,
were—

From	No.	Tonnage.	From	No.	Tonnage.
Africa	2	273	Brought forward.	654	307,328
America	15	10,594	Hamburg	26	6,961
Amsterdam	7	2,740	Java	175	46,029
Arabia	3	2,005	Madras and coast	7	2,669
Arracan	4	3,048	Malacca	13	1,786
Australia	25	10,414	Malay Peninsula	25	5,637
Bally	15	3,120	Malta	3	3,962
Bombay and coast	47	37,784	Manila	9	4,545
Borneo	75	10,923	Mauritius	10	6,200
Bremen	3	1,000	Moulmein	5	1,904
Calcutta	58	33,999	New Zealand	3	1,803
Cape of Good			Penang	175	36,924
Hope	7	7,229	Rangoon	45	15,659
Celebes	16	2,327	Rhio	5	1,422
Ceylon	9	5,553	Siam	116	31,119
China	213	100,593	Spain	1	1,301
Cochin China	64	26,556	Sumatra	5	1,018
France	15	5,915	Tringanu and		
Great Britain	76	43,245	coast	2	214
Carried forward.	654	307,328	Total	1,279	471,441

The nationalities of these one thousand two hundred and seventy-nine vessels were:—

—	No.	Tonnage.	—	No.	Tonnage.
American	81	61,240	Brought ford....	590	224.462
Arabian	6	2,504	Oldenburg	1	616
Belgian	1	800	Portuguese	9	2,347
Bremen	23	11,372	Prussian	4	865
Chinese	2	290	Russian	4	2,023
Danish	30	7,151	Spanish	5	2,170
Dutch	279	70,401	Siamese	54	15,549
French	74	43,041	Swedish	4	2,583
Hamburg	58	22,310			
Hanoverian	4	1,103		671	250,615
Native States	29	3,181	British	608	220,826
Norwegian	3	1,069			
Carried forward..	590	224,462	Total	1,279	471,441

Such is the actual trade of Singapore, and such the channels through which it is conveyed. It will not be difficult to gather, from a comparison of the imports with the exports, confirmation of what was pointed out at starting, namely, that the consumption of the island is insignificant as compared with its imports, and that its production is even more disproportioned to its exports. It may be roundly stated that 90 per cent. of the European manufactures and Indian produce which are landed there, are again re-shipped further eastward, and that not 5 per cent. of the products exported to Great Britain, America, the Continent of Europe, and India, are of local

13

growth or manufacture. To no other port in the
world therefore can the designation of entrepôt be
more justly applied; and with this important fact,
and all its consequences prominently before their eyes,
it is impossible that either local or imperial legislators
can ever seek to encumber its free trade without being
guilty of the most wilful disregard of the national
interests.

And it must be borne in mind that imposts which
would produce no damaging effect upon the trade of
a European port, might have the most fatal effect
upon the trade of Singapore. A harbour due, a tonnage due, wharfage or anchorage charges, are all fair
enough means of reimbursing a Government for its
outlay on harbour improvements and facilities, and are
ordinarily understood and willingly acquiesced in. But
at Singapore it is very different. The native traders are
men altogether unable to distinguish the causes of a
particular impost, and fly from them all as from oppression; besides this, they know nothing of our
language or of our rules and regulations, and would
possibly have to entrust the agency of their shipping
business to some sharper of their own nationality, who
might practise fraud and extortion on them to any
extent.

The port of Singapore must not only be free from
burden, but the forms of business must be maintained
as plain and simple as possible.

Of the commerce of Penang and Malacca I am
unable to give the same details as I have given of
that of Singapore, and must deal more generally.

The imports at Penang for the year 1862–63 were
from the following countries and to the values opposite
each :—

IMPORTS.

	£
Great Britain	117,960
North America	4,850
Europe	26,956
Calcutta	197,741
Madras	52,574
Bombay	7,074
China	84,519
Siam	275,343
Sumatra	172,183
Malayan Peninsula	98,582
Miscellaneous, including Singapore, Malacca, and British Burmah	647,366
Total	£1,684,598

In kind they do not differ materially from those
of Singapore. From Great Britain, America, and
Europe, the imports are comparatively insignificant—
the manufactures of these countries for the greater
part finding their way through Singapore, the imports
from which amount to fully a third of the gross values
from all the other countries put together. It will
be seen, that the imports from Sumatra, consisting
chiefly of pepper, are nearly double the value of those
received from the same country at Singapore; but
they are nevertheless considerably smaller than they
were in previous years. This falling off is attributed
to the policy of the Dutch, who, it is suspected, are
pushing their way in Sumatra somewhat unfairly.
By the treaty between England and Holland of 1824
we evacuated our possession of Bencoolen, and gave
up all right and title which we might have to the

13—2

island of Sumatra to the Dutch, receiving Malacca
and the hitherto disputed supremacy of the Malay peninsula in return.   But by the 3rd article of that treaty
it was stipulated that no fresh treaties should be made
by either power with the native princes of the respective territories, exclusive of the trade of the other, or
imposing unequal duties thereupon.   It is strongly
suspected, however, that exclusive treaties have not-
withstanding been lately made by the Dutch in
Sumatra—and the suspicion receives confirmation
not only from the diminished imports of that island's
produce at Penang, but from various reports, more
or less reliable, from the native princes themselves.
All the protests, however, which may be made by the
Straits' merchants in the dark, must, from the terms
of the treaty of 1824, be unavailing; but it is certainly
high time that the Government of the Hague should
be asked for copies of whatever treaties their East
Indian authorities may have concluded in Sumatra.
Copies of these the Netherlands Government is bound
to furnish in terms of the 3rd article of the treaty
of 1824, and if they are found to be restrictive of
our trade, they should be at once disavowed.   If,
on the other hand, the terms are consonant to
all the articles of the old treaty, copies of them
should be placed in the hands of the Straits authorities, that their true intent and meaning may be made
known to the traders who still flock into the English
ports in the Straits, and thus be disseminated throughout the produce districts of Sumatra.

From Siam the imports, which exceed those from

the same country to Singapore, have consisted chiefly
of rice, a great portion of which crosses over for
consumption to Province Wellesley and the Native
States on the north-west coast of the Peninsula.

The exports from Penang for the same period as I
have given the imports, were as under :—

EXPORTS.

	£
Great Britain	453,623
North America	111,026
Europe	51,153
Calcutta	101,667
Madras	36,687
Bombay	13,228
China	155,046
Siam	253,155
Sumatra	310,496
Malayan Peninsula	236,562
Miscellaneous, including Singapore, Malacca, and British Burmah	669,466
Total (sterling)	£2,392,109

It will be seen that while in Singapore the exports
fall short in value of the imports, in Penang they
are nearly one-half more. There is also this difference between the ports, that while in Singapore the
local consumption and the local production are quite
insignificant as compared with its imports and exports; in Penang, on the other hand, the imports
are, with some trifling exceptions, consumed on the
island, in Province Wellesley, or in the adjacent Native
States, and the exports are entirely the production of
the same territories.

To Great Britain, America, and the Continent of
Europe, as indeed to most of the countries named

above, the chief articles of export are pepper, gambier, nutmegs, and sugar. The cultivation of pepper is not so extensive as it was in former years, and owing to the blight which has extended all over the Straits, it is probable that nutmegs will before very long cease altogether to be exported. The production of the other articles, especially of sugar in Province Wellesley, appears to be on the increase. Cotton is produced in small quantities, but according to the best authorities it is never likely to become a staple article of export. Indigo and nilam have also at times been exported in small quantities, and cocoanuts, siri, and betel-nut (the nuts of the Areca palm, or Penang tree, from which the island takes its name), are produced in tolerably large quantities, but chiefly consumed in the ports of the Straits.

The arrivals of square-rigged vessels in Penang have been for the years 1862–63 :—

From	No.	Tonnage.	From	No.	Tonnage.
America	3	1,373	Brought ford.....	98	44,404
Amsterdam	1	300	Great Britain	15	6,767
Arabia	8	4,048	Goa	2	607
Arracan	15	4,164	Hamburg	2	1,040
Australia	2	1,522	Madras and coast	31	7,043
Bombay and coast	12	6,574	Malacca	8	1,083
Bremen	1	238	Moulmein	21	2,991
Calcutta	17	9,188	Rangoon	94	9,848
Coringa	5	953	Siam	10	1,339
Ceylon	6	2,292	Spain	1	216
China	24	12,393	Singapore	177	54,591
France	3	1,259	Sumatra	56	6,603
Carried forward..	98	44,404	Total	514	136,434

Their nationalities being :—

—	No.	Tonnage.	—	No.	Tonnage.
American	18	7,999	Brought ford....	54	22,815
Arabian	6	8,680	Hamburg	4	1,670
Belgian	1	444	Native States	11	925
Bremen	5	1,200	Portuguese	15	4,578
Danish	3	758	Siamese	5	422
Dutch	11	2,329	British	425	106,015
French	15	6,414			
			Total	514	136,434
Carried forward..	54	22,815			

The proportion of trade carried by junks and native prahus is even greater at Penang than at Singapore.

The trade of Malacca, which at one time might be said to comprise the sum of European intercourse with the far East, is now comparatively unimportant. But the decline has not been under British rule ; on the contrary, since our final acquisition of the territory, the trade, as will be seen on reference to the comparisons made at the beginning of this chapter, has steadily progressed. Still, however, the commerce of Malacca is far from satisfactory and far from what it might be. The imports for 1862–63 were :—

IMPORTS.

	£
Calcutta	1,950
China	713
Sumatra	8,217
Malayan Peninsula	81,894
Jeddah	—
British Burmah	3,050
Miscellaneous, including Singapore and Penang	356,830
Total (sterling)	£452,654

The exports on the other hand were :—

	£
Calcutta	—
China	—
Sumatra	15,228
Malayan Peninsula	61,752
Jeddah	18
British Burmah	1,744
Miscellaneous, including Singapore and Penang	281,098
Total (sterling)	£359,840

The arrivals of square-rigged vessels at Malacca for the same year have been :—

From	No.	Tonnage.	From	No.	Tonnage.
Arabia	2	1,284	Brought ford....	92	16,331
Bombay	2	794	Rangoon	8	1,962
Calcutta	4	1,626	Singapore	152	26,733
Ceylon	1	192	Sumatra	2	284
Penang	83	12,435	Total	254	45,310
Carried forward.	92	16,331			

Their nationalities :—

	No.		Tonnage.
American	1	....	869
Arabian	6	..	3,954
Dutch	3	...	619
Native States	3	.....	210
Portuguese	1	...	220
British	240	.....	39,940
Total	254	.....	45,312

The number of junks trading to Malacca is not large.

It will be seen that the amount of the exports of produce is a fourth less than that of the imports; and this, for such a possession as Malacca, must I think be deemed an unwholesome state of trade. With an extensive tract of territory and a soil not only fertile but rich in mineral wealth, and a numerous population, the station is still unable to return to Singapore produce sufficient to pay for the value of the manufactures and other goods imported from it. The articles of import to Malacca consist chiefly of cotton manufactures and opium, received through Singapore and Penang; its exports are chiefly of tin, tapioca, and sago, besides fruit, fowls, and live stock, which, though they do not appear among the exports, are pretty regularly supplied to Singapore by a fleet of small schooners plying between the two ports. It was for many years thought that the prosperity of this station was retarded by the unsatisfactory nature of the land tenure, but about three years ago a new land bill was introduced which entirely removed whatever objections had previously been thought to exist, and yet no extension of cultivation resulted. Perhaps as tin is the chief article of export, the royalty on metal still reserved to the Crown should be abandoned, with a view to the further development of the metallurgic resources of the station.

Such is a brief epitome of the trade of the Straits. I have been careful that all the figures which I have given should be accurate and reliable, and for this purpose have taken the sum of the entries during the years indicated at the import and export offices of the three stations. But as there is no law to compel correct entries being made, or rather to punish those who neglect to make such, it is more than probable that these records fall somewhat short of the actual trade; especially so with that portion in the hands of native merchants. But gauged even by these records, the commerce of the Straits of Malacca assumes a magnitude which, resting as it does on but a precarious foundation, entitles it to all the solicitude which I have claimed for it at the outset of this chapter. The prosperity and progress of no country ever lay so completely at the mercy of its rulers. It is possible by one year of port imposts utterly to ruin the settlement; it is also possible by a liberal, enlightened, completely free-trade policy not only to maintain its present prosperity, but to make its progress keep pace with the development of the countries around it.

CHAPTER VIII.

OF the past Government of Singapore and the Straits
Settlement very little need be said; and that little
not all evil. Doubtless, the affairs of the Straits
have occupied but a small share in the deliberations
of the Council of India, and have systematically been
set aside to give place to the more pressing and
the undoubtedly more important concerns of the
Continental empire itself. The causes of this neglect
were manifold. The Straits formed an outlying station
fifteen hundred miles away from Calcutta, of a completely different character from India itself, unaffected
alike by its prosperity or misfortune. The races by

whom it was peopled were numerous and distinct, chiefly gathered together by immigration since it became a British possession, from whom no revolt was to be anticipated, and on whose account there was no anxiety felt for the safety of the settlement. Besides all this, the legislators of India being entirely ignorant themselves of what could benefit or what would injure the Straits, and unwilling to trust too implicitly to the representations of the individual whom they from time to time placed there as Governor, preferred pretty well to refrain from legislating altogether.

It must be admitted, however, that at no time has the Indian Government sought to derive a profit out of the Straits. The most it has done was to endeavour to raise the revenue to a sum sufficient to cover the military as well as the civil expenditure, and though the former is not a just charge to impose upon the Straits, not at least to its full extent, still it is one for the cost of which the Indian Exchequer has every right to be refunded. For protection against internal revolt the military are not needed, and if retained for any other purpose the cost of their support ought to be matter for adjustment with the Imperial Government, not a charge upon India. But, not to anticipate, it is only in the last year, 1863-64, that the endeavour has really been carried out, and that the revenue has been raised by fresh taxation, in the shape of a stamp duty, to a sum equal to refund India for the military expenditure. During the long years that preceded this last, India has suffered and suffered patiently a yearly drain upon her treasury on account of the Straits settlements of over 30,000*l*.

With respect to the want of legislation, too, it may be doubted whether the Straits has really suffered much on this account.   Certainly there is less risk to a country in men who are ignorant of its wants abstaining from legislating altogether, than in hurrying enactment upon enactment with ill-directed haste. So I think it has proved with Singapore.   Founded and its earlier development watched over by men of the enlightened policy of Sir Stamford Raffles and Mr. Crawfurd, it only required to be allowed to grow up unmolested to maturity to present the picture of prosperity which it now does; and perhaps had the zeal even of those on the spot most interested in its progress, been permitted at all times to display itself in multitudinous reformatory enactments, the result would not have been so satisfactory.   Indeed, I consider that when the Government becomes local, it will require to carefully avoid hasty or revolutionary legislation.   Stability lays claim to first respect in the native mind, and any policy that would seek to be constantly altering the laws and administration of Government even for the sake of improving them would be a disastrous one.

When the Indian Government hands over the Straits settlements to the Crown, it will deliver a trust honestly kept and well deserving the solicitude of its new guardians.   It has shown, too, an example of high-minded forbearance in abstaining to check the growth of a promising colony to save its own

treasury, an example which, though owing to impai
resources it need not now be followed by the Imp
Government, should nevertheless be set down wi
colony's history against any day of unforeseen cal
With the new colony, the Indian Government
also hand over to the Crown a revenue ready
ample in all respects, and gathered in a manner
leaves trade and industry unburdened, and lays
pressure chiefly upon native vice and luxury.

From the time of its foundation till 1805, Pe
was subordinate to Bengal; from that date till 1
it ranked as an independent presidency. During
first four years of its settlement, Singapore was
dependency of Bencoolen; for the next two year
was placed under the Bengal Government, and
1825 both it and Malacca, which had in that
come finally into our possession, were united
Penang, and formed for the first time "the
porated settlement of Prince of Wales' Island,
gapore and Malacca," by which title the three
are still officially designated. For four years
incorporated settlement continued the fourth presid
of India, but in 1829 it was deprived of the
expensive distinction, and placed once more und
Bengal Government, in which condition of depen
and with no alteration whatever in the form
administration, it has remained down to the pr
day.

The Governor, who is placed with supreme
control over the three settlements, is the appoi
and representative of the Bengal Government.

a long time after their incorporation the chief seat
of government was Penang, but now and for many
years back, the Governor's residence is in Singapore,
and he spends only about three months of each
year between the two other stations. Under the
Governor, there are three Resident Councillors: one
at Penang as sort of Lieutenant Governor; another
at Singapore as secretary and treasurer to Government;
and the third at Malacca as the Governor's representative there. In each station there is either one or
two Assistant Resident Councillors, who, except in
the absence of their chiefs, discharge the duties of
police magistrates or other appointments of a similar
nature. The Governor and the Resident Councillors
may be said to comprise the executive government,
collecting and disbursing the revenue, registering the
trade, conducting the diplomatic and political corre-
spondence, and having supervising control over all
the other departments.

The Public Works Department is under a chief
engineer and an executive engineer. The municipal
works of each station are under separate and partly
elective commissions. There is a Commissioner of
Police with a deputy and staff at each station, under
the executive of course, but partly paid from the
municipal funds. There is also at each station a
police magistrate, a marine magistrate and master
attendant, and a Court of Requests with a commissioner
to adjudicate on civil suits of trifling value. The
military throughout the Straits consists at present of
two regiments of Madras Native Infantry, and three

garrison batteries of European artillery, under the
disposition of a brigadier resident at Singapore. The
incumbents of nearly all the chief offices of Government are military men of the Indian army; there
is no covenanted civil service as in India, but I do
not propose to consider here either the personnel of
the Government, or particularly the nature of the
various offices. Further on will be found a list of
the salaries attached to all the chief Government
appointments. My object is to get as directly as
possible to the revenue and expenditure; the former
a matter of paramount interest just now to the
Imperial Government, and the latter involving some
questions of great importance both to the settlement
and to the mother country, such as the military
defence and fortifications.

Before passing on to these, however, I ought perhaps to notice here the singular advantages which
the Straits settlement has always possessed in the
administration of justice. From their establishment
each of the stations has possessed a supreme court
of judicature, in which English law, civil and criminal,
has been administered as in the courts of Westminster.
Up till 1855 only one judge presided at the three
courts, upon circuit, but in that year an additional
judge was appointed. The courts of Singapore and
Malacca are now presided over by one, and that of
Penang by the other. To the non-official community
these courts have served the purpose of a representative institution, and have always been a wholesome
check upon the mal-administration of Government.

In earlier times, when the Company's servants, responsible only to an indifferent council at Calcutta, paid little regard to the interest and little respect for the opinion of the mercantile residents, the supreme court remained as a place of appeal where the grand jurors might from time to time raise their voice in such a manner that it could not well be disregarded. The judges have always been men of standing and ability, barristers of the courts at home, whose acquirements were such as to obtain for them from their sovereign the distinction of knighthood, in addition to the honour of an appointment of no small value. They were completely secured from the Indian authorities, and, by supporting the presentations of their grand juries, have done good service to the settlement independent of the value of their ordinary duties.

The sources of revenue, while they are certain, have the advantage of being few. The excise farms alone, being more than two-thirds of the gross income; the following being the revenue derived from all sources for the past official year; that is, from 1st May, 1863, to 80th April, 1864 :—

	£
Excise and other farms	137,521
Land and forests	6,705
Stamp tax	26,175
Law and justice	9,957
Public works	4,222
Marine	4,300
Miscellaneous	3,029
Total	191,909

The system of excise farming, or yearly selling

14

out to the highest bidder the excise sources of revenue, is one, I believe, peculiar in a great measure to China and the European settlements in India and the Archipelago. It was first adopted by the Dutch, who early found it the only practicable method of collecting a revenue derived from a restriction tax upon the consumption of luxuries. It was copied from the Dutch by the English at Penang shortly after the occupation of that island, and has ever since continued in operation in the Straits. In later years it has been imitated by the King of Siam, by Rajah Sir James Brooke at Sarawak, and by the French at Saigon; and no one at all acquainted with the actual working of this revenue system will doubt its many advantages in a country where a small dominant race have the government of an extensive mixed population.

The frauds to which any European Government would be subjected were it attempting in such a possession as Singapore to exact an excise revenue by a paid establishment, would be so serious as to reduce the product by one-half, and at the same time, expose to corruption its own servants. Even could the men be spared, no staff of purely European officers could contend against the trickery and evasions of the Chinese and other elements in the populations. "Set a thief to catch a thief," and set a native to detect fraud on the part of his countryman. But unfortunately native constabulary in Government pay are notoriously incompetent to resist temptation, and what would be gained in some cases by their greater skill and cunning would be lost in others by their dishonesty. With the farmers—usually Chinese of large capital—it is otherwise. They employ men of their own country and caste against their own countrymen, on a principle of gradually descending responsibility, which renders fraud difficult; or, as is frequently the case, subdivide their farm and ensure themselves against imposition by selling the subdivisions to smaller farmers under them for sums certain. The profit obtained by the farmers above the amounts paid by them to Government is often considerable, but it is not more than would be the cost of collection by a paid establishment, and the taxes yield their full product, which I think they would fail to do under any other treatment. Indeed, a system of descending responsibility in the collection of revenue is adopted not only by the Chinese but by most of the native rajahs throughout the Archipelago, though not in the nature of farming. When in the Island of Lombock some years ago, I became acquainted with a rather singular method of detecting the abuse of this responsibility adopted by the rajah of that populous and important island. The rajah's revenues, derived from a head tax, were falling sadly short, apparently without any decrease of the population. After sore tribulation as to the probable cause of the deficit and the means of detecting it, he hit upon an idea which he wisely kept to himself. It was the custom of himself and his forefathers to repair every year to the summit of a high mountain and sleep there alone one whole night, during which slumber God was believed to reveal any important

14—2

danger that threatened the country or people, as also the means of averting it. This year when the day came round, the mountain was ascended in great pomp by the entire court to within a hundred feet of its summit. When nightfall came, the rajah leaving his attendants behind, proceeded alone to the summit, and having spread his mat lay down to sleep. In the morning at daybreak he rejoined his courtiers and announced that he had been vouchsafed a most wonderful dream. God had appeared to him and told him that a desolating plague would that year overrun his and the neighbouring countries; but all who chose might be protected from it by sending in to the palace a single steel needle, not more or less, for himself and his wife and each of his children if he had them. Of these needles the rajah was to have two large swords made and to hang them in the temple, and they would be a protection to all those who had contributed towards their material. Needles came pouring in by the bushel; each chief sending those from the people of the district over which he ruled. When the contributions were announced as complete, the wily rajah, instead of having them melted down had every one carefully counted over, and in his hall of state confronted each chief with the number of needles received from his district in one hand and the poll-tax returns in the other. The dream was a useful one to the rajah, next year his revenue increased by more than one-half.

European houses of business or individuals never compete for the purchase of the Government farms

in the Straits, as the difficulties in the way of the
direct collection of excise by Government would be
opposed to them in even a greater degree; for while
they would have to rely upon a native excise service,
they would lack that respect which the authority of
Government gives its officers. The Chinese are the
only other class who have capital, energy, and system
sufficient for the successful management of a revenue,
and from the beginning, the chief farms have continued
in their hands.* The policy of letting out the revenue
in this way has frequently been called in question on
the grounds that the servants of the former might
take advantage of their quasi authority and become
oppressive and extortionate; but there would be the
same chance of this with Government excise officers,
and against oppression on the part of the farmers,
the people know they will much more easily find
redress in our courts than against similar treatment
on the part of Government officers. Besides, all fines
for the infringement of the farmers' rights must be
recovered in the magistrate's court, and no illicit opium
or spirits can be seized except through the instru-
mentality of the police. For my own part, I think
that almost every source of revenue from taxation
might, in a country peopled as Singapore is, be farmed
out with advantage, provided the tax in no way
affected trade or commerce. The farms in the Straits

---

* The only farm which is not held by Chinese, is the excise upon
toddy and baing; these two articles are consumed in the greatest
measure by natives of India, and the farms have generally been purchased by people of that nationality.

are now four in number; they are sold in April each
year to the highest bidder either for one or for two
years according to the nature of the farm. During
the year that closed on the 30th of April last the
farms at Singapore brought the following yearly
rentals respectively :—

	£
Opium	64,829
Toddy and bāng	1,196
Spirits	25,852
Pawnbrokers	5,491
Total	96,868

The gross returns of the same farms at Penang
and Malacca for the same period was 40,953l.

The opium farm, which is essentially a tax on the
Chinese, gives the exclusive right to prepare and
retail that drug. In the condition in which it is
imported from Calcutta and Bombay, opium is a very
different article from that which administers to the
sensual enjoyment of the consumer, and the conversion
of the imported article to chandoo, or the treacly
consistency required for smoking, is one of the mono-
polies secured for the protection of the farmer. The
opium is received from Calcutta in boxes containing
forty balls each of the size of a 32 lb. cannon shot.
These balls have an outer husk of compressed poppy-
leaves, and contain a certain quantity of moist opium
inside, but which in this state is unfit for consumption;
so that, as long as the privilege of reducing it to
chandoo remains with the farmer, he is tolerably safe
in the enjoyment of his exclusive privilege to sell
for consumption. The method of reducing the drug

is thus described in an interesting paper on the habitual use of opium in Singapore :—*

Between three and four o'clock in the morning, the fires are lighted. A chest is then opened by one of the officers of the establishment of the opium farmer, and the number of balls delivered to the workmen is proportioned to the demand. The balls are then divided into equal halves by one man, who scoops out, with his fingers, the inside or soft part, and throws it into an earthen dish, frequently during the operation moistening and washing his hands in another vessel, the water of which is carefully preserved. When all the soft part is carefully abstracted from the hardened skins or husks, these are broken up, split, divided and torn, and thrown into the earthen vessel containing the water already spoken of, saving the extreme outsides, which are not mixed with the others, but thrown away, or sometimes sold to adulterate chandoo in Johore and the back of the island.

The second operation is to boil the husks with a sufficient quantity of water in a large shallow iron pot for such a length of time as may be requisite to break down thoroughly the husks and dissolve the opium. This is then strained through folds of China paper, laid on a frame of basketwork, and over the paper is placed a cloth. The strained fluid is then mixed with the opium scooped out in the first operation, and placed in a large iron pot, when it is boiled down to the consistence of thickish treacle. In this second operation, the refuse from the straining of the boiled husk is again boiled in water, filtered through paper, and the filtered fluid added to the mass to be made into chandoo. The refuse is thrown outside and little attended to. It is dried and sold to the Chinese going to China, for three to five dollars per picul, who pound it and adulterate good opium with it. The paper that has been used in straining contains a small quantity of opium—it is carefully dried and used medicinally by the Chinese in hæmorrhoids, prolapsus ani, and a few other complaints.

The third operation : the dissolved opium being reduced to the consistence of treacle, is seethed over a fire of charcoal of a strong and steady, but not fierce temperature, during which time it is most carefully worked, then spread out, then worked up again and again by the superintending workman, so as to expel the water, and at the same time avoid burning it. When it is brought to the proper consistence, it is divided into half a dozen lots, each of which is spread like a plaster on a nearly flat iron pot to the depth of from half to three-quarters of an inch, and then scored in all manner of directions to allow the heat to be applied equally to every part. One pot after another is then placed over the fire, turned rapidly round, then reversed, so as to expose the opium itself to the full heat of the red fire. This is repeated three times; the

---

* By R. Little, Esq., M.D.

length of time requisite and the proper heat are judged of by the workman from the effluvium and the colour, and here the greatest dexterity is requisite, for a little more fire, or a little less, would destroy the morning's work, or 300 or more dollars' worth of opium. The best workmen are men who have learned their trade in China, and, from their great experience, receive high wages.

The fourth operation consists in again dissolving this fired opium in a large quantity of water, and boiling it in copper vessels till it is reduced to the consistency of the chandoo used in the shops, the degree of tenacity being the index of its complete preparation, which is judged of by drawing it out with slips of bamboo.

By this long process many of the impurities in the opium are got rid of, and are left in the refuse thrown out, such as vegetable matter, a part of the resin and oil, with the extractive matter, and a little narcotine. By the seething process the oil and resin are almost entirely dissipated, so that the chandoo or extract, as compared with the crude opium, is less irritating and more soporific. The quantity of chandoo obtained from the soft opium is about 75 per cent.; but from the gross opium, that is, including the opium and the husk, the proportion is not more than from 50 to 54 per cent.

Opium-smoking is undoubtedly a vice, and to some over sensitive minds the deriving of a revenue from it may appear a moral dereliction; but it is a subject which must be dealt with in a practical spirit, and there can be no question that unless we are prepared to interdict the use of opium altogether in our possessions in the Straits, and to double or treble our police to keep the interdict effective, we can work no improvement whatever on the present system. Now in the first place, I question seriously if we, a small, foreign, though governing race, have the right to suppress in a large people the indulgence of a vice of this sort provided it does not directly affect good order; certainly to exercise that right with any show of justice we must first close our public-houses and stop our imports and manufacture of strong drinks; and in the second place, no settlement such as the Straits could spare the cost of a police sufficiently strong for this suppression without a taxation seriously trenching upon the industry of its people.

Next to the suppression of the vice is its regulation and confinement within reasonable bounds, and for this purpose the farming system is I think well suited. I cannot go the length, as I notice some local writers on this subject have gone, of saying that the main object of the farm at its establishment was the restriction of opium consumption. With the East India Company revenue was a matter of considerably greater solicitude than the moral condition of the large populations under their rule; and there can be very little question that the opium farm had its origin in the necessities of the local exchequer. But the fact that it has continued to contribute fully one-half of the revenue of the settlements has not deprived it of its beneficial influence. By greatly enhancing the cost to the consumer the consumption is kept within narrow bounds. To the labouring classes it is all but banned and forbidden fare, and even to the rich its indulgence to excess would be a serious item of expenditure. Besides this, the consumer is supplied by the farmer, though at a high price, with good sound opium free from the baneful adulteration to which so precious a drug would be subject if an unrestricted traffic were allowed. Altogether the opium farm is a source of revenue to the Straits of which no friendly councillor will seek to deprive it.

Toddy and baáng are purely native indulgences. Both are intoxicating, and therefore may fairly be

subjected to a tax on the consumption. This
however realizes but a small sum, generally
speaking, from the fact that the farmer's duty is
large and that the consumption of both is
to a small section of the inhabitants. Toddy, the
sap of the cocoanut-tree, drawn by an incision in
the upper and greener part. It possesses
property; it is a fine wholesome refreshing
when newly collected, is strongly stimulating a
hours afterwards, and when kept for twenty-four
a very small allowance indeed will suffice to
the most hardened drinker. Baáng is obtained from
a small bush not unlike the flax-plant, and is a
harsh narcotic like tobacco; it is both chewed and
smoked by the natives of India. The toddy and
baáng farm is, as already stated, the only one not
rented by Chinese.

The spirit farm, which is next in value to that of
opium, deserves no particular allusion; it confers a
right to tax at a certain rate the retail of all liquors
containing alcohol, except toddy and baáng. The
nature of the pawnbroker's farm may be gathered
from its name; it confers the exclusive right to
advance small sums of money upon pledged articles;
but it is strongly illustrative of a feature in the
character of the native population, that in Singapore
alone, where there are not 100,000 souls, the farmer
can pay a premium of 450l. a month for the monopoly
of the pawnshops. Buying and selling it is said is
an indication of fair civilization; and mortgaging,
which followed long afterwards in mercantile history,

one of positive refinement. If this be so the native population have carried their refinement to a high point.

The Government farms were not always confined to their present number. In the earlier days of the settlement there were several others; some of them were trifling and unimportant, but there was one which ranked next to, if indeed it did not take precedence of, that of opium—this was the gambling farm. It was established at the same time as the others, and abolished in 1829 on a presentment of the grand jury of Singapore. Some of those grand jurors have lived to bear witness to the error they committed when, yielding more to the influence of official blandishments than to their own convictions, they recommended the Supreme Government to sacrifice a large revenue, and at the same time withdraw the most wholesome restriction which it is possible to impose upon a popular vice. The preponderance of public opinion now is certainly in favour of the farm, and several agitations have been begun with a view to urge its reintroduction upon Government; but the fact that no additional revenue was acknowledged by the community to be required has doubtless prevented public opinion taking such a decisive form as it might have done under other circumstances.

Gambling is an inherent vice in three-fourths of the population of the Straits. Legislation has done all that it can to suppress it, and that all has been futile. It has increased steadily with the population. The interdict we have placed upon it has only served to drive it from daylight to darkness—from open, life and moderate gaming to surreptitious, stolen, and unbounded indulgence, where the simple can be victimized by the crafty with impunity, and where violence and bloodshed may be resorted to with little fear of detection. As with the use of opium, no police that the settlement can afford to maintain will be able to do more than drive the vice into hiding-places. The cases which are brought before the magistrates, indicate a very fair activity on the part of the police; and though the fines inflicted after conviction are as heavy as they can be made consistantly with the nature of the offence, yet they and the exposure, fail altogether of their effect as a deterrent to others, and the charge-sheet of the magistrates' court continues to show an undiminished daily crop of offenders. Indeed, the vice would appear to gain strength from the very difficulties we oppose to it. It has frequently come to light that fines which are levied upon individuals have been refunded by subscriptions made over the next night's gaming-table. The chances of detection and of fine seem to be well calculated, and to be looked upon and provided for simply as a premium on the play—just as a farmer's tax would be. Those who question the morality of a gambling-farm, therefore, would do well to reflect that, in point of fact, the settlement now derives a very heavy addition to its revenue from gambling. The money collected in the magistrate's court in Singapore alone from fines on gambling for the first four months of the present year (1864), and handed over to the court

cipal fund for public purposes, was, in round numbers,
6,112 dollars, or 1,370*l*., and the only practical difference between swelling our revenue with these fines,
and drawing the produce of a gambling farm, is that,
in the one case we heavily tax those few unfortunates
only whom we detect in the indulgence, and, in the
other, we should tax all who actually do indulge in
the vice.*

It is amusing the stratagems to which some of
the wealthier if not of the better classes resort to
obtain peaceable enjoyment of a good day's gambling.
Invitations, often printed, are issued ostensibly for a
picnic to be held in some lonely district of the jungle,
where the police would have no little difficulty to find
them out. One of these printed circular invitations
was placed in my hands by the Commissioner of Police
at Singapore. It is an amusing document, and I give
it in facsimile. Where or by whom they had got it
printed it is difficult to say.

Mr. Quang Coon Lee presents his best Compliments to Mr. Tan
Gee Wok, and requests the pleasure of his Company to Pic-Nic
Entertainments, on Sunday next the 20th Instant at Salang Tiga, Bukit
Timah Road, Plantation of Kim Tiang Hoo, next door of Beng Lee's
Plantation, and also be requested all his Amiable invitors will start at
5 A.M. punctually on that day.

The favour of an answer is obliged.

SINGAPORE,
15th March, 1864.

---

* Not only are these fines appropriated to public purposes as stated,
but they have actually come to be calculated upon as a part of the
revenue. That I am not mistaken in this, the following extract from the
annual report of the president of the Municipal Commissioners for 1863
will show. The president in this case was also resident councillor, or
next in authority to the Governor. After alluding to the items of revenue

If it was only at those picnic entertainments that
illicit gambling went on, there would be little to fear
beyond what evil there is in the vice itself; for though
surreptitiously indulged in as far as the police are
concerned, there is sufficient openness and generally
honour in such gaming to secure against foul play or
violence. But the great bulk of gambling is carried
on by those who cannot afford to send out printed
invitations, and indulge for a whole day in a country
picnic. These are forced for concealment into hidden
dens in the lowest slums of the town, where, if they
are secure from the police, they need place no limit
of time or money on their play, and may fearlessly
resort to any extremes which may be prompted by
the fortunes of the game. Indeed, there is something
in the necessity for concealment which of itself re-
moves a natural and wholesome restraint upon the
gambler; for if to gamble is to break the law, he
must feel that as a law breaker he has already placed
himself beyond the social pale; and it is well known
with this consciousness how reckless in other respects
such men become. It is beyond all doubt, too, that
to be secure against interruption, these town gaming
parties extensively bribe the police. In the entire
police force of Singapore, numbering over 400 men,
there are only six Europeans, and the native races
of which the bulk is composed are notoriously weak

which showed an improvement. the report says:—" The increase of
revenue from the above sources is, however, unfortunately counterbalanced by a heavy decrease in magistrates' fines and fees—a falling off
equivalent to a fourth of the revenue derived from this same source last
year, a sum of more than 5,000 dollars."

against bribery. A case was brought to light about four years ago where a systematic receiving of bribes was proved to have been practised, and this not by the native police only, but by some of the European as well. To the gamblers it is a simple calculation what their chances of detection and fine against an unfriendly police amounts to, and if they can compromise the risk by payment to the constables of a lesser sum beforehand, they gladly do so.

The consequences of the present system as compared with that under the farm, may shortly be summed up to be an even greater practice of the vice—a clandestine indulgence without stint or regulation, and a corrupt police. With a farm—such as that which was abolished thirty-five years ago—the vice would be heavily and evenly taxed; it would be forced within reasonable bounds—would be fair and open, and free from scenes of violence. There would be a certain number of gaming-houses in each district; these would be open at certain hours only, and subject to rules and regulations, for the observance of which the farmer would be responsible. A number of police peons might be present at each gaming-house as a guarantee against violence; and the public would have free access to them at all times, and habitual gamesters thus become marked men. By such a farm the police would not only be kept pure, but be relieved of a very large part of their present labour. The farmer would have an organized system of espionage, independent of, though subject to, the general supervision of the police. It is possible that illicit gambling

might still go on, and that the officers of the farmer
would be bribed, as the police are under the present
system; but though possible, it is very unlikely. The
premium charged by the farmer would probably amount
to less than would be the cost of bribery; and, besides,
even if such bribery did take place, it would have a
very different consequence from the corruption of the
police upon whom the settlement must depend otherwise for so much.

Nor do I think there is any good reason why such
a question should not be openly and seriously considered from a revenue point of view, and some estimate be made of the amount likely to be realized when
a gambling farm is re-introduced. The same maudlin
morality that would, with a knowledge of all the
relative advantages of the farm, reject such a source
of income to the state, must, to be consistent, reject
also every excise possessed by the settlement. Indeed
it almost appears to me that, strictly speaking, there
are better grounds for abandoning a revenue derived
from the licensing of spirit-drinking and opium-smoking
than from a tax on gambling; for whereas the
former vices permanently injure the constitution, the
latter, directly at least, affects the pocket only.
With regard to all such taxes, I would set it down
as a rule, that where a government finds itself either
without the right or without the power to suppress
a popular vice, the taxation of that vice becomes a
much more legitimate source of revenue than a
burden laid upon honest industry.

Of the probable returns of a gambling farm

very accurate test can be obtained by a reference to those years in which it was in operation. In Singapore the farm existed from 1820–29, and during those nine years it took precedence of all other sources of revenue. The returns in dollars for that period of the three principal farms at Singapore were :—

— —	Opium.	Spirits.	Gambling.
	Dollars.	Dollars.	Dollars.
1820-21	7,345	3,305	5,275
1821-22	9,420	5,115	7,335
1822-23	14,200	7,700	9,500
1823-24	22,830	8,270	15,076
1824-25	24,000	9,600	25,680
1825-26	24,030	12,000	33,657
1826-27	24,600	12,000	30,390
1827-28	24,720	12,180	32,616
1828-29	32,640	15,600	33,864

·It will be seen from these that the gambling farm increased with the population more steadily and in a greater ratio than either that of opium or of spirits; so that the increase which it would if continued have made up to the present day, may at the least be taken as equal to that made by the opium and spirit farm. From the table of farms first given, it will be found that in 1863–64 the produce of the opium farm is nine times, and that of the spirit farm seven times, greater now than they were respectively in 1828–29; taking the mean of these rates, the sum realized from the gambling farm in 1828–29 has to be multiplied eight times to give its present value, which would therefore be for Singapore 205,000 dollars, and adding a third for Penang and Malacca 273,000 dollars, or equal to 61,000*l*. for the entire settlement yearly. Here then

15

lies a sure and legitimate source of income, equal to close upon one-third of the present gross revenue, ready to pour into the Colonial exchequer when occasion shall require and when her statesmen shall have the power and shall grow bold enough to legislate according to her best interests, independent of the clamour of a distant sect alike uninformed and uninterested.

The revenue derived from land and forests is not great, nor can it be expected materially to increase. It comprises not the sums derived from the sale of unoccupied land, but only rents, quit-rents of land conditionally alienated and the amounts paid for commutation of quit-rents, together with a small sum for the right to cut timber on waste lands. The sums received for the sale of land are carried to a deposit account against the public debt and do not appear at all as revenue. In the early days of the Company the fee simple was seldom parted with; and both town and country lands were sold for a term of years only, subject to a small annual payment. From official carelessness and other blunders, however, some grants, both at Penang and Singapore, appear from the first to have been held in perpetuity, and in later years, when the giving to purchasers a permanent interest in the soil became an acknowledged principle in good government, the sales were made in fee simple or next thing to it, and every facility offered to previous holders to convert their leases to the same tenure on equitable terms. As this process of conversion is still going on, and as no new rents are now being reserved, the land revenue so far must gradually decline, but the increased value of the unsold lands as they are brought to market will probably compensate for this in another way.

According to estimates drawn up by the surveyor-general in 1860, it appears that in Singapore there were at that time about 25,000 acres under cultivation and about 120,000 lying waste, of which probably five-sixths or 100,000 acres remained in the hands of Government. In Penang there were in the same year 7,500 acres, and in Province Wellesley 50,000 acres, available for sale. In Malacca the territory is much more extensive, measuring over 1,000 square miles; and of this 250 are calculated to be under cultivation, and the remaining 750 to be disposable in the hands of Government. When we came into possession of Malacca it was found that nearly one-half of the territory had been granted away by the Dutch some fifty years before to private hands on somewhat peculiar terms. To buy up these rights our Government granted annuities to the aggregate value of nearly 2,000l., and also agreed to the somewhat extraordinary condition that these lands should, in the event of the settlement being abandoned by our Government or transferred to any other Power, be returned to the representatives of the annuitants. This condition long remained a stumbling-block in the disposal of these lands, it being impossible for our Government to grant them in fee simple. This difficulty has now been removed however—somewhat arbitrarily it is true—by the late Land Act, so that the whole of the waste lands of Malacca may be said to be at

15—2

the disposal of Government. The disposable land then in the British possession in the Straits of Malacca is as under :—

Singapore	100,000 acres.
Penang	7,000 ,,
Province Wellesley	50,000 ,,
Malacca	400,000 ,,
Total	557,000 acres,

which, valued at the minimum selling price of five rupees, or ten shillings per acre, gives a sum of 278,000*l.* as a standing capital to the settlement, either to be gradually gathered in at improved rates, or ready at any moment to be pledged for its necessities.

The stamp-tax, which is now a considerable source of revenue, was only introduced at the beginning of last year. Great outcries were made against it by the mercantile community, who based their remonstrances first on the assertion that no further revenue was required, and that the settlement already paid all her legitimate expenses; and secondly on the nature of the tax itself, which they declared was an infringement of that free-trade policy which it is so essential to maintain in the government of these dependencies. The first objection however was unreasonable as applied to India, for though the existing revenue was equal to the civil expenditure, still it left the military almost entirely unprovided for; and however small a share the settlement ought to have to pay of its military defence, India ought certainly to have to pay none, as it derives no advantage therefrom; and, if there are only the two pair of shoulders on which to lay the burden, those of the settlement ought certainly to bear it. So at least thought the Indian authorities, and those at home too it would appear, for the remonstrances of the Chamber of Commerce to both were alike disregarded. As to the nature of the tax itself the objections were scarcely better founded, because a stamp duty has always been found a very fair means of raising a revenue and not particularly burdensome upon mercantile transactions, as on all but legal documents it amounts only to a fractional percentage. At all events it has not as yet, after eighteen months' operation, proved any perceptible restraint on the business of the Straits; and the merchants have done their best to turn its burden away from themselves by making it a regular recognized charge upon their constituents at home.

The product of the tax during the year 1863-64, for which I have stated the general revenue, has been so regular from month to month as to permit it to be taken as a tolerably certain index of its value in time to come. The following are the monthly returns at Singapore during the year :—

		£
1863—May		1,672
	June	1,322
	July	1,670
	August	1,636
	September	1,972
	October	1,583
	November	1,526
	December	1,681
1864—January		2,308
	February	1,460
	March	1,879
	April	1,919
	Total	£ 20,637

The returns of Penang and Malacca are mainly as regular, and bring the gross amount realized for the year up to 26,175*l*.

The fourth item I have set down in the account of revenue includes all fees received by the registrars of the two divisions of the Supreme Court of Judicature, the Commissioners of the Courts of Requests, and the Deputy Sheriffs; all unclaimed property of intestates, also all fines and forfeitures except those levied at the police courts which go to the municipal funds. The fees of the Supreme Court form perhaps the largest part of the sum set down under this head; these were, until lately, the perquisites of the registrars, who received them in lieu of salaries; they were very large, and it is asserted that the incomes of the registrars were, at one time, greater than those of the judges of the court. However this may be, there is no doubt that the change to fixed salaries was ill relished by them. I have certainly heard one of the registrars talk bitterly of the Act that "robbed him of his fees." Litigation appears to be a weakness with some sections of the native population, and there is no lack of business for the court in its civil jurisdiction, nor does there appear to be any lack of agents to conduct it, the number of practitioners authorised to plead at the bar of the court numbering no less than thirteen in Singapore alone.

Under the head of Public Works are included the rents of public markets, that are let out yearly by public auction at the same time as the farms, rents of Government bungalows and other buildings. Under

Marine, are placed rights of Government steamers, light dues, hospital charges recovered, and sale of coals and stores to H.M.'s steamers, &c. As to light dues, though no European ship-owner would ever grudge to pay such a tax, they might, I think, if the revenue could spare it, be abolished; the sum they yield is not great—barely amounting to 2,000l. annually—and they interfere with that absolute freedom of the port which it is desirable that the Straits settlement should maintain in name as well as in substance.

In addition to the ordinary revenue, but distinct from it, is the municipal fund of each station. These are supplied by assessment upon dwelling-houses and carriages, supplemented also to a large extent by the fines recovered at the magistrate's courts. In Singapore the municipal receipts for last year amounted to 25,207l., of which sum 22,233l. was derived from assessment and other sources, and 2,974l. from the magistrate's court. From these funds are defrayed the entire cost of the maintenance of the police force at each station, the cost of maintaining the public roads and bridges within a certain radius of the towns, and all other expenditures connected with municipal affairs. The administration of them is entrusted to committees, consisting partly of nominee or official members, and partly of members elected by a majority of the rate-payers. The expenditure of the Singapore fund for last year was 22,963l., of which 9,990l. was for the police establishment.

Such are the purely local sources of the revenue of the settlement, and they could scarcely be more satis-

factory. The yield of the Excise duty, two-
thirds of the gross income, can be ad.....
increase or decrease of the population.....
favourably and adversely by the latter, and .....
of Government will probably rise or fall by ......
causes, so far the revenue will be self-adjusting .....
stamp-tax, which forms the next largest source .....
be affected chiefly by commercial prosperity or .....
tion, and it is worthy of remark that the present .....
for which its returns have been given, has, owing
the American war and other causes, not been a
bright one. The other sources are so legitimate
their nature, and even taken together, comprise ....
so small, that by no combination of unfavourable
cumstances can a falling off in them seriously affect
the financial condition of the settlement.

The general expenditure of the Straits for the last
official year ending 30th April, 1864, may be set
down under the following heads :—

	£
Collection of revenue	7,585
Allowances under treaties	8,279
Public works	27,388
Salaries and expenses of departments	25,861
Law and justice	22,564
Marine	14,908
Retired allowances and grants in charity	8,402
Education	2,289
Miscellaneous	2,744
	114,932
Military	81,073
Total	£ 196,005

The expenditures under these heads embrace every
charge civil and military at present incurred on account

of the Straits, and except only the cost of maintenance of the Indian convicts, which, though paid out of the treasury here, is clearly an item for reimbursement.* The cost of the post-office is also omitted, as the receipts under that head I have not carried to the credit of the revenue; but I may mention that the cost of the post-office is only 2,124*l*. annually, while its receipts on collection of postage was 14,280*l*. for last year. Taking, then, the gross outlay comprising as it does every possible charge against the settlement from the revenue as stated at page 209, there is left a deficit of only 4,096*l*., and this after paying the monstrous sum of 81,000*l*. or very nearly one-half of the entire revenue, for the support of military, in addition to the sum of 15,000*l*., the cost of the local marine. In no year previous to this last has the military expenditure exceeded 50,000*l*., and had it remained at this figure, instead of now showing a deficit of 4,000*l*., the public accounts of the settlement would have displayed a surplus of 26,000*l*.

The cost of the collection of revenue is necessarily small from the nature of the taxes themselves. The

---

* The labour of the convicts, it has been maintained by some, more than recompenses the settlement for the cost of their support; and I find that public works are for the future to be charged with the wages of the number of convicts employed, at two-thirds the rate paid to free labourers, and the amount then charged will, it is expected, cover a large portion of the outlay on their maintenance. But this is scarcely fair to the settlement; for though some of the men may be worth that rate of wages, all are not, and besides it is hard that the settlement should have several hundred felons forced upon it for whom it is bound to find work, or, at all events, whom it is bound to support. Labour of this sort will always be lavished, and comparatively needless works undertaken simply to find it employment.

farms bring in their returns net, so that of the sum
set down here, 3,884*l.* is for the cost in salaries, &c.
of gathering in the land-rents, and 2,749*l.* the expenses
and salaries of the stamp offices.

'Allowances under treaties are: first, at Penang,
10,000 dollars a year to the Rajah of Quedah, his
heirs and successors, for the cession of that island
and Province Wellesley; second, at Malacca, a pension
to Syed Sahaney; to the family of the Captain China
of Dutch times, who possessed an important magis-
terial post, and to some few others; third, at Singapore,—

	£	
To Sultan Ali and family........	649	per annum.
To Toonkoo Mahomed.............	134	,,
To Toonkoo Sleyman	134	,,
To Tumongong and family	943	,,
Total	£1,860	,,

These pensions are paid according to treaty, and
were part of the consideration given by the Government for the cession of the island. The payment
at Penang to the Rajah of Quedah must continue a
permanent burden upon the resources of the settlement; but the pensions at both Malacca and Singapore
will be considerably reduced and ultimately extinguished
by the effluxion of time.

The expenditure under the head of public works
has of late years been a heavy one in the Straits,
and it may be doubted whether the settlement has
reaped any benefit at all commensurate with the
outlay. In the first place, an extensive system of
fortification for Singapore was devised about seven

years ago, and is now barely completed, after having been tortured by a long series of modifications and enlargements according to the fluctuations of military tactics, and according to the different opinions of the officers who have held the appointment of chief engineer; so that whether or not such works may be fairly debited to the local instead of the imperial revenue, it is just ground of complaint that they should be put down at three or four times their proper cost. Further on I shall have more to say of these fortifications, and of their value as works of defence. In the next place, with respect to public works of a non-military character, the Straits settlement has been unfortunate, in so far that these have been undertaken quite as often to develop the plans of the department as to provide for the necessities of the place. The appointment of chief engineer, which has continued since 1857, has had much to do with this; it has been held by officers of some rank in the Royal Engineers, who draw large salaries from the local treasury in addition to their military pay and allowances, and feel bound in honour to project some work worthy of their professional status, and on a scale corresponding to the large emolument they receive. Fortunately these projections have seldom lately taken a substantial form, and it was determined to abolish the office in April this year; but the Indian Government had apparently some difficulty in finding another post for the incumbent, and so instruction was afterwards sent down that the appointment was to continue another year. The chief engineer's salary, and the expenses of his establishment, are debited under the head of public works. Some creditable and useful undertakings, however, have been carried to completion under the direction of the chief engineer's department. Among others an extensive range of public hospitals; a new sea-wall on the western side of the river, which reclaimed some valuable town land; a fine granite-built lighthouse at Cape Rachado, and the imposing pile of St. Andrew's Cathedral.

The salaries and expenses of public departments call for no special remark; the former, with perhaps one exception, are in every respect ample for the duties performed, and the latter quite as great as they are likely to be under any other form of government. The exception I allude to respecting salaries is that of the governor. Even now—but especially if he has entrusted to him powers as her Majesty's plenipotentiary—it is most desirable that he should be in a position to entertain largely and liberally. From its central position, Singapore is the calling place of her Majesty's ships and of her Majesty's representatives on their way to or from China, Japan and the Archipelago; and its governor should be well subsidized, that he may without trenching on his private resources display that liberal hospitality which undoubtedly goes a long way to secure good feeling and respect. It is scarcely creditable, at all events, that her Majesty's representative in Singapore should be found to study economy so much more than the Dutch governor-general in Java, or the Spanish capitan general of the Philippines. It should be borne in mind, too, that the residents of Singapore for the most part indulge in a somewhat lavish hospitality, which often threatens to eclipse that of the governor.

The principal officers of Government, and the salaries they at present receive, are as under. Their salaries are not all debited under the same head, but many are charged to their respective departments; such as the chief engineers and executive engineers to public works, surveyor general to land revenue, recorder, registrar, &c., to law and justice, &c. &c.

GENERAL.

	£
The Governor	4,200
Secretary and A.D.C., exclusive of Staff-pay	420
Chief Engineer (including military pay)	1,180
Senior Surgeon	960
Surveyor General	864

SINGAPORE.

Resident Councillor	1,800
Magistrate of Police	840
Executive Engineer (including military pay)	1,240
Commissioner of Police	1,200
Commissioner of Stamps	960
Master Attendant	600
Postmaster	400
Commissioner of Court of Requests	540
Deputy Commissioner of Police	528
Chaplain	960
Assistant-Surgeon	504
The Recorder	2,500
Registrar of the Court	1,200
Sheriff	300

PENANG.

Resident Councillor	2,400
Magistrate	720
Magistrate, Province Wellesley	720
Executive Engineer	480
Harbour Master	480

	£
Deputy Commissioner of Police	528
Chaplain	960
Assistant-Surgeon	564
The Recorder	2,000
Registrar of the Court	1,080

MALACCA.

Resident Councillor	1,200
Magistrate	720
Surveyor	600
Assistant-Surgeon	564
Missionary Chaplain	420
Registrar of the Court	600

The amount charged under the head of law and justice in the general table of expenditure it will be seen is far in excess of the salaries given to the recorders, registrars and sheriffs; for it includes, besides the court establishment, the expenses of the jail and house of correction, the Court of Requests, &c. Under the head of Marine is comprised the cost of some small steamers, and which are noticed further on. The sums spent on account of education, retired allowances, charities, and those set down under miscellaneous, are unimportant, and call for no special remark.

The military expenditure is one of the largest, and probably the most unsatisfactory of the items that appear in the public accounts. It is one against which the residents have protested for a long time back; and though these protests may appear to have been sometimes carried to unreasonable extremes, yet they are based upon indisputably good grounds. It is not so much the extent of the sum charged upon the local revenue—though in the last year it has swallowed up nearly one half of the revenue—which has caused dissatisfaction,

as the fact that the military strength it pretends
to secure is no defence at all.   Against internal revolt
or disaffection the Straits settlement needs no such
force as it at present maintains.   An additional police,
perhaps better armed, would in such an event serve
this purpose, and be otherwise useful besides.   And
though the local resources would be ungrudgingly contributed towards an efficient outward defence too ; yet,
against external attack—that is, against the assault of
a European force, on such a place as Singapore, what
could 400 or 500 sepoys do ?   Why, as far as any
infantry is concerned, the town could be laid in ashes
by an enemy from his ships without the exchange of
a single musket-shot.   The military strength in infantry
of the Straits is, and has been for a long time back,
two regiments of Madras native troops—numbering
about 1,000 bayonets, 400 of whom are stationed
at Penang, 100 at Malacca, 100 at Labuan, and 400
at Singapore.   Scattered in this way, it is not difficult
to appreciate the value of the protection they would
afford.   In Singapore the 400 men do little more than
furnish the ornamental guards to the treasury, the
Government offices and other public buildings.

There are forts, it is true, which have cost the
Indian Government and the settlement large sums of
money, and which give Singapore the empty reputation of being a stronghold.   But since these
have been constructed, they have never yet been
manned ; far from this, there have not been men
enough to keep the guns in order.   On the Queen's
birthday, some two years ago, it was determined

to fire the royal salute from the big guns at Fort
Canning. At sunrise, the military and the volunteers
were drawn up in order on the plain beneath, and
they were to wait the firing from the fort to commence
their evolutions. I was at the time standing with
some others on the ramparts overlooking the southern
battery of the fort; from the seven sixty-eight
pounders mounted on which the salute was to be
fired. The guns were manned by a detachment
of European Artillery. At six o'clock the royal
banner was unfurled, and run up to the mast-head of
the large flagstaff in the centre of the fort. This was
the signal for the firing of the first gun, but unfortunately it hung fire, and would not go off—the trigger
of a second was pulled with similar result; a third
also failed, and only the fourth, sixth, and seventh
guns of the battery could be discharged. New tubes
were tried on the guns that had missed fire, but it was
no use, and the salute had to be bungled through with
the three guns only, much to the astonishment of the
disconcerted infantry and volunteers on the plain
beneath.*

The fortification of Singapore consists of four
earthworks — Fort Canning, Fort Fullerton, Fort
Palmer, and Fort Faber. Fort Canning is a redoubt,
following the contour of the top of Government Hill,

---

* I have been told that the cause of the guns not going off was that
the junk wads which had been placed in them after last drill practice
were not withdrawn before loading; but I can scarcely think a detachment of Royal Artillery could neglect such a precaution, and I prefer
rather to blame the guns than so seriously to call in question the efficiency of the Artillery.

which stands near the centre of the town about half a
mile back from the beach. The hill rises abruptly
from the level land around, in the shape of a cone, to
the height of some 200 feet. Its apex is of considerable extent, the ramparts measuring nearly 1,200 yards.
It mounts at present seventeen heavy pieces, namely,
seven 68-pounders, eight 8-inch shell guns, and two
13-inch mortars; there are also in course of construction, platforms for eight more heavy pieces. Besides
these, the ramparts of this fort are furnished with a
number of 14-pound carronades. Within the ramparts
are barracks, hospital, and accommodation for 150
European artillerymen. Fort Fullerton is a battery
à fleur d'eau, built on the promontory at the western
entrance of the Singapore river, containing barracks,
&c., fit to accommodate about half a garrison battery
of European artillery, or about 40 men; it mounts
nine 68-pounder guns, and one 13-inch mortar, with
platforms ready for five more big guns. Fort Palmer
is a small earthwork overlooking the eastern entrance
to New Harbour, and contains merely a guard-room
with magazines, &c., and mounting five 56-pounder
guns. Fort Faber is also an earthwork, half way up
the hill of that name, overlooking New Harbour, with
guard-room and magazine, and mounting only two
56-pounder guns. At the summit of the hill two
mortars are also placed in position. The total of
these guns and mortars actually mounted and supposed to be available in case of emergency in the
defence of Singapore, is thirty-six; and if to this is
added the fifteen for which platforms are ready made,

16

and which only want lifting into their places, there is
a total of fifty-one guns of the largest calibre independent of smaller mounted ordnance.   Until September
last year the European artillerymen to work these
fifty-one guns was exactly seventy; at that time the
number was increased to 120, which now gives the
somewhat more liberal allowance of two men to each
gun—the other duties of the forts being left to look
after themselves.   Garrisoned in this way, it is easy
to understand of what value the best of fortifications
can be.   But unfortunately there are good reasons to
believe that the forts themselves are so placed that,
even if fully garrisoned, it would be unwise to use
them against an enemy's ships in the roadstead.

They have all, with the exception of Fort Fullerton,
been constructed within the last seven years, and Fort
Fullerton itself has been so extensively remodelled as
almost to be considered a new work.   It was in 1857
that the plan of this modern defence was first drawn
out.   At that time local disturbances among the
Chinese and the rebellion in India, pointed, it was
thought, somewhat ominously to the unprotected condition of the settlement.   The object at first in view
was to provide rather for the safety of the European
residents in event of an outburst of local disaffection,
than for defence against an outside enemy; at the
same time to combine as much as possible the one
with the other.   But before the works had been
commenced, the renewal of hostilities in China, the
unsatisfactory condition of the foreign relations of
the Imperial Government at the time, and the opera-

tions of other European powers to the eastward, determined a wider range to be given to the system of defence, and new plans were drawn up by which, if carried out, the place might be considered safe in event of a European disturbance. It was at this time too that the Imperial Government directed barracks to be constructed for the accommodation of a full regiment of European infantry.

The war in China however came to a speedy close, the position of affairs in Europe became settled and satisfactory, and the French did not seem inclined to push their advantages in Cochin China to a dangerous extreme. In fact, immediate danger appeared to have passed away, and with it it was thought the necessity for the extended works contemplated. Piece by piece the system of fortification was reduced until all that remained of it were the works described. They had been from the first a compromise, and by extension here and contraction there, by the desire to serve two purposes at the minimum of outlay, they have proved ill-suited for the one and inefficient for the other.

Fort Canning, which is much the largest of the forts, from its position must be used with great disadvantage against an enemy's ships at sea. It is placed right in the centre of the town, and would of necessity draw his fire upon the chief buildings of the place. Besides this, its distance from the beach is so much loss of power. A vessel with guns of the same calibre as those mounted on the fort, might so anchor as not only to be able to blow up all the

16—2

merchantmen in the harbour, but to destroy the greater part of the town itself, and yet be by a quarter of a mile beyond the reach of the fort. With even the powerful weapons now mounted upon it, this is painfully apparent. At the last shot and shell practice I witnessed, the target was placed just in the range of the anchorage of the larger ships. The distance was about a mile and a quarter, and the elevation required by the guns was so considerable, that together with the height of the fort the balls went plumping into the water at such a great angle that a ricochet was impossible. If they had hit the deck of a ship, they might have gone through her bottom; but they would require to be fired with extraordinary accuracy to drop in this way on to their mark.

Fort Fullerton possesses the advantage of stretching out on a slight promontory for some few yards into the harbour, and its embrasures being only some fifteen feet above the sea level, the shot from its guns, if even moderately well directed, would, owing to the ricochet, seldom fail to hull an enemy. But the fort is placed right in line with the densest and most valuable part of the town, and an enemy, in the attempt to silence it, would sweep away one-half of the richly-stored godowns of the port.*

The two small works at Mount Palmer and Mount Faber are well enough; they are clear of the town, and command two important portions of the harbour,

---

* Since the above was written, the dismantling of Fort Fullerton has actually commenced, for the reason assigned in the text.

but would of course be useless unless supported by
extensive batteries bearing on the other unprotected
points. In event of a war between Great Britain
and any Power possessed of territory and of fleets
and forces to the eastward of the Straits of Malacca,
the safe possession of Singapore would secure an
incalculable advantage in a strategetic point of view
alone, and quite irrespective of its commercial value.
It guards indeed the highway of steam navigation
between India and the western world and China and
the far east. With the Straits of Malacca in her
possession, and with Singapore as a half-way house
to provision, recruit, and repair her expeditions, Great
Britain is sure of ascendancy in the far east. For from
the vast military resources of India, she could pour
in the very shortest time an overwhelming force upon
any given point, and also so rapidly transfer them
backwards and forwards as never to endanger the
continent itself from which they were withdrawn. It
is on this account that I have been so particular in
dealing with the fort defences, and to prevent any
false reliance being placed upon them. It is not
unusual in China, Java, at Saigon, and in India itself,
to hear people talk of the extensive fortifications of
Singapore, which have been built and heavily armed
to render the place a military stronghold. I do not
know whether such a belief is shared by the War
Office at home, but I hope not, for it is a very false
one, and might prove a very fatal one.

Singapore is in no condition of defence whatever,
and the town might be shelled and knocked to pieces

with impunity by a vessel mounting modernly heavy ordnance; or a couple of regiments of infantry might be landed at some point a few miles from the harbour and quietly marched from behind into the heart of the town. It ought here to be borne in mind that the destruction of the town is synonymous with the destruction of the station, which has no agriculture and no inland resources to fall back upon, but being an entrepôt, has its entire wealth stored up in its merchants' warehouses. It is not that the forts are ungarrisoned, though by being left so they are even placed at the mercy of any powerful local rising did such take place, but that they are unserviceable. Except from Fort Fullerton* not a shot could be fired into an enemy lying securely at anchor some two miles from shore and pouring broadside after broadside with deadly effect upon the warehouses of the town from guns of no greater strength than those mounted on the forts; and as to the landing of a body of infantry, I may mention that there is not a single heavy gun mounted on any of the forts capable of being turned to deliver its fire inland.

Nor does it appear that any system of fortification could be carried through that would prove by itself a satisfactory defence. The town might perhaps be rendered safe from the fire of an enemy's ships; but it must be borne in mind that the wealth which floats in the trading ships at anchor in the roadstead must at most seasons represent one or two millions sterling,

---

* When Fort Fullerton is dismantled an enemy's ship in such a position would be completely secure.

and owing to the gentle curve of the bay there is no point of land on which we could erect forts whose guns would be able to protect these.   The best military and naval authorities whose opinions I have been able to obtain now agree that the protection of Singapore and its shipping in case of a European war can be best secured by the presence in the Straits of one or two of H.M.'s heavily armed ships.   The position of the island is exceedingly favourable for a defence of this sort.   At its western extremity the navigable channel of the Straits is not more than ten miles broad; at its eastern extremity, which with Bintang to the southward forms the eastern entrance to the Straits of Malacca, the navigable channel is barely eight miles, and admission here by night time could in an extremity be rendered highly perilous, if not impossible, by the extinction of the lighthouse which guards an important danger in the centre of the channel.   The blockade of the Straits therefore either to eastward or westward of the island of Singapore could be easily maintained, and the distance from the one point to the other is so small, barely thirty miles, that the squadron, of whatever it might consist, could in case of danger be concentrated at either extremity at the shortest notice.

In no other way do I think could the safety of the shipping in the roadstead be secured, or the town protected against the possibility of an attack from an enemy's infantry landed at an unprotected part of the island and marched up on its rear.   Efficient fortification might, as I have said, secure the town itself against destruction from an enemy's ships, but

it could never secure the ships in harbour nor prevent
such a landing as that indicated. And, therefore,
whether or not it be necessary to keep up the fortification of Singapore to a certain standard, the first
and chief reliance must be placed upon a sea defence;
which while it is the best will also be found the
most economical to the State.

Some years ago it was resolved by the Imperial
Government to construct a royal dockyard, arsenal,
and coal depôt at Singapore for the use of the China
fleet. I believe the intention has not been abandoned,
though the carrying of it out has been delayed. The
site has been selected, and contracts were only a few
months ago entered into for the construction of substantial stone piers along the length of the water
frontage; these are progressing, and the Government
on entering upon the land came into possession of
coal-sheds, a half-finished dock, and other premises
ready made, the property of an unfortunate squatter
who has up to the present moment received no recom-
pence whatever. If these works are carried out on
a scale commensurate with the requirements they are
devised to supply, they will of themselves render the
defence of the island an imperial necessity. And
though some land batteries for the greater security
of the dockyards themselves may require to be thrown
up and kept garrisoned, yet the general defence must
be by sea, and this will in part be secured by the
very vessels that in the ordinary course of events
must resort to the docks.

With regard to infantry, as I have said, it is not

required for the security of any of the stations in the Straits against internal revolt.   Nor could it come into service against an outside attack until the very last extremity; and then no such paltry detachments as at present of 400 or 500 men could avail.   But it seems to me that there could be no better point at which to keep a reserve of European infantry for general imperial purposes.   By recent medical returns of the army and navy, the China station has proved by a long way the most unhealthy for European troops; and it is almost certain that for a considerable time to come, Great Britain must continue to back her influence there by the occasional display of military strength.   Singapore is but six or seven steaming days from Hong Kong, and ten from Shanghai, even in an unfavourable monsoon; its climate has been established beyond all doubt to be kinder and more genial to the European constitution than any other in the east.   It has no pestilence, no epidemics or endemics that extend themselves to Europeans.   Invalids, broken down and exhausted, from China and Bengal alike seek its shores, and after a sojourn of six or seven weeks leave it in health and vigour. Why, then, not station in the Straits one moiety at least of the troops intended to be available for China and Japan ?   At Singapore about five years ago under orders from the Home Government, a magnificent range of barracks and cantonments were erected in the midst of scenery rarely equalled in its beauty, destined for and capable of accommodating 1,200 European soldiers and their officers, which have never been occupied, and are now going fast to wreck and ruin simply from the want of tenants. What a saving there would be in the mortality, and what a difference in the condition of the troops detailed for the China service if, instead of being all hurried on to the cholera and fever swamps of the Yangtze, one-half were maintained in health and vigour in the luxuriant quarters of Singapore, and allowed to exchange from time to time with their less fortunate comrades at their post. Far more efficiency than would be lost by reason of the fortnight's or three weeks' delay (for it could not be more) in the appearance of the section of the forces left at Singapore on China soil in case of emergency, would be gained by the superior condition in which they would arrive. Besides this, it is apparent that any body of troops stationed at Singapore would be available not for China only, but for India; and that within a period so short as to meet any emergency which is almost possible to arise, nine days would serve to convey both men and baggage to Calcutta, Madras, or any point on the east coast, or in Burmah. Indeed, I think that, irrespective of the China force and in regard to India only, Singapore might with great advantage be used as a health re-cruiting or reserve station for European infantry.

There is another reason why it should be the object of the Imperial Government to carry out such arrangements as I have indicated, both with respect to the naval and the military forces of the east. It is that they would dispense with the necessity for any local force naval or military, and what sums now are, or were proposed to be, spent from the local exchequer under these heads, could be handed over to the Imperial Government in the way of a subsidy. Determined to have some sort of marine available when need be for the suppression of piracy and other local purposes, the Government of the Straits have obtained three steamers, the yearly cost of which may be noted in the table of general expenditure. Unfortunately this marine is little better than a name only; one steamer is a wooden vessel of 400 tons, going at full speed probably five knots, and carrying two old 32-pounders and two swivels, useless for all purposes in India, and sent down to the Straits on that account. The other two are old Thames river-boats, of about 100 tons each, carrying no arms at all, which were sent first out to Calcutta, and then up with the last China expedition for conveying messages between the larger ships in the rivers.

This lilliputian fleet is officered by gentlemen in the uniform of the Straits marine, but barring the uniforms of the officers, its appearance is too ridiculous to have any moral weight, and as to its usefulness that can be understood from the description of the boats, and from the fact that with some very few exceptions where they have conveyed diplomatic despatches, they have been used for nothing else but passenger traffic. Even in this last capacity they have proved sadly insufficient. It is not many months ago that the Government medical officer of Malacca had the misfortune to fall from a height and fracture his leg so seriously as to necessitate amputation; no

doctor besides himself however was at the station, and
as he was suffering great agony one of the two little
steamers which happened to be there was despatched
for the residency surgeon of Singapore. The distance
between the two ports is barely 100 miles. Late on
the night of the accident the steamer left Malacca and
got into Singapore on the following night. She was
despatched again early next morning with the necessary assistance on board and got back to Malacca that
night, having occupied altogether two days for a
passage which could have been completed there and
back by one of the Malay sampans if well manned
in thirty-six hours. When the steamer reached
Malacca the patient had died after helplessly suffering
the most excruciating agony, and when it was believed
that amputation would have saved his life. What
steamers of this sort could do against pirates or anything else with means to fight or means to run, must
be left to conjecture only, for though especially destined
for the purpose, as far as I can learn none of these
vessels have ever yet been able to obtain more than
a fading glimpse of a pirate and that while there were
many reported to be about. There appears to me no
public purpose which can be served by a local marine
that could not be equally well secured by H.M.'s
ships, except it be that Government officials, instead
of travelling free of expense by the colonial boats,
would like other people have to engage their passages
by the regular opportunities.*

---

* The Court of Judicature on its circuits to Malacca, and the
Governor on his yearly visit to Malacca and Penang, could be conveyed
in any of H.M.'s vessels which might be stationed in the Straits at the
time.

The advantages of making Singapore a constant station for at least a full regiment of European infantry and doing away with the Madras troops or any local corps, would be shared alike by the Imperial Government and the colonial. In addition to the available position of Singapore its good climate and magnificent ready-made barracks before alluded to, a very considerable part of the cost of such a force might be defrayed by the subsidy drawn from the colonial resources. The sum set down in the public accounts of the past year for the support of the Madras regiments stationed in the Straits is no less than 80,000*l.*, and it has always before averaged close upon 50,000*l.* The cost of the local corps, which dissatisfied with the expenditure on the Madras troops it was at one time, I think unadvisedly, recommended by the residents of the Straits to raise, was set down at 44,000*l.* for 1,050 men. The Imperial Government then might safely calculate, I think, on a contribution from the local treasury of about 50,000*l.* yearly towards the military stationed at Singapore, and this ungrudgingly. An infantry regiment of Europeans would be many times more worth paying for than any local corps which could be organized.* Indeed, I consider under any circumstances a local corps is to be avoided. No such

---

* The out-door non-military guards, such as those to the Treasury and other public offices, might be furnished by a body of the native police, specially armed for the purpose. The few purely military guards which it would be absolutely necessary to maintain in the day-time could be protected by a covering, which, while it would shelter from the sun, need not interfere with efficiency ; the periods of the guards, too, might be made half the ordinary duration.

force composed of any elements within reach in the
Straits would be worth maintaining. With years of
training they would fail to attain that discipline which
would enable them to share effectively with regular
troops in the defence of the place against a European
attack, and besides lacking skill they would lack
prestige and fail to obtain respect. Considered as
a local defence merely, and if kept distinct from the
police they will have nothing to do but to furnish
guards for the public offices, to turn out on State
occasions, perhaps in the absence of artillery to fire
a few salutes, and so to consume the public money.
If, on the other hand, they share in any way police
duties they cannot be maintained as a separate body
without leading to endless jealousies and frequent
collisions between them.

I am strongly opposed both to a purely local land
force and to a local marine being maintained at a
point which must, if it is to be maintained in time
of war at all, be defended by H.M.'s troops and H.M.'s
ships; and which even in times of peace will in all
probability continue a place of resort for both. All
that it remains for the local government to do is
to support an efficient police for the security of
internal quiet, and to contribute in money to the
general defence secured by the imperial ships and
forces. The measure of this contribution must be
calculated according to the peculiar circumstances of
the colony, of its being both an imperial stronghold
and a commercial emporium; but it would in all
probability be less than the amount hitherto drawn

from the colonial treasury to pay the Madras troops, or than the residents proposed as the cost of a local corps and the present local marine, or in round figures 60,000*l.* annually.*

---

* It may be remarked that I have made no provision for the defence of Penang and Malacca. I have purposely omitted to do so, because I think neither of these stations is entitled to have regular troops stationed at it; unless, perhaps, at Penang a small shifting detachment might be maintained, but more for the purpose of affording change to the troops themselves than of securing defence to the island. To both Penang and Malacca, in a strategetic point of view at all events, may be safely applied the proverb, " Cantabit vacuus coram latrone viator."

CHAPTER IX.

DURING even the short period of its history in con-
nection with our rule, Singapore has not been without
its excitements, sometimes of national, though more
frequently of local interest; but of these, very few
have been of a dangerous character.

Although the native population numbers 300 to
one of the European, no attempt has ever been made
to use this fearful disproportion as a means of coercion
or menace. There are 13,000 Malays, whose country
we have occupied; there are 60,000 Chinese, with
whose empire we have been twice at war, and there
are nearly 10,000 natives of India of the same castes
as those who rose up against us there, and yet with

but 500 European residents, and some 400 sepoy soldiers to protect them, there has been no display antagonistic to our rule, the most thorough good order has been maintained and the most complete obedience to our laws secured.

Some have attributed this long security entirely to the mixed and opposite elements of which the population is composed, and to the jealousy entertained by one section towards the other. The Chinese would certainly find no co-operation in any disturbance they thought fit to raise, from the Malays or Indians, or *vice versâ;* each stands distinct by itself, speaking another language * and writing another character. But though this condition of the population may be unfavourable to a combined insurrection, still it would be quite possible for any section, moved by a sense of injustice or by a sudden love for power, of itself to overthrow the existing Government. It is true that no usurpation of the kind could be long maintained among a population more than half antagonistic, but still it is proverbial that people worked up to the revolution point do not stop to weigh consequences, and a few days of such a revolution would be sufficiently appalling to make up for the limited length of its duration.

It is, I think, to the thorough feeling of good-will which subsists between every section of the population and the European residents, that the long immunity

---

* Malay is the language generally used by Europeans in their transactions with all sections of the native population alike, yet, among themselves, each section speaks its own tongue.

17

from serious disturbance is due.   There may be
hatreds between one native nationality and another,
but all agree in looking up to and respecting the
English community.   The Government is respected
too, for it has always been mild and just ; but it
would be quite possible, as has been too often seen
already, for a small dominant population such as the
English are in Singapore to render themselves so
obnoxious that the mere possession of an abstract
right to justice and equality would fail to establish
contentment or good-will amongst the masses. But the
conduct of the European residents of the Straits is
rarely, if ever, domineering or oppressive, and the
superiority which it is necessary for them to maintain
has nothing assuming or arrogant about it.   So proverbial indeed has this become, and so favourably
does it contrast with the bearing of the Dutch in their
Eastern possessions, that throughout Java and in every
island to the eastward of it, there is no better introduction to native kindness and protection than the
English name.

Like other countries inhabited by Malays and
Bugis, Singapore is subjected occasionally to the
dangerous practice of amok running.   In apparent
obedience to some sudden impulse, a Malay, or Bugis,
will arm himself with two large *krises*, or daggers,
one in each hand, and rushing from his house along
generally the most crowded street in the neighbourhood stab at random all who come in his way.   As
many as fifteen persons have been killed or seriously
wounded, and many others slightly hurt by one of

these amok runners before he was slain, but the killed always bear a small proportion to the wounded as the strokes of the infatuated man fall promiscuously and are ill-directed. As soon as an amok runner makes his appearance, a warning cry is raised and carried on in advance of him all along the street. On hearing this cry a general rush into the houses is made of all the women and children and of all the men who are not armed—no attempt is made to capture the maniac alive, but he becomes a mark for the musket, spear, or *kris*, of every man who can obtain a favourable opportunity for attack. He ceases to be viewed as human and is hunted down like a wild beast, yet it is surprising how long he will escape the death which is aimed at him from every side. Some of these unfortunate wretches have run the gauntlet of nearly a mile of street that was up in arms against them, and have temporarily evaded destruction, some for hours, and others for days. But the end is inevitable, they refuse to be captured, and are ultimately shot down or stabbed.

The first instance of running amok in Singapore occurred more than forty years ago, and Colonel Farquhar, then resident, narrowly escaped becoming a victim. It was in the time when the residency bungalows stood along the beach, where the esplanade is now, and the man was descried coming tearing down within the palisade that enclosed them, brandishing a weapon in each hand. The cry of alarm was raised, and Colonel Farquhar, who was at dinner at the time, ran out to learn the cause. He just got out as the man

17—2

was rushing past, and received a deep flesh cut on the shoulder ; an instant afterwards, however, the infatuated wretch was run through the body by the sepoy guard on watch close by.

At the time of the Chinese riots, about ten years ago, an amok was run by a Bugis who made almost miraculous escapes from death before he was captured. The town was under guard at the time, the streets being patrolled by the troops and the volunteers, and fortunately few of the inhabitants were abroad. Towards evening the man was seen by his friends, with whom he had lived quietly, to arm himself and leave the house. A few moments afterwards he had commenced his work, and was rushing madly along one of the busiest streets. Many shots were fired at him both by the troops and volunteers, and repeated attempts made to arrest his progress; but though badly wounded and bleeding profusely he reached the side of the river alive. A large force was now after him and it was thought that his escape was impossible. It was getting dusk however, and the man throwing away one of his swords, placed the other between his teeth and plunged into the water. Some of those in pursuit got into the boats which lay around and gave chase, while others blazed away from the banks; but the man, who kept swimming up the river under water, only appearing now and then to take breath, evaded all attempts to take or shoot him and disappeared. An hour afterwards a dark slimy object was seen to creep from one of the small muddy canals in the upper part of the town. Those around went up to it, and as they approached recognized the form to be that of a man evidently in great pain. No sooner however did the man see that he was watched than he started up, brandished his *kris*, and made a rush towards them; but his strength failed him, and in a moment afterwards he lay stretched powerless on the ground. On examination the man was found to be the late amok runner, and was conveyed to the hospital where he died the same night.

It is impossible to give any explanation of the motives which lead to these fatal frenzies. Some have written that they most generally arise from the dejection succeeding an over-indulgence in opium. But the Malays are seldom addicted to the use of that drug, and nearly all the amoks that have occurred in Singapore were run by men who had never tasted it. It seems to me that they are those who from some cause have become disgusted or tired of life and are determined to die, but that as their religion and super-stitions prohibit suicide they resolve to provoke death at the hands of others. This may not account for the efforts they apparently make to escape when they have once started, but I would put these efforts down as unpremeditated, and as an obedience to an after-felt yet irresistible instinct of self-preservation. Not many years ago an amok, in which several lives were lost, was run in Campong Java by a Bugis who was known to be a peaceable, well-to-do, industrious man. He was also a very devout Mahommedan, and for nearly twenty-four hours before he started on the amok was intently perusing the Koran. He was not killed, but was stunned by a blow from behind and taken prisoner. He was condemned to be hanged, and suffered death with the greatest indifference. When asked a few minutes before his execution regarding his motive, he said that he had felt his time was come, and that he was irresistibly impelled to seek death in the manner which he did.

So numerous at one time were these amoks in Penang, and so little did the punishment of hanging such as were taken alive appear to act as a deterrent, that Sir William Norris, the Recorder there, resorted in one case to the extreme measure of accompanying the ordinary sentence of death with orders that the body of the condemned man should after death be cut up into small fragments, some of which were to be cast into the sea and others exposed in public places of the town. No little indignation was felt and expressed by the more sensitive portion of the English community regarding this sentence; undoubtedly it was rather a bold exercise of judicial functions, but it apparently had the desired effect, for amoks were afterwards of much rarer occurrence. Mussulmen, while they pay little regard to death, have a horror of the mutilation of their dead bodies. Sir William Norris most probably knew this and resolved to turn it to advantage.

About twenty years ago an evil began to show itself in Singapore which threatened to extend to somewhat formidable dimensions. Up to that time thefts and robberies had been committed, and had increased pretty much in the same ratio as the population, but had never been distinguished by any approach to combination. Then however what were termed "gang robberies" began to be perpetrated— at first by perhaps only ten or twelve men and directed against the houses and property of natives, but by and by the robber bands grew much stronger in numbers and open attacks were made upon the residences of Europeans. In one case the house of a merchant,* only about two miles from the town, was surrounded by a gang of forty to fifty, who were evidently under the belief that a large sum of money was concealed in the proprietor's bed-room, for they broke into this first. The proprietor had been aroused and met the intruders with a couple of loaded pistols which he levelled at the foremost; the weapons however missed fire, and were immediately knocked out of his hands, and he himself cut down and left for dead. The house was pillaged, and the robbers escaped with impunity. The owner was shortly afterwards picked up by his own servants still insensible, with a deep gash extending across one side of the face. It is said that his life was only saved by the presence of mind of a Chinese female servant, who, after he had been knocked down and when one of the robbers was proceeding to cut his throat, cried out, —"What! are you going to waste your time cutting the throat of a dead man while his house is yet unplundered?" the appeal succeeded, and the robber turned his attention to pillage.

* Mr. McMicking.

Not long after this a gang robbery of even a more alarming nature occurred to the house of a resident in Orchard-road.* The attack was made between ten and eleven o'clock at night, and about 250 men were engaged in it. The roads approaching the house were guarded, and every precaution taken to prevent interruption. Intimation of the intended attack, however, had by some means been conveyed to the inmates a few minutes before the arrival of the robbers, and some measures taken for the safety of life; the doors of the upper part of the house were barricaded, while arrangements were being made to carry the females of the family up to the roof of the building. The robbers first entered the lower part of the house and drove out all the servants they could find. Here they stayed for some time. They lighted all the lamps of the billiard-room, and burned on the table a plenteous supply of joss paper, apparently to conciliate the fates. This done they commenced to pillage, and then attacked the upper part of the house. This was defended for a considerable time, during which a good many shots were fired among the robbers. At last the windows and doors were broken in, but the whole family had got on to the roof, and, though the house was pillaged, no injury was done to the occupants.

Many other cases occurred, but these two were the chief; at least where European residents were attacked. The gang robberies were ultimately suppressed by a very decided action on the part of Government, who

* Mr. Hewetson.

gave liberty to the police and to the residents to challenge all bodies of men going about at night in larger numbers than ten; and if the challenge was unattended to, to fire into them. Several men were shot in this way, and a wholesome dread of attempting combined robberies implanted. One of the Chinese hoeys, or secret societies, too, gave up twenty of the men engaged in the second attack I have described, no doubt with the view to conciliate Government, and this also had a salutary effect. At the time these societies possessed great power among the Chinese; and though there was no direct evidence of the fact, it was strongly suspected that at the courts they were known to hold, they frequently awarded and had carried out the sentence of death. Many murdered bodies were found about the country, each mutilated in a peculiar manner: generally with either the right or left hand chopped up into a certain number of parts, left hanging together by the skin; and in these cases Chinamen never were the informants, nor could they ever be induced to give evidence.

There have been two great riots among the Chinese, both of which created for the time a good deal of un-easiness—not so much regarding the safety of the English residents, as from fear that the disturbance might spread and prove destructive to order, and fatal to large portions of the Chinese themselves. The first occurred in 1854, and was entirely a war of nationality between two of the largest divisions of the Chinese population—the Tu Chews and the Hokiens. Its origin was very insignificant. A man of each clan had a bazaar dispute about some plantains, upon which blows followed. On this the clansmen of each belligerent who were in the neighbourhood joined the battle, which gradually grew in extent and spread from street to street. All the shops and houses were quickly closed and barricaded, and the fight became general throughout the town. The military were then called out, and they succeeded in clearing the streets; but the spirit of clanish jealousy and hatred had been roused. None of the shops would open, and when any of the streets were left unguarded the men on both sides would rush out and have a fight. This state of things grew gradually worse, and when the clans found they could only fight at short intervals and in small numbers in town, they each marched out in large bodies to the country, determined to have an uninterrupted trial of their respective strengths. Many battles took place and large numbers of men were killed on both sides, the heads of the dead men being cut off and carried on the spears of their adversaries. All the merchants' godowns in town were closed and business completely suspended. The residents were sworn in as special constables, as also many of the captains and officers of the ships lying in harbour, and detachments of these sent all over the country; the military being principally left to guard the town. Very little resistance was made by either of the belligerents to the Europeans. One position in the country had been palisaded by about 150 of the rioters. Here they made some stand, but after a little firing they abandoned it and fled; they were pursued, and it is

to be feared were not treated with much humanity
by their pursuers. Several were shot, and among
those brought into town as prisoners some were old
men with broken arms and severe flesh wounds received in their retreat. Many of the dead bodies,
too, that were afterwards picked up, contained what
were undoubtedly bullets from the muskets of some of
the special constables.*

After about a fortnight of this work both parties
began to quiet down, and the most influential Chinese
merchants, who suffered severely from the interruption
to their trade, used their best efforts to cement matters.
In ten days from the commencement of the riot 600
prisoners were accumulated in the lock-ups of the
central police station, and as this was far in excess
of what they could well hold, the authorities were
anxious to allow the matter to blow over in the easiest
manner possible. In three weeks all was quiet, and
the shops began to open again and trade go on as
before. No great efforts were made to capture the
ringleaders, or single out those who had taken life;
and though several hundred lives had been lost, only
two men were hanged for murder committed during
the riots, and in these cases the circumstances were
too glaring and the evidence too strong to allow the
matter to be passed over.

It was in this year and in a great measure owing

---

* It is worthy of notice, too, that not one of the troops, police, or
specials was seriously hurt, much less killed. · Colonel Butterworth,
the Governor, was struck on the head by a brickbat while walking
through the streets with a view to quiet the riots by his presence, but it
may be doubted whether the missile was intended for him.

to these disturbances that the volunteer rifle corps sprang into existence. Some necessity was felt for an organization among the residents that would enable them effectively to supply the deficiency of the military in case of any sudden insurrection among the natives, and the idea was warmly supported, few refusing to join in such a praiseworthy movement. For the first seven years of its existence the corps was maintained with enthusiasm and deserved to be esteemed as a part of the colony's defences. The breaking out of the Indian mutiny in 1857 and the reports that were then continually going about regarding the disaffection of the Indian population gave the volunteers an importance which was acknowledged by the Government of India. This flattered the vanity of the corps, which afterwards carried on its banner (and with justice) the motto : *In Oriente primus*. But the chivalry of other days has passed away, and one decade has been the measure, if not of the existence, at least of the efficiency of the " Singapore Volunteer Rifles."

The second Chinese riot broke out in 1857, but was not marked by the party feuds or by the violence which distinguished the one of three years before, for it had entirely a different origin. A new municipal Act had just come into operation, and it was dissatisfaction with, or rather a misunderstanding of its terms that determined the Chinese to make the demonstration they did. One section of the Act gave the police magistrate power to inflict for certain minor offences fines not exceeding 500 rupees. The Chinese overlooking the discretion which was left with the magistrate concluded that the extreme penalty was in all cases to be exacted, and judging that the offences mentioned (one of which was gambling) were those which they could not long avoid, determined to make a stand against it. Some collisions did take place between the Chinese and the troops, volunteers, and police, but they were not serious. It was rather a passive resistance which the Chinese had resolved to offer; they closed their shops to a man and absolutely refused to do business or carry on their daily avocations; but though passive it was a powerful resistance, for all the bakeries, groceries, and provision trades are left in the hands of the Chinese.

It was a short time before the real cause of disaffection became known to the authorities, and in the interval a collision took place. The military and the volunteers were called out and distributed over the town, and the streets patrolled as they were in 1854. Some of the residents, too, afraid lest it might be the prelude to an outburst similar to that which was brewing in India, sent their wives and families out of the settlement, some to Sarawak and others to Java. But the Chinese who had no cause of quarrel amongst themselves, and who are tolerably well impressed with the uselessness of open resistance to the English Government, kept close to their houses; and the few encounters which occurred were, it is believed, provoked by the over-zeal or over-officiousness of the volunteers, who, warmed up to a taste for adventure in one or two instances, forcibly broke into the blockaded houses and

dragged out the inhabitants. Some of these adventurous parties met however with a rather warm
reception. The leader of one who had penetrated
further than his comrades found himself surrounded
by twenty or thirty Chinamen, and after a short and
ineffectual resistance was knocked on the head and
tumbled down a well, but he was not seriously hurt
and was spared to fight another day. It is stated
too that on one occasion the captain of the corps
himself was seen together with two or three of his
subalterns to come tumbling over the wall of a Chinese
temple with rather indecorous haste.

But beyond a few of these escapades, which rather
afforded the bases of after-tales of adventure than any
cause for present alarm, this riot passed quietly over,
and business was not suspended for more than a week.
The Governor, Mr. Blundell, got a few of the most
respectable of the Chinese merchants together and
explained to them the exact nature of the Act, that
though power was given to the magistrate to impose
fines to the full extent of 500 rupees, yet the power
would not be exercised unless there were peculiar circumstances calling for it. Notices were then circulated
among the Chinese to meet at the police-office. A
large concourse assembled and the Governor read out
the Act from the roof of the building, and had it
interpreted with the necessary explanations of the
objectionable section. After this the crowd dispersed
quietly, and that same day all the shops were open
and business going on as before.

These appear to me the only events out of the

common which have in any way threatened the public safety, and after all the excitement they created had very little of real danger in it. Some of the harmless excitements which have from time to time been felt I have casually alluded to in the first chapter while glancing at the history of the settlement, and also elsewhere. There was the first China expedition, and the gaiety and bustle it created. There was the first appearance of tigers on the island. There was the agitation created by the Indian mutiny, and by the second expedition to China. There have also been the excitements attending the visits of great men to the place, and the changes of the respective governors.

Nor must I omit to mention the excitement into which the people of Singapore were thrown by the arrival of the renowned Confederate cruiser *Alabama*. Her appearance at Cape Town, and her subsequent destruction of three American ships in the neighbourhood of Sunda Strait, had brought her prominently into notice, and it had been confidently prophesied by the newspapers that she would ere long visit Singapore. A considerable time had passed away, however, since her appearance in the Java Sea, and there had been so many false alarms that people grew doubtful and were in a condition to receive with great distrust any further reports concerning her.

She arrived at dusk on the evening of the 21st December. A few made her out as she came to anchor, but as the larger part of the residents had retired to their houses in the country, the news did not spread.

Early next morning however, for the despatch of the Europe mail commercial Square were clustered groups inquiring faces learning the particulars of the renowned cruiser. The effect was heightened by the appearance, here and the strange grey uniform of the Confederate ment. There was no longer any doubt about *Alabama* was lying in the roads in full view of godowns facing the beach, and here, knocking talking in an unconcerned yet affable manner the men who had held the torch to many a merchantman, and who had taken not a few out of the pockets of some of the very with whom they were standing side by side.

From the beach, a considerable way out, low black hull, with its raking masts and funnel, could be seen. There was no doubting identity; and how other vessels could so often been mistaken for her by those who had once seen it is difficult to understand. At ten o'clock in the morning she proceeded from her anchorage off to one of the wharves at New Harbour to take supply of coals; she moved with great rapidity, and made but a ripple in the water. The promontories the land soon shut her out from the view of the town, and Captain Semmes caused a notice to appear in the newspapers that visitors could not then be received, as his ship was coaling, but that all who chose to inspect her on the following day would be gladly welcomed on board.

New Harbour is three miles distant from the town by the road, and next day carriages were at a premium, for natives of all classes, as well as the European residents, had determined to avail themselves of the opportunity to inspect a ship that will possess some place in the history of the present age. The excitement among the natives was the more remarkable; for they generally display no interest in events which do not purely relate to themselves. Seven years ago, at the time of the Chinese war, the town batteries were constantly saluting the arrivals of important plenipotentiaries in the finest ships of the British Navy, and yet seldom was even an inquiry ventured by the natives as to the cause of these unusual proceedings. All however, from the smallest boy to the grey-headed old patriarchs, could tell that the *Alabama* was in. They had learned her name, and flocked in crowds to see her. What their conjectures were concerning her, or what they could see about her more attractive than about the war-ships of three times her size and armament, which arrive in the roadstead at all seasons of the year, it is somewhat difficult to say. Some had doubtless learned her story, but the great mass must have been ignorant of it. Perhaps a clue to the interest they displayed might be found in the often repeated exclamations,—" Hantu, Kappal Hantu— ' Ghost—ghost ship.' "

The *Alabama* is in appearance a small vessel, I should say barely of 1,000 tons register; she looks trim and compact, however, and likely to prove a match for a much larger enemy. She is very long

18

and very narrow : I paced her length as she lay along
the wharf, and made it 210 feet. her breadth is barely
27 feet : and she is extremely low in the water. She
is bark. but not full bark rigged, with long raking
spars ; and has the greatest spread of canvas in her
fore and aft sails. which are of enormous size. I
was assured that with canvas alone, under favourable
circumstances. she has gone thirteen knots per hour;
whether this be exaggerated or not, she must have
great sailing powers, for one of the officers on board
told me that she had only coaled three times since she
had been in commission. before coming to Singapore.
Her deck appeared to me slightly crowded for a fighting
ship. but while she was taking in stores was not the
best time to judge of this.   Her engine-room is large,
and her engines kept in beautiful order.   She has
made. they said. as much as fourteen knots under
steam. but her ordinary speed was ten to eleven knots.

Her mounted armament consists of six 32-pounder
broadside guns. and two large pivots, one 100-pounder
rifled Blakely. placed forward, and the other a smooth
bore 68-pounder.   She is not a slimly built vessel as
has been frequently represented, but is of thorough
man-of-war build.   The only action in which she had
yet been engaged was off Galveston, when she was
chased by the *Hatteras*.   The action was a longer one
than is generally believed, for it took eight broadsides
of the *Alabama* to sink her enemy. and not one, as
was reported.   Her officers pointed me out several
places where she had been damaged by the fire of
a *Hatteras*. one was just under the main chains

where the shot had gone right through her side
and lodged in the opposite timbers; one ball had
hulled her a little before the foremast—low down
—one struck her on the deck, close to her middle
starboard broadside gun, nearly killing a number
of the crew who were working it, and another shot
went clean through her funnel. These are small scars
for a ship eighteen months in commission during war
time; but I could see that they were carefully
cherished. Round the wheel, inlaid in large brass
letters, I noticed the rather remarkable motto, "Aide
toi, et Dieu t' aidera."

I was anxious to ascertain the loyalty of the crew,
of which, according to late accounts, there were good
reasons to doubt. When I went on board they were
washing decks and cleaning up after coaling, by no
means an occupation calculated to foster the most
agreeable spirit in a sailor; and yet I must say I
could remark no sign of impatience, much less of
insubordination. Nor could I attribute this contented
behaviour to fear of the officers, who were far from
rough or domineering in their manners; so that I
conclude whatever may be their hardships or the precarious nature of their pay and emoluments, the crew
of the *Alabama* would stand by her in case of danger.
The officers were all Americans, except two, an
Englishman and a German. They were all fine men,
and seem enthusiastic in the service on which they
had adventured. Some of them admitted to me, however, that the capture and destruction of merchantmen
had begun to lose its excitement, and I should not be

18—2

surprised, were the officers left to ....
that the *Alabama* had risked ....
armed ships of her enemy; her commander ...
should say was a man slow to move ....

Captain Semmes is in appearance ....
character a remarkable man. He is ....
and rather bilious-looking, and would ....
more readily to the picture of a *Georgian* ...
planter than to that of a sailor. He speaks very ...
but when he does allude to the Confederate .....
is with a bold confidence as to their future fate, ...
what surprising in these latter days of ....
reverses. When the somewhat disheartening ....
for the Confederate cause just received by the ....
mail was handed to him on his quarter-deck ....
Harbour, he simply replied, pointing to the Con-
rate ensign above him,—" It is no matter; that ...
never comes down." Time will tell whether ....
his boast be a true one.

Whatever may be one's impressions ....
sedately views the mission of the *Alabama*, it ....
possible in the presence of the trim little ship ....
not to be momentarily carried away by a sympathy
for her cause; and perhaps some more tangible pal-
liative than momentary enthusiasm may be urged
in her favour. " You must remember, sir," said one
of her officers to me, " that we but retaliate on our
enemy that destruction of property which he has
been the first to inaugurate in this war. His power
at sea was by a simple chance too much for us to
cope with from the first, or we should by this time

have had a small navy of our own, built in our own
dockyards; and as we have been content to fight him
in the field with a disparity of numbers, so we should
have attacked him at sea with a weaker force. Such,"
he continued, "has not been our fortune; but it has
been our fortune to obtain this and some few other
ships, and to bring them to bear on our enemies' most
salient point. General Gilmore himself, when he
uses the advantage which the Federal ships have
placed in his hands to destroy from his batteries the
warehouses and mansions of Charleston,* endorses
our course as legitimate. It is true, Charleston has
its forts and batteries which do their best to protect
these defenceless buildings, but does this alter the
parallel? Is it confessed that the merchant shipping
of the Federal Government can find no protection in
the Federal navy? and if it is so confessed, is it
urged that we should therefore hold back from the
advantage which our enemies' defencelessness gives us
in one particular, while he advantages to the full by
our insufficiently protected state in another? No!
when the Northern hordes pause on their onward raid
by the consideration of the inability of the Confederate
Government to afford protection to its cities, then may
we too pause on our course, for the reason that the
Federal Government cannot or will not spare ships
from the blockade of Southern ports to protect her
foreign shipping." It was a strong argument—as
strong probably as could be urged, and it did not

* The news of the shelling of Charleston with Greek fire had
reached Singapore by the previous mail from Europe.

lose its force from being put on the deck of the *Alabama*.

There the renowned ship lay, in calm unruffled water, making with a background of the beautiful green islands of New Harbour as pretty and as peaceful a picture as the eye could wish to gaze on.

On the morning of the 24th, at about ten o'clock, the *Alabama* proceeded out of New Harbour, to the westward, and her long low dark hull, raking spars, and short stumpy funnel, rapidly faded from the view of the green island of Singapore—probably for ever. But like Dundee and his blue-bonnets of old, if Singapore had seen the last of the *Alabama*, it certainly had not heard the last of her and Captain Semmes and his grey-coats. On the night of her departure from New Harbour, scarcely thirty miles off, she came up with and destroyed the British, or at least British registered barque *Martaban*; two days later she burned the American ships *Sonora* and *Highlander*, as they lay at anchor in the Straits of Malacca. Captain Semmes found means, too, to send back to Singapore a justification of his destruction of the first ship which appeared in the newspapers there three days after the event.

In very few foreign ports could the proximity of the *Alabama* have created a more visible effect than it did at Singapore. At the beginning of the present year there were eighteen large American ships, aggregating over 12,000 tons' measurement, lying idle in the harbour, when there was a brisk demand for shipping. Fully one-half of that number changed owners

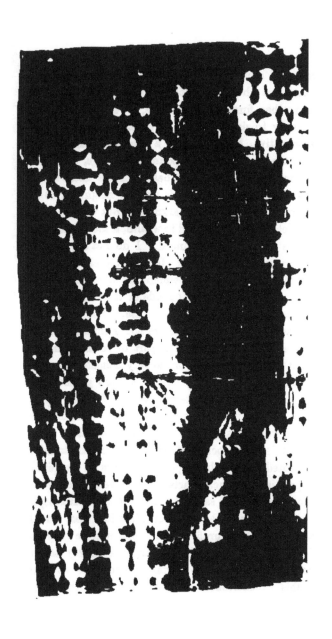

times of animadversion. Faultless, it certainly is
not. But that it has faults in any greater degree
than other foreign settlements, I am inclined very
seriously to doubt. It may be said to be strongly
conservative, but it is not a conservativeness built
upon the low standard of pounds, shillings, and pence.
The man of narrow means has often the doors thrown
wide open to him, while his wealthy neighbour is left
to grope about in utter darkness. But while a nearly
complete disregard is paid to wealth, a too great watch-
fulness of position is evinced. I do not say that the
line drawn at Government House is too circumscribed,
but all the distinctions which are necessarily made
there need not be made outside of it; nor need fresh
ones be drawn, as is often the case. The community
is a very small one. There are not, I think, even forty
families who aim to form a part of society, and if I
might offer an opinion on so very delicate a subject,
it would be that, among so few, a more general, even
though less intimate, intercourse should spring up.

Whatever it may be under the new regime, the
official world has certainly not hitherto taken a prominent lead in social affairs. But this is doubtless
accounted for by the expensive nature of hospitality
as practised in these parts. To Government officers
who receive fixed salaries, the cost of housekeeping
must be a more serious consideration than to the
merchants whose profits on a single venture may out-
bid the highest salary in the land. Probably nothing
has served to preserve certain distinctions so much
as this expensiveness of hospitality, and the extent

…which it is practised. To an extreme it must be …dulged in but by few, and as it cannot long live …less it is reciprocal, it degenerates too often into …tle better than an account current system of enter-…ainment. Latterly, there has been apparent some …proach to improvement in this respect, which it is …be hoped if of slow will be of sure growth. The …people of Singapore must come to appreciate what …long experience taught the Dutch in Java, that heavy …dinner-parties are scarcely suited either to the climate …or to the purses of settlers anxious to push their way …to fortune. In Batavia dinner-parties are now of rare …occurrence; the much more sensible fashion prevails …of giving occasional evenings "at home," at which …people can reasonably enjoy themselves without danger …of morning attacks of indigestion.

Society may be said to be composed of the chief Government officials, the merchants and bankers with their assistants and clerks—the lawyers, the doctors, and the military,—at least, any of those positions *primâ facie* give the necessary social status. Unfortu-nately however, here as elsewhere, circumstances occasionally combine to render the best of these positions unavailing, and it is not always owing to the faults of those who are excluded, but sometimes to their misfortunes. One of the chief of these impedi-ments appears to be an insuperable, though a some-what over-sensitive objection taken to all who are descended in any way from the people of India, no matter how remote the descent; and it has happened more than once at a ball, that one lady has refused to

dance opposite another because her vis-à-vis was
slightly darker than herself in complexion. There
can be no real necessity for such extreme sensibility
as this.

It is to the merchants chiefly that Singapore is
indebted for the introduction of its very expensive,
though very pleasant style of hospitality. Their
dinners are affairs of every week; they possess the
charm of being at once magnificent and unrestrained,
and they do much to maintain a spirit of emulation in
household luxuriance. It is wonderful how perfect,
too, is the knowledge possessed of the measure of
hospitality of each house, and how soon new arrivals
and visitors become acquainted with the comparative
degrees of excellence in this respect. The discreet
bachelor scarcely allows a week after his landing to
pass by before he makes his calls upon the residents,
and it is remarkable how closely they follow in the
ascertained order of hospitality. The military, however,
have the credit, and with every appearance of justice,
of being the most accurate and rapid in their discovery
of this desirable information. They scent the quarry
from afar off, and come down upon it with singular
good success. In addition to household hospitality,
picnics to various parts of the island are of frequent
occurrence. As can be inferred from the description
I have given of its scenery, the island is in every way
favourable to these, and so, also, is the weather, in
spite of the extreme noon-day heat. A few good
balls, too, are scattered throughout the year—on the
occasion of the races, of the opening of a public

building, or the arrival or departure of some important personage.

But even the ordinary style of living in Singapore may be set down as luxurious, and this to a degree that could not well be indulged at home on similar means. Any distinction, too, in this respect between one class and another is merely of degree. All have alike that exemption from the necessity of positive exertion in domestic concerns, which a large supply of native labour gives. There is also an abundance of what at home would be termed rare delicacies, and with which even on the spot, the taste never completely palls. Neither are the substantials of the table so expensive as to render an economy of these necessary. The tables of the wealthiest are to be distinguished from those of the poorest, rather by the lavish supply of European preserves and condiments—and, of course, by a draft from a choicer and more extensive cellar, than by any greater abundance or variety of dishes. Again, every one has his stable—though the poor man may have but one steed, and the rich man a dozen.

To give a correct idea of the everyday life of the European it is necessary rather to distinguish between the unmarried and the married, than between the man of narrow and the man of extended means. Most of the bungalows, as I have before mentioned, are about two miles from town; nearly all, at least, are within hearing range of the 68-pounder gun on Fort Canning, the discharge of which each morning at five o'clock ushers in the day. This is the accepted signal of all

old residents to start from bed, the younger however,
usually indulge in an extra half-hour's slumber. Still,
six o'clock generally sees all dressed and out of doors,
to enjoy a couple of miles walk or ride through the
lovely country roads, in the delicious coolness of
morning, before the sun's rays become disagreeably
powerful.

The air at this hour is of that temperature which
may be described as a little colder than cool, and
it has a sharpness which I have experienced only in
the early mornings of tropical countries, or on a frosty
day at home. A slight mist, too, rises from the
ground, that, whether it does in reality lend any
measure of coolness, certainly by association gives a
frosty aspect to nature. Indeed I have often, when
setting out on my walk at sunrise, been positively
startled by the resemblance of sharp frost. All over
the grassy patches of lawn, on the shrubs and bushes,
and on the roadside hedges, a species of spider work
their fine cobwebs upon which the dew is caught and
held in minute pearly drops, giving exactly the appearance of hoar frost; add to this, the rising mist, the
sharp air, and the red sun just showing his upper limb
above the hills, or peering through a low-lying bank of
clouds, and the illusion is tolerably complete. I may
remark that, throughout the year there is barely
thirty minutes difference in the hour of the sun's
rising. In June and December it dawns about quarter
past five, in March and September at a quarter to six.

I have already partly described the appearance of
the country or suburban roads, but if beautiful at any

time, they are certainly much more so during the two first hours of morning. The rich, green, wall-like bamboo hedges which generally line those parts of the roads which border the various residences, sparkle with large drops of dew, and from many of these that have been newly clipped may be seen shoots of over a foot in height, the growth of a single night. The trees, which are almost all evergreens, have also their large leaves wet and glistening with the refreshing moisture. Here and there, too, a strip of jungle-covered land is passed, from which breathes forth the last fragrant airs of the night blossoms. Everything living seems to share the vigorous freshness; the birds that are hushed in shelter during the mid-day heat now chirp and carol forth their short and musical notes.

Nor are these morning walks always given over to solitary commune with nature. At no other hour of the day are the roads out of town so lively with Europeans. One can always depend upon picking up a companion, and getting and giving all the little gossip of the night before; or more seriously discussing the last China or Europe mail news. During these walks, too, may be encountered pretty nearly the entire rising generation of European parentage—the heirs and heiresses, to be, of Singapore's merchants, who with their ayahs or native nurses are sent to "makan angin"—literally, "eat" the morning air.

Than this practice of exercise in the early morning, there is, perhaps, none to which the inhabitants of

19—2

Singapore are more indebted for their singularly good health. It has an effect quite opposite to fatigue; and whether it be considered as a corrective of the previous evening's dinner and its accompaniments, or simply as a means of bracing up one's nerves for the day's labour, it is invaluable. Most people limit their walks to two miles, or about half an hour; but this is by no means a rule. Some go as far as four, five, or six miles in a morning; these are the early birds who start at gun-fire sharp, and they are in the minority. I know one gentleman, now nearer seventy than sixty years old, who is out of doors at five each morning, goes a round of six miles, and comes back to his tea at about half-past six. He has kept up this practice during forty years of residence, and has reaped his reward in still robust health, strong nerve, clear head, and a yet lively enjoyment of the good things of life.

During the training season for the races, it is at this hour that the horses are taken their rounds, and the course then forms to a great many the limit of their walk. As early as half-past four the syces or native grooms are up preparing their horses, and start a little after gun-fire for the course, a distance of about two miles. At sunrise the horses commence to go their rounds, and as they wait their turns, it is generally half-past six before all have been exercised. As the distance is to most a tolerably long one, the stewards provide tea on the course, so that it is altogether a very favourite resort for about six weeks before both the spring and autumn meetings. Very little training takes place privately; but still some horses have occasionally been met returning from the course before daylight. The Malays however have a superstition connected with this "moonlight training," which is not favourable to it. A few years ago an owner, anxious to test his horse's strength and speed in secret, had him taken to the course about two o'clock in the morning; some Malays who lived on the borders of the course saw the horse saddled, mounted, and started. He went round, they aver, once, twice, thrice, gaining in speed each time; the fourth time he passed like a bird, the fifth time like lightning, and the sixth time nothing but a blast of wind went by. Certainly the horse was never seen on the course again, and so the Malays think he must have been translated into the spiritual world, where both horse and rider are still going their rounds with undiminished velocity.

On coming home from these morning rounds, the custom is to get into loose, free and easy attire, generally baju and pajamas. A cup of coffee or tea, with biscuit or bread-and-butter and fruit, is then consumed, and the next two hours spent in reading, writing, or lolling about in the verandahs which front each apartment of a house. I have said reading, writing, or lolling about; but, more correctly speaking, the time is devoted to a combination of the first and the last. In the daily avocation of most, the pen is pretty actively handled; and unless at mail times, or by those of a literary turn of mind, it is seldom taken up out of office. Reading is generally accomplished in the extremely reclining posture for which the verandah chairs of Singapore are so admirably adapted; and no doubt a deal of " quiet contemplation " must be gone through in the same attitude, in fact, perhaps, more than is generally conceded. The "dolce far niente" has its charms here as well as elsewhere, and what is more, it has a good excuse.

At half-past eight the breakfast dressing gong or bell is sounded. A gentleman's toilette in this part of the east is not an elaborate one, and half an hour is ample time for its completion. The bath is its chief feature. Attached to the dressing-room of each bedroom in almost all houses is a bath-room, with brick-tiled floor, containing a large bathing jar holding about sixty or seventy gallons of water. The orthodox manner of bathing is to stand on a small wooden grating close to the jar, and with a hand bucket to dash the water over the body. This is by no means such an unsatisfactory method as to the uninitiated it may appear. The successive shocks to the system which are obtained by the discharge of each bucketful of water, seems to have a much more bracing effect than that of one sudden and continued immersion. Every gentleman has his native boy * or body servant, whose sole duty it is to attend upon him personally. While bathing, these boys lay out their master's apparel for the day; so that on coming from the bath a gentleman has little trouble to get himself attired. As to shaving the process is

---

* The term boy is applied to all servants of this class, whatever their age. Some of these " boys " are grey-haired men of over sixty.

generally performed by itinerant Hindoo barbers, who for the small charge of a dollar or a dollar and a half per month come every morning round to the residences of their customers. The charge is so small, and the saving in trouble so great, that almost all avail themselves of the convenience.

The universal breakfast hour is nine o'clock, and when the bell then rings the whole household assemble, and should there be ladies of the number this is the first time of their appearance. Singapore breakfasts, though tolerably substantial and provided with a goodly array of dishes, are rarely dwelt over long, half an hour, being about the time devoted to them. A little fish, some curry and rice, and perhaps a couple of eggs, washed down with a tumbler or so of good claret, does not take long to get through and yet forms a very fair foundation on which to begin the labours of the day. After breakfast the conveyances drive round to the porch or portico and having received their owners hasten in to town. No matter how many may reside together, each bachelor has generally his own "turn-out;" and for half an hour every morning the two bridges leading across the river into town present an endless string of these rather motley vehicles—by no means an uninteresting spectacle. On the whole both the private conveyances and horses of Singapore are creditable to it, though the same cannot be said for the miserable pony hack-gharries that are let out on hire. A large number of horses are brought up from Australia, not less I should say than 100 each year, and all find a sale at what must be remunerative prices. None are ever exported again, and where they all go to it is difficult to conjecture, for the European population who chiefly make use of them increases but slowly, and yet horseflesh is not subject to greater mortality here than elsewhere. The climate seems to agree well with them; they grow fat and sleek and live long, though they can scarcely go through the same amount of work as in their native country; each horse has its groom and grass-cutter, and probably the additional attention they receive compensates for the exhausting temperature.

Arrived in town, ten minutes or a quarter of an hour are usually spent in going the rounds of the square to learn the news of the morning. These commercial square gatherings are quite a characteristic of the place and of the community, and whatever channels they may open to the flow of local gossip, or it might even be scandal, yet they are so far useful that they serve the purpose of an open air and non-commercial exchange. Differences of position are in most cases left behind in office, and all meet here on a footing of equality, or if there is any ascendancy at all it is that which is obtained by the readiest wit or perhaps by the greatest measure of self-assurance. As scarcely a day passes without the arrival of a steamer with news from England, China, India, or from some interesting point in the neighbourhood, there is always ample material for an animated exchange of ideas and information on leading topics, whether they be European politics, the war in America, the position of affairs in China, the com-

bined action at Japan, the affairs of India, Java,
Borneo, the administration of the local Government,
or the condition and prospects of the adjacent markets.

This sort of congress takes place between the first
arrival in town and ten or half-past ten o'clock. At
that hour business has commenced and continues in
full force till tiffin time, or one o'clock; and certainly
it is gone through in quite as smart and active a
manner as at home. The climate, though it may
produce a greater languor in the evening, has apparently no such effect during the day. There is not
much out-of-door bustle; but still when occasion
requires the folks post about the square under the
midday sun at a lively pace and with apparent
impunity.

Tiffin time does not bring the luxurious abandonment to the table which it does in Java; people in
Singapore are more moderate in their indulgence,
yet some show of a meal is in most cases made; a
plate of curry and rice and some fruit or it may
be a simple biscuit with a glass of beer or claret.
Half an hour's relaxation too is generally indulged
in, and as the daily newspaper comes out about this
hour, there is a goodly flocking either to the exchange
or the public godowns in the square for a perusal
of it.

Two o'clock is the exchange hour, and though
I do not think there is really much intercommuni-
cation on commercial subjects, yet as a rendezvous
and a place where the leading men of the mercantile
world can have an interchange of ideas even on

irrelevant matters, it has the good effect of promoting
and maintaining a more general intimacy than might
otherwise prevail.   Unlike the chamber of commerce,
from which it is distinct, the exchange as a body
assumes no political influences, and is thus no doubt
saved many a humiliating experience which it has
fallen to the lot of the former body to encounter.
The exchange is rather distinguished for its hearty
and mixed co-operation in all that tends to ameliorate
or enliven the condition of life in the settlement.

Business hours are not particularly severe, and
by half-past four or five o'clock most of the mercantile houses have got through their work.   But only
a few proceed direct home at this hour; the greater
number, at least of the younger members of the
community, resort to the fives-court or the cricket-
ground on the esplanade.   The former is an institution of long standing in Singapore; as far back as
thirty years ago it was erected, and at no time since
then has the interest taken in the game subsided.
On the contrary, about two years ago it was found
necessary to build another court out at Tanglin about
two miles from town in the vicinity of the residences,
so greatly had the number of members increased.   The
game is well-known at home, and I need not describe
it further than to say that it is a kind of rackets, but
that the hands instead of bats are used to play up the
ball and that consequently the exercise is much more
severe.   It is really surprising, in a temperature seldom
ranging at the hour the game is played below 82°,
to see those who have gone through a fair day's work

at the desk come here and doff their vests, coats, and shirts to an hour or an hour and a half of about the most severe exercise in which it is possible to engage; and this too in an unroofed building with the rays of the sun if not directly beating down, at least reflected in fierce glare from the whitewashed walls. And yet medical men attribute the extreme good health of the residents to this continued exercise indulged in, begun by the morning walk at sunrise and ending with cricket or fives at sunset. Cricket is of course precisely the same game in Singapore as it is at home.

But there are two evenings in the week when the whole European community may generally be seen upon the esplanade, whether or not they be fives or cricket-players, and these are band evenings, generally Tuesdays and Fridays. The band, which is that of the regiment on the station at the time, or from one of the men-of-war which occasionally visit the port, plays on a raised mound on the centre of the esplanade green. The chains which protect the green on ordinary occasions are on these evenings let down, and carriages, horsemen, and pedestrians are alike admitted to the greensward. Gathered round the band in a tolerably broad circle are the beauty and fashion of the place. The ladies, to whom almost all the other out-door amusements are denied, partake at least in this, and though the ruddy glow of the colder latitudes has fled from most cheeks, still there supervenes a languid softness which is more interesting and perhaps more beautiful. The pretty pale-faced European children too may on these occasions be seen tripping about in

playfulness a little less boisterous, but quite as cheerful
as is witnessed at home. The band plays from half-
past five till half-past six, at which hour it is all but
dark, when the carriages make for home in a long
string, gradually falling off one by one as the various
residences are reached.

Except on band nights however, most of the commercial and all of the official world retire home a little
before six o'clock. Arrived there, probably a glass of
sherry and bitters will anticipate the refreshing process
of dressing for dinner. A slight difference as to
dinner-hour prevails; some dine at half-past six, some
at seven; the former however is the time most commonly adopted. There is one advantage here which
is too seldom to be found in other parts of the world.
Whatever may be the hour, a clock-work regularity
and punctuality is observed, and this not with respect
to dinner only, but with respect to all other meals.
No doubt this regularity also has its share in the
maintenance of the good health of the European
community.

Dinner in Singapore is not the light airy meal
which might reasonably be imagined from the nature
of the climate; on the contrary, it is quite as substantial a matter of fact as in the very coldest latitudes.
The difference is not that the substantials are fewer,
but that the luxuries are more numerous. Indeed the
every-day dinner of Singapore, were it not for the
waving punkahs, the white jackets of the gentlemen,
and the gauzy dresses of the ladies, the motley array
of native servants, each standing behind his master's

mistress's chair, and the goodly display of argand lamps, might not unreasonably be mistaken for some more special occasion at home. Soup and fish generally both precede the substantials, which are of a solid nature, consisting of roast beef or mutton, turkey or capon, supplemented by side-dishes of tongue, fowl, cutlets, or such like, together with an abundant supply of vegetables, including potatoes nearly equal to English ones grown in China or India, and also cabbages from Java. The substantials are invariably followed by curry and rice which forms a characteristic feature of the tables of Singapore, and though Madras and Calcutta have been long famed for the quality of their curries, I nevertheless think that those of the Straits exceed any of them in excellence. There are usually two or more different kinds placed on the table, and accompanying them are all manner of sambals or native pickles and spices, which add materially to the piquancy of the dish.

During the progress of the substantials and of the curry and rice, the usual beverage is beer, accompanied by a glass or two of pale sherry. The good folks of Singapore are by no means inclined to place too narrow restrictions on their libations, and it has been found in the experience of older residents that a liberality in this respect conduces to good health and long life. Besides this the American Tudor Company keeps up a tolerably regular supply of ice, and as it is sold at three cents, or less than $1\frac{1}{2}d.$ per lb., it is within the reach of all, and is an invariable adjunct to all beverages.

To curry and rice succeeds generally some sort of pudding or preserve, but sweets have not the same temptation here as at home. Very good cheese however is obtained in fortnightly supplies by the overland steamers, and, as good fresh butter is always to be had, this part of dinner is well enjoyed, accompanied as it is by no illiberal allowance of excellent pale ale. But it is in the luxuriance of the dessert perhaps more than anything else that the tables of Singapore are to be distinguished, and it is little wonder that it should be so; for there is no season of the year at which an abundance of fruit cannot be obtained. Pineapple may be considered the stock fruit of the island, and one or two splendid specimens of these generally adorn the table. There are plantains, ducoos, mangoes, rambutans, pomeloes, and mangosteens; the latter fruit is peculiar to the Straits of Malacca and to Java, and so great is its fame that to India or China no present or gift from Singapore is more acceptable than a basket of them. It is of a somewhat singular genus; it is round, of the size of a small orange, is covered with a thick woody purple bark in place of rind, which has to be cut or broken off, and inside are the snowy-white cloves of the pulp, sweet and with a very delicate but delicious flavour, unlike anything else I know of. But though dessert generally makes a finer display than any other part of dinner, it is not that to which most attention is directed. A cigar and a glass or two of sherry after the ladies are gone, and dinner is over.

Many of the residences have billiard-rooms attached.

in which case the usual custom is to retire there after dinner. Where no billiard-room is within reach, a chat in the verandah, a little meditation, or perhaps a book passes the hours pleasantly enough until bed-time. And as dinner is seldom over before eight o'clock, and the usual hour for rest is ten, it is not a very long interval between them that has to be disposed of.

As I have remarked before I think it is to be regretted that the people of Singapore so determinedly set their faces against every sort of entertainment which does not include a dinner. I am quite sure that much of the after-dinner time, that is under the present system in a manner thrown away, might be more agreeably, and at the same time more profitably spent, if the custom were to set in that people should meet occasionally after dinner, and pass their evenings in the same sort of social intercourse as is usual at home, and in most other parts of the world.

Such is the everyday life at Singapore. It is true, I have taken rather an uncommon method of describing it, and one which might be thought more to become the pages of a journal or diary, than a book such as this, but it appears to me that by thus detailing the various acts of the day as they succeed one another, I shall have carried out more effectually the object I have in view, and presented a clearer picture of the nature of the European's life there to the people at home, than had I confined myself more to generalities.

(304)

CHAPTER XI.

PENANG: SETTLEMENT—PROGRESS—SCENERY.

Introduction—Object of the Settlement—Founded by Mr. Light in 1786 —Its formal Inauguration—Early Contentions between the Officials and Merchants—Death of Mr. Light—Proposed Abandonment— Major McDonald — Continued Contentions — Contumacy of the Merchants—Death of Major McDonald—Sir George Leith succeeds —Extension of Establishment — Annexation of Province Wellesley —Penang becomes a Presidency in 1805—First Recorder arrives— Rapid succession of Governors — Eccentricities of the Recorder —Deficiency of the Revenue—Lord Bentinck's Arrival—Scenery —Approach— Town and Shipping — The " Valley "— The High Lands—The Waterfall — View from Government Hill — Climate —Society.

PENANG, the earliest British possession in the Straits of Malacca, though its importance is cast into the shade by the magnificence into which the younger settlement of Singapore has grown, retains, nevertheless, an interest of its own. Its history is the history of the first great efforts made by the East India Company to obtain a footing in the native States of the Malay peninsula, and to set up a commercial and naval depôt, that, while it would prove of incalculable service to them as a midway station between their seat of Government and China, would also enable them to exercise a wholesome influence in the affairs of the Eastern Archipelago, from which the Dutch seemed to be rapidly excluding them.

Nor is it in point of historical interest only that it claims notice; a commerce of fully four millions sterling annually is too considerable an item in British trade to give the dependency that possesses it no commercial significance. And it must also be borne in mind, as was stated in the previous chapters of this book, that the trade of Penang stands on a far more secure basis than that of Singapore, its exports being chiefly the production of its own soil, and that of Province Wellesley, which is incorporated with it; while, on the other hand, its imports are of equally local consumption. The cultivation of these products, too, which brings its exports up to so considerable a figure, forms of itself a matter of interesting study.

In point of size the island of Penang is considerably less than that of Singapore, being some 13 miles long by 10 broad, and containing an area of about 70,000 acres. It lies on the west coast of the Malay peninsula, in lat. 5° 24′ N., and long. 100° 21′ E., and having the northern point of the island of Sumatra lying to southward and westward of it at a distance of less than 100 miles, may be said to guard the northwestern gate to the Straits of Malacca. It is separated from the mainland of the peninsula by a small belt of sea at its narrowest point, not wider than three miles. The territory opposite, for some years after the island of Penang was in the hands of the Company, continued the property of the Sultan or Rajah of Quedah,

20

from whom Penang itself had been purchased; but in
1800 a strip of this territory measuring twenty-five
miles long by four or five broad, and fronting Penang,
was purchased and added to the settlement under the
title of Province Wellesley.

Penang was founded in 1786, after the Company
had held Bencoolen on the south-west coast of Sumatra,
near the Straits of Sunda, for just one century. Bencoolen had never been a satisfactory station however,
costing far more for its government than was returned
to the coffers of the Company from its own produce,
or the trade it created. It seems indeed to have been
held merely as a supplement to the Company's power
in the far east, and as a counterpoise to the growth of
the Dutch ascendancy in the Archipelago. But even
these objects it failed to secure to any extent, as
it offered no facilities for the provisioning or repair of
the Company's ships, and was removed out of the
highway of the China and Indian trade. It was with
the view therefore, in a great measure, to obtain what
Bencoolen failed to give that Penang was founded.

As far back as 1771, in the time of the great
Warren Hastings, the settlement of the island was
first contemplated. Mr. Light, its founder, in a letter
dated 1787, says,—"So long ago as 1771, I wrote to
Mr. Hastings particularly concerning the country of
Quedah, and the utility of Pulo Penang as a commercial
port, recommending it as a convenient magazine for
Eastern trade. I had then an idea of a naval port
being necessary on this side of India, and before the
commencement of last war was convinced of the

jealousy of the Dutch, and their endeavours to exclude the British entirely from any part of the Eastern commerce." A plan was not long afterwards formed to carry out a settlement as indicated, but the breaking out of the war with France delayed it, and it was not till 1786 that Pulo Penang came formally under British dominion.

Mr. Francis Light who thus early contemplated the occupation of the island was the master of a merchant-man who had traded a great deal with the native States of the peninsula, and more especially with that of Quedah to which Pulo Penang belonged. A story was for a long time told by the early settlers in Penang that during his intercourse with the State of Quedah, Mr. Light had wooed and won the affections of the Rajah's daughter, one of those comely maidens who are still beautiful though of dusky hue, that he had married her according to the rites of her country, receiving from her father as dower the jungle island of Pulo Penang which then contained but a few fishing huts on its eastern shores, and that he afterwards sold his wife's dower to the Company for the comfortable annuity of 10,000 dollars. The story however has no good foundation. Mr. Light was a man of high prin-ciple and unselfish in nature ; and, besides, the annuity of 10,000 dollars is received to the present day by the Rajah of Quedah, to whom in Mr. Light's lifetime it also appears to have been regularly paid.

It was on the 16th of July, 1786, that the Com-pany's ships, *Eliza*, *Speedwell*, and *Prince Henry*, first anchored opposite the sandy point where Fort Corn-

wallis now stands, and they came with all the men
and material necessary to lay the foundation of the
new settlement. Early on the morning of the 17th
Mr. Light disembarked with the marines and Lascars
and the small body of European officers who had
accompanied him. On landing they found extending
down to the strip of sand on which the boats had
grated nothing but a dense jungle with an impenetrable
undergrowth of shrubs and creepers. Immediately
skirting the sand at one or two points where a few
fishing-huts stood were some clusters of the tall
slender areca palm-tree, the Penang of the Malay,
and from which the island takes its name. The
reduction of the jungle was immediately commenced,
but it seems to have been no easy task. In his diary
of the 29th July Mr. Light records that, "In cutting
the trees our axes, hatchets, and handbolts suffer much;
the wood is so exceeding hard that the tools double
like a piece of lead." In the end the work had to be
chiefly entrusted to the Malays who gathered around
them from the mainland. It is said that even
their patience frequently gave way and they were
often on the point of abandoning the work, but that
Mr. Light, on several occasions when their spirits were
at the lowest ebb, administered a somewhat novel
incentive by loading a cannon with a small bag of
dollars in place of grape and discharging it right into
the thick of the uncleared jungle; in the search for
these dollars the undergrowth at all events was sure
to be cleared away.

About a month after landing a considerable patch

of land in the locality of the present fort and esplanade
was cleared, and a few temporary barracks and houses
erected. On the 10th of August two of the Company's
ships, the *Vansittart* and the *Valentine*, anchored in
sight of the clearing and sent their boats on shore
with despatches from Madras. It was now that
Mr. Light inaugurated on the island that hospitality
which so long characterized it while in the Company's
possession, and we find him modestly chronicling in
his official diary of that day that, "I wrote to the
captains and requested their company ashore for a
few hours in the evening." What was the nature
of their evening entertainment in the temporary shed
that served for a Government House, with the newly-
hewn jungle all around, is not mentioned; but it
must have been satisfactory, for the captains returned
again on the following morning and Mr. Light fixed
upon that day for taking formal possession of the
island. He records the event in his faithful journal
in the following words: "August 11th.—Captains
Wall and Lewin came ashore with several passengers.
Saluted them with nine guns. Thought this the
most favourable opportunity for taking a formal
possession of the island. At noon assembled all the
gentlemen under the flag, who unitedly hoisted the
flag, taking possession of the island in the name of
His Britannic Majesty and for the use of the Honourable East India Company; the artillery and ships
firing a royal salute, the marines three volleys."
Such was the manner of the establishment of a
dependency which has come through many vicissi-

tudes and many alternatives of good and bad government, but has survived them all, and at the present
moment, nearly eighty years afterwards, possesses a
trade of nearly four millions sterling annually.

From 1786 till 1794 Penang continued under the
government of Mr. Light. During those eight years
the progress made was considerable, and a compact
little township stood with its fort and public buildings
on the once jungle-covered point upon which the
expedition had first landed. Up to this period the
European residents, official and non-official, had continued very much as one family; though, from the
old records still extant, there appears to have been
no lack of family quarrels and dissensions. From the
Governor, or Superintendent, as he was then called,
downwards, all the officials dabbled in trade and
might be seen between the discharge of their official
duties haggling with the natives about the prices of
all sorts of produce and merchandise. It seems also
that they traded at some advantage over the other
residents, for all produce brought to the island for
sale had first to be submitted to the Government
officers before it was taken to the merchants. This
was a constant source of bad feeling; and though
the advantage appears to have been very moderately
used by the officials, yet the bare existence of such
a state of matters was sufficient to drive away
all ordinary commerce. Mr. Light in his letters to
the Government at Calcutta urgently requested that
the public servants of the Company, himself among
the number, should be deprived of this trading privilege

and receive extended salaries instead ; but his recom-
mendations were disregarded.

In 1794 Mr. Light died, and it was then seriously
contemplated to abandon the island, and perhaps to
form a settlement on one or other of the Andamans.
Major Kid was directed to report upon the relative
merits of the old, and the newly-projected settlement,
and his report seems to have been so favourable to
the retention of Penang, that the idea of its abandonment was laid aside.   It does not appear however that
any successor to Mr. Light was appointed for three
years after his death, and it is probable that the duties
of superintendent were during that time discharged by
one of the inferior local officers.   In 1796 Major
MacDonald became superintendent, though it is not
recorded from whose hands he received the reins of
Government.   Early in his administration he experienced the evil effects of that rivalry in commerce
between the officials and the merchants which had
so disturbed Mr. Light, and he addressed long remonstrances on the subject to Calcutta.   His very first
letter contains the following remarkable but quite
characteristic passage :—" The history of the island
since its establishment under the British flag, is only
to be gathered from the journal and ledger of a certain
mercantile house, which indebted for its uncommon
prosperity to the preponderating weight it derived
from having as its principal and most ostensible head
the Company's superintendent, and the convenient
command of the public treasury, is too much interested
in defeating all retrospective inquiry to allow more

to transpire than what the publicity of certain mercantile transactions forbid it to dissemble, or to be
gleaned with caution from its equally anxious although
less favoured competitors, who are not backward in
their attempt to prove by no scanty store of anec-
dotes that to the accomplishment of its interested
views was, too frequently for the general good, most
avowedly sacrificed the real interest of the infant
settlement."

Major MacDonald however appears to have been a
man of more firmness if not severity of disposition than
Mr. Light, and he went heartily to war with the difficulties that surrounded him.   Under the somewhat
friendly administration of the first superintendent,
and the three years interregnum which appears to
have followed, the merchants had grown as the major
terms it "a most contumacious body," and he directed
his attention first to the reduction of these traders to
a proper understanding of their position.   In virtue of
powers entrusted to him by the Government at Calcutta, he addressed a circular letter to all the non-
official residents somewhat in the nature of that which
Mr. Fullerton long afterwards resorted to in Singapore,
demanding to know the authority or permission by
which they resided there, and requesting them to
report their names and characters, that the propriety
of withdrawing or continuing such permission might
be determined on.

The replies to this general interrogatory form a
very fair confirmation of the charge of contumacy,
and show anything but a respectful or even conciliatory

disposition on the part of the merchants. One of the replies is sufficiently characteristic to be singled out; it is from a Mr. Mason, and is addressed to Major MacDonald :—

"Sir,— . . . . I beg leave to inform you for the information of the Governor-General in Council that my authority or permission to reside in India is from his Majesty King George the Third—*God save him !*—also from Superintendent Francis Light, Esq., the public faith being pledged for that purpose. . . . . And as to my character I shall take particular care that it be laid before the Governor-General in Council." When the writer of this letter was afterwards asked regarding the nature of the Royal authority which he pleaded, he is said to have referred Major MacDonald for particulars to his Majesty King George the Third.

It does not appear, however, that much good came of this warfare, and Major MacDonald ill pleased with the result of his labours and the position in which he felt himself placed, and broken in health, obtained leave of absence, and died in 1799 while away from the island. But in spite of these bickerings between the mercantile and the official world, the substantial prosperity of the island had been steadily progressive ; both its commerce and its revenue had increased ; and in 1800 the Earl of Mornington, who was then Governor-General, sent down Sir George Leith in the exalted capacity of lieutenant-governor and commander-in-chief, with Mr. Phillips, his secretary, and Mr. Dickens, a barrister of some reputation, as judge;

Mr. Caunter, who had acted as superintendent after the death of Major MacDonald, became first assistant under Mr. Phillips. A few months after his arrival Sir George Leith, having purchased from the Rajah of Quedah the tract of land opposite Penang, now known as Province Wellesley, took formal possession of it on the 7th of July, by planting the British colours on the point at the mouth of the Prye river. The amount of purchase money, 2,000 dollars, for nearly 150 square miles of territory, was not great, but it was probably the full value. The chief object of adding it to the Company's possessions was to extirpate piracy in the neighbourhood of Penang, by depriving the marauders of their favourite and most convenient resort.

At this time the brilliant prospects of nutmeg and spice planting which had just been introduced afforded a strong stimulus both to the exertions of Government and private individuals. In 1801, too, a ship of some 800 tons was completed and launched on the island, and it was hoped by many that ship-building might ultimately be a large source of wealth to the settlement. The revenues rapidly improved, and in the year 1805 approached for the first time to within 2,000 dollars of the ordinary expenditure. Altogether the Council at Calcutta looked with hopeful satisfaction on the settlement, and were inclined to sanction a somewhat lavish expenditure upon it. In 1805 more than 70,000 dollars were expended upon the forts, and in the same year it was resolved to supersede Mr. Farquhar, who had administered the Government since the retirement of Sir George Leith in 1808, by a governor and council, and to constitute Penang into a regular presidency.

In September, 1805, Mr. Dundas, the first independant governor, arrived with his council, which consisted of two members, besides himself and commandant; the other functionaries of the new establishment numbered twenty-seven individuals. Mr. Dundas administered for two years, when he died at the early age of forty-five; it was a painful coincidence that he, his wife, and the first member of his council, Mr. Montague, were all carried to the same cemetery within a fortnight. Colonel Macalister succeeded to be Governor in 1807, and in the same year Sir George Stanley came out as first Recorder of Penang. In the following year the destruction of the fort at Malacca, which had come into our possession in 1805, was completed; and a great fire swept the commercial division of Penang, and destroyed over half a million dollars' worth of property. Part of the force destined for the capture of Java arrived at Penang in 1810, under Lord Minto, and the value of the island in a military point of view, was for the first time recognized. The expedition for the capture of the Moluccas took place shortly afterwards. In these years, too, there was a change of governors, Mr. Bruce assuming control. Indeed, it is remarkable the frequency with which the supreme authority was passed about from hand to hand. Mr. Bruce was succeeded by Mr. Seaton in 1811, Mr. Seaton by Mr. Petrie in 1812, who continued in power till his death in 1816,

when Mr. Phillips, who had at many intervals been
acting Governor, exercised supreme authority for a
year, until the appointment of Colonel Bannerman as
Governor in 1817.   Colonel Bannerman continued to
administer the Government till 1820, when he died,
and was succeeded by Mr. Phillips, who shortly after
assuming power was confirmed in the appointment of
Governor, retaining it until he was succeeded by
Mr. Fullerton, in 1824, and of whose administration
of the incorporated Settlement of Penang, Singapore,
and Malacca, I have spoken in the first chapter of
this book.

During those years over which I have passed so
hurriedly many of the little jealousies which characterized the earlier administration were still at work; but
the Executive had become so strong as to form a
circle of its own, and maintain complete independence
of the mercantile body.   In the Recorder, Sir George
Stanley however, a new source of trouble to the
administration arose; as this functionary claimed,
and with some justice too, the right of independent
action.   Sir George appears to have been of eccentric
character, and thought proper at times, especially
when opposed by the Executive, to push his authority
to somewhat obnoxious extremes.   On one occasion
he had a Captain Cookson of the Royal Artillery
arrested and cast into prison, because he had taken
out probate of a will of a deceased relative which was
said to contain some libellous reflection upon his
administration of justice.   In this he had acted without the knowledge, much less the co-operation, of the

other officials; and having vindicated what he considered to be the respect of his position, he determined to act equally alone in the display of his leniency, and proceeding early one morning to the gaol, he released the prisoner himself. It was somewhat singular, that during the ensuing night the roof of the gaol fell in, killing several persons, and in such a manner that it would have been impossible for Captain Cookson to have escaped, had he still been in confinement. Not very long after this, much in opposition to the remonstrances of the local Government, he seized and placed in gaol a Malay chief named Syed Hussein, on the charge of having excited a rebellion in Acheen, and driven out its king. Probably in this instance convinced of his error, he proceeded late one night to the gaol, by himself as on the previous occasion, and peremptorily ordered the gaoler to release his prisoner, the Syed.

But in addition to the little dissensions that occurred on the island itself, a gradual dissatisfaction with the condition of affairs was growing up in India. The heavy establishment which was introduced in 1805, had gone on increasing, and this without effecting any proportionate improvement, either in the revenue or commerce of the island. In 1818, the disbursements were 90,900*l.*, the receipts only 43,200*l.*, and ten years afterwards affairs had got still more unsatisfactory, the expenditure for 1827-28, being 137,000*l.*, while the receipts ere only 63,000*l.* It was this continual deficit whi h seemed to grow and not disappear with the growth of the settlement that led to the arrival of Lord W. Bentinck's mission in 1827, to remodel the Government, and as this brings me at present to the point at which I have treated of the history of the three stations together in the first chapter, it will not be necessary to consider that of Penang any further apart, especially as after this period the island came to hold a secondary place. Indeed, I have only given so much of its early history, because it may not prove uninteresting to learn the long-suffering and unselfish policy of the East India Company in the management of at least some of its acquisitions.

Penang has high claims to beauty of scenery. The island, with the exception of a narrow belt of plain on the eastern shore, is a mass of hills rising steeply from the water's edge in little cones, and gradually increasing in height towards the centre, where three distinct mountains compete for the extreme altitude. The bases of all these hills, and the valleys running between them are clothed in jungle brushwood, with here and there a patch of the tall forest trees that once covered the entire island. The slopes are in most cases cleared, and smile out in healthy culti- vation of pepper vines and fruit-trees, and on the summit of many stand the neat bungalows of the residents, belted often by a fringe of cocoanut and areca palm, or Penang trees; the latter being the tree from which, as already stated, the island takes its name, though it does not seem that it was indigenous, or that it even was produced in great quantities. Malacca is named in the same way after a tree that

cannot now be found, or at least is no longer distinguished by that name. Penang has probably more
title in later days to the name it bears, than it had in
the time of the Malays; for it now exports more *penang*
or *betel-nut*, as it is termed in commerce, than any other
eastern port, receiving as it does not only the collection
of Province Wellesley, but of the whole western coast
of the Peninsula.

The point where the European residences or warehouses are collected together is called George Town;
but except in official papers it is seldom distinguished
by that name, claiming like Singapore the name of
the island itself. It is built upon a level sandy point
running out on the south-eastern extremity of the
island, and separated by a narrow channel of less than
three miles from the mainland. The approach to the
town from the southward is, as may be inferred from
the nature of the island, very beautiful. Between
the south-eastern point of the island, which rises in
a bold wooded promontory, and the opposite shore
of Province Wellesley, the distance is about eight or
nine miles; this is some twelve miles south of the
town, and the intermediate water has more the appearance of a deep bay than of an open channel. The
northern part of the island and the mainland close in
together, and shut out the view of the northern outlet.

At the entrance of this bay some pretty green islets
are passed, wooded in some parts to the water, and at
others encircled by a sparkling beach of white sand.
The main island itself towers majestically up on the
one hand, and on the other the low mangrove shores

of Province Wellesley stretch along, backed in the distance by the blue mountains of the Peninsula. So land-locked is this passage, that as soon as the southern point of the island is passed, the sea assumes a placid lake-like appearance; and indeed it is seldom at any season disturbed by more than a ripple. About four miles up to right of the usual passage rises the lofty island of Pulo Jeraga thickly covered with wood, and the tall *Poona* trees which were long ago, in 1787, recommended to the directors, and it is believed actually collected for the purpose of furnishing masts and spars for the Company's ships. Between the island and Penang there is a deep though narrow channel, but which is seldom made use of by large vessels. The considerable native village of Jamestown, surrounded by cocoanut and other palm-trees, can just be seen peering out from behind Pulo Jeraga. Further up on the Province Wellesley side the mouths of the Juru and Prye Rivers are passed; on the northern bank formed by the confluence of the latter stands Prye town, the chief village of Province Wellesley.

The shipping of Penang rides at anchor right opposite the town, the chief feature of which is the stone fort which surrounds a small promontory running out into the sea. There is no wharf or pier at which large ships can lie, the landing and discharging being effected by means of lighters. The town is said by the residents to lie in the " valley" of the island as distinguished from the high land further back. This " valley" is in the shape of a triangle, the points of which are the fort on the east, Mount Erskine on

VIEW OF A COUNTRY ROAD IN CEYLON.

Published by Thomas Tegg, 73 Cheapside, 1837

the north, and Sungie Glugor on the south, and comprising about ten square miles. The town, with its suburbs, covers perhaps a square mile of ground, and besides the sea frontage has one principal street, with others branching off from it. The houses present the same Oriental appearance as I have remarked of Singapore, but they are perhaps less compact and more diversified, small attap-covered native huts being frequently close up against handsome European buildings; besides, the residences are removed only a very short distance from the business part of the town. The bustle in the streets is also considerably less, though the character and appearance of the people that wander through them are very much the same, except perhaps that there the natives of India are more numerous.

The roads that intersect the "valley" from the limit of the town to the base of the high lands are numerous and well made, and lead through some very beautiful country. They are for the most part planted upon either side by rows of angsana or other umbrageous trees, which afford a grateful protection from the fierce heat and glare of the noonday sun. One of the finest of these roads is that leading to Government Hill, and which passes close by the largest of the two beautiful waterfalls for which the island has a local celebrity. For some distance from town, neat little Malay cottages with enclosure of fruit-trees, cocoa-nut and sugar canes, are passed; and further on, though lying back from the road, are the large nutmeg plantations of the Ayer Itam and Ayer Rajah districts, which though severely

21

shaken by the same blight as has ....
of cultivation in Singapore, are ....
attended to.

The soil of the "valley," which is ....
near the town, gradually improves as the ....
approached, and is capable of producing ......
nary culture almost any species of inter....... ...
or grain. The hills themselves, however, are ....
reasons esteemed the most valuable for ....
the soil is deeper and richer, being made ....
disintegration of granite in which felspar ....
have predominated. From their height they ....
a constant supply of moisture in the shape ....
and mist, and have also a cooler and more ....
temperature than the valley below. These ....
were early seized upon by the first settlers, ...
summits and slopes of all the smaller hills were .....
cleared of the tall jungle with which they were ....
ginally clothed and laid out in gardens of ....
clove and cinnamon trees, interspersed with ....
pepper and sirii vines, sugar canes, tobacco, ...
and indigo. Fruit-trees have now on many ....
taken the place of the clove and nutmeg, and .....
products have greatly fallen into neglect, as Province
Wellesley opposite has been found better suited both
in point of climate and soil; and the greater facilities
of obtaining land there have also served to draw away
from Penang the attention of the planters of all descriptions of eastern produce.

About three miles out on the road to Government
Hill, a small bridle-path diverges towards the valley

through which runs a stream. This stream, higher up,
falls in a series of cascades over the granite rocks and
dead and dying vegetation of a deep gorge between the
high backland hills of the Ayer Rajah districts. The
waterfall itself is in comparison with the cascades of
colder and sterner lands little worth remarking upon ;
but the denseness and luxuriance of the vegetation by
which it is surrounded, the beauty of the flowers and
mosses and the strange character of the creepers, lichens
and parasitical plants that abound in its neighbourhood,
must be sought for in vain in any colder clime. And
added to these beauties, this waterfall secures around it a
coolness which in the "valley" below is unknown,
and its neighbourhood is sought as much by those
in search of health and relaxation as by the lovers
of the beautiful. Within the last year an hotel has
been built on the road to Government hill a few yards
before the path leads off to the falls. Its bath-houses
have been so planned as to collect the waters of the falls
before they have become heated by a long exposure
to the sun; and combining with the advantages of
those cool and refreshing waters all the requisites
of a quiet retreat surrounded with great beauty of
scenery, it will I think be largely made use of.

Passing the gorge of this mountain torrent the
ascent to Government Hill becomes steep and winding,
and the hack or palanquin must be here exchanged for
the saddle, a sturdy breed of Sumatra pony being
generally "well up" to the weight of travellers of
ordinary bulk. Sometimes the "valley" and the
town are completely shut out of view by the inter-

eye. At its mouth can be traced the outlines of
the native village to which the river lends its name,
and where in former times stood a gun battery of
the honourable Company. Its broad course upwards
as it reflects the morning's sun presents the aspect
of a stream of molten silver meandering tortuously
through the dark green moss of some shady dell.

As the clouds and the mists continue to clear
away the channel between stands out like a mirror
to repeat the beauties that surround it. Then the
shores of the island itself, with the town and shipping
in front of it, become distinct—Pulo Jeraga and Pulo
Kra away down to southward like watchers of the
channel. Between the shore and the point of view
is the long sweep of plain or "valley" already alluded
to, and the little minor hills which intervene having
their slopes and their summits green with cultivation
and the passes between them clothed in jungle. The
prospect on the other side is confined to the hilly
ranges to westward, which though inferior in height
to Government Hill, shut out from it the view of the
Indian Sea behind them. The peaks of many of these
ranges are crowned by neatly built bungalows, and
have their slopes covered with various fruit-trees.

These hills and the retreats which they afford, are
the chief charm of Penang, and have made for it a
reputation quite independent of its commercial importance, and give it rank as one of the sanitaria
of India. The lowland or "valley" of Penang does
not compare advantageously in point of climate with
either of the other stations in the Straits. Its tem-

perature is nearly two degrees higher than that of
Singapore, and more than one degree higher than
that of Province Wellesley opposite, or of Malacca;
besides this there is a disagreeable heaviness or sultri-
ness about the atmosphere. But these disadvantages
are more than counterbalanced by the easy access to
the high lands of the hills, where a climate is obtained
differing but little from a mild summer in Europe.
While the mean temperature of the "valley" ranges
throughout the year at about 81°, that of the Government or Flagstaff hill, which is the highest, averages
about 72°; the rain, too, is much more considerable
on the hills, for whereas the yearly fall on the plain
rarely exceeds 65 inches, that on the hill generally
measures over 100 inches. To the summit of the
highest of these hills is just six miles, so that it is
no wonder Penang is so frequently sought by the
invalids of other parts of India, and that the residents
there are well content to broil away in the heated
plains below with the knowledge that an hour's ride
will at any time secure them a relief which neither
Singapore nor Malacca can offer.

CHAPTER XII.

PROVINCE WELLESLEY—TOPOGRAPHY—AGRICULTURE.

Fertility of the Soil—Climate—Sea Frontage—Rivers—Early Piratical Nests—Roads—Culture—Rice—Malay and Siamese Farmers—Intermixture of the Races—Malayan Tradition of the Origin of Paddy—Siamese Account—Harvest Ceremonies and Amusements—Sugar Culture—Advantages of the Province—Early Chinese Cultivation—Their Method of Milling—European Planters—Varieties of Sugar-canes—Manner of Planting—Principal European Estates—Future Prospect of Sugar Culture—Other Products—Wild Animals—Tigers—Elephants—Rhinosceros—Bison, &c.

PROVINCE WELLESLEY is interesting almost entirely in an agricultural point of view. Purchased in the year 1800 for the small sum of 2,000 dollars, with the view to deprive of their principal rendezvous the piratical marauders who in these early times committed extensive damage to the native trade that began to pour into the new entrepôt of the Company at Penang, the province has now come to be the only satisfactorily productive possession held by the British in these parts. The causes that have led to this agricultural development are manifold, though a long time elapsed after the settlement of the province before they were properly appreciated or acted upon. In the first place the soil at least of the low-lying level lands available for cereal products was richer, more plentiful, and

consequently cheaper than in the limited " valley" of
Penang. The climate too was better suited to most
kinds of cultivation; the temperature was lower and
more equable; rain fell in quantities nearly as great
as on the hills of Penang, and at night-time in the
hottest weather and during the longest drought a
heavy and refreshing dew could always be depended
upon. And last though not least the province when
it came into our hands possessed a tolerably large
indigenous population, which has ever since continued
to be augmented by an easy immigration from the
bordering states of the peninsula, whose peoples are
not unwilling to exchange the arbitrary and uncertain
rule of their native princes for the security and justice
to be obtained on British territory; and as a consequence of this, abundance of labour could be obtained
by the European planters at a very moderate rate,
besides furnishing an abundance of native ryots for
the cultivation of rice and other products which
leave no room for the skill or capital of Europeans.

Though the province has only a little more than
twenty-five miles' frontage to the sea, it is irrigated
by four rivers of considerable volume. The Muda
river forms the northern boundary of our territory; it
is well defined and has high banks, but is not navigable for boats of any draught of water. Between the
Muda and the river Prye, which disembogues nearly
opposite to the town of Penang, there are several
creeks or streams which permit small boats to reach
the native villages that line their banks. The Prye
itself is over 200 yards wide at its mouth, and though

They then both went forth to the plain and called on their missing children by name, bidding them return. The two other children, who had followed them out, answered, 'We are coming.' Adam and Hawah now beheld with wonder the wide plain, waving with a golden harvest. On a sudden the whole grain became *samangat* or instinct with life, and then rising in the air like dense swarms of bees, poured onwards with a loud buzzing noise, until it entered the habitation of the first man and woman from whom it had its birth. Hence it is incumbent on cultivators to treat paddy with respect."

The Siamese farmers, and such of the Malays as retain the Buddhistic faith pure, have a different legend respecting the origin of paddy. They affirm that its growth has always been presided over by a goddess—equivalent to the ancient Ceres, and "that of old when mankind were yet in a state of innocence, grain grew spontaneously on the earth. At length the women began to steal, and men compassionating their weakness pardoned their error four successive times. It then became necessary to have a king to control the evil now just appearing in the world. The men however soon followed in the steps of the women, and they even ventured to show every degree of disrespect to the goddess of grain, by the rough manner in which they cultivated the corn. At length disgusted with the insults heaped upon her, and at the crimes of the human race, she fled and took refuge in a deep cave on a high mountain. Famine now ravaged the earth. To avert this calamity holy men were sent in the act was so sudden, vigorous, and altogether so unexpected that the pirates gave way in disorder. Simultaneous with the attack by sea three companies of sepoys, a body of native artillery, and some twenty-five Europeans were landed on the beach of the province, and attacked and after some hard fighting at great odds took the stockades from their pirate defenders.

About four miles south of the Prye is the mouth of the Juru river, which is about 100 yards wide; but this breadth grows rapidly less until at a mile from the sea it becomes a very small narrow creek quite unnavigable. Four miles further south behind the two steep islets of Pulo Kra, and skirting the northern slope of the small promontory of Batu Kawan, is the stream of the Junjong river, which is navigable to small boats about a mile up to the base of Bukit Tambun. The Krean river, which forms the southern boundary of the province, has a volume of water more than equal to that of any of the other rivers I have described, and is navigable for a considerable distance beyond the British boundary, affording a valuable outlet to the products of the native states of the interior. Following the windings of this river for about ten miles from its confluence with the sea, though only six miles distant in a direct line, is the boundary pillar that was long ago erected to mark the south-east limit of the province. Close to this pillar a police-station has been placed to protect the freedom of the river and afford security to the settlers on the confines.

the level plain-like formation of the land offered much
greater facilities for cultivation than the more hilly
districts of Singapore.   The chief cause, however,
that led to the rapid and continued increase of sugar-
planting in Province Wellesley, and the early suspen-
sion of it in Singapore, was, that shortly after the
cultivation had commenced at both places, it was
decided by the Imperial Government to admit the
sugar and rum of Province Wellesley into the home
market at the reduced colonial duties, while the same
products of Singapore were to be charged foreign
duties.   This was a death-blow to the early efforts
at sugar-planting in Singapore; but it was after all
a fair measure on the part of the Imperial Government, for Singapore was even then an entrepôt for
the collection of sugars from China, Java, and Manila,
to ten times the value of what could have been produced upon the island for many years to come, and
it would have been very difficult to have distinguished
between the transhipment of foreign sugars and the
exportation of bonâ fide local produce.

In Province Wellesley a kind of coarse sugar had
been brought to market by the Chinese settlers long
before the cultivation was undertaken by Europeans;
but whatever might be thought of the tact and industry
of these people in raising the canes, their manufac-
turing process was a very primitive one and little calculated to extract the full value of the product.   Their
mill consisted generally of a pair of vertical rollers,
either of stone or of very hard wood, resting on a
sort of bason platform raised at the rim and having

an outlet leading to a large barrel sunk in the ground, and which collected the juice of the canes; the rollers were set in motion by bullocks and the canes passed between them by the hand. Close to the mill and under the same shed a large fire-place was built of mud or mortar, with three separate shallow boilers embedded in it. The juice was carried in buckets from the barrel at the mill to a reservoir close by the boilers and within reach of the sugar-maker, who ladled it in as required. No stated temperature was maintained, but the fire merely increased or diminished so as to keep the juice always bubbling. A jar of cocoa-nut oil was kept close at hand, and any sudden ebullition was checked by pouring a little oil into the pan. After the juice was sufficiently boiled in the first pan it was poured into a flat-bottomed wooden reservoir, where it cooled and left behind it many of its impurities. From this reservoir it was conveyed by means of a syphon into the second boiler, when nearly the same process was gone through. Finally it was led into the last boiler, where it was boiled with a little shell-lime and then poured into a cooler. From this cooler, when reduced to the proper temperature, it was slowly drained off into conical, porous clay jars, one layer being allowed to partially crystallize before a second was added. These jars were arranged on a wooden platform, and the molasses which oozed from them collected thereby into a large barrel. In twelve or fifteen days the molasses had generally drained away, and the surface sugar of each jar was then scraped off and placed in the sun to dry. This scrap-

ing was repeated every few days until only the refuse
at the bottom was left, which was thrown in with the
molasses.

It may be readily understood that the planters of
the present day have found little to imitate in this
rude process of manufacture; but it is nevertheless
probable that the present extensive sugar estates in
Province Wellesley owe their existence there in a great
measure to it. It was very easy to see that if, under
a rude and imperfect milling, which lost it was estimated nearly one-third of the juice of the canes, and
required twice the amount of labour needed for the
finest West India mills, enough sugar could yet be
brought to market to recompense both for the planting
and milling, the prospects of remuneration on the introduction of modern machinery were more than favourable. By the early Chinese planters, too, the suitability
of the soil was demonstrated; and it is somewhat remarkable that the European sugar-growers have as
yet effected but little improvement in the manner of
cultivation; and though the examples of both Java,
Manila, and the West Indies are before them, they
have been content very much to adopt the system
previously prevailing among the Chinese.

There are several varieties of sugar-cane at present
produced on the estates under cultivation : different
species both from the West Indies and from Mauritius
have been also tried, but it may be said that only the
indigenous plants, or those which were early introduced by the Malays themselves, have come into anything like extensive or remunerative production. The

varieties in common use in the province are thus stated
in Colonel Low's dissertation on Penang.

1. The large cane or Tubboo, which is comparatively free from the ashy powder found on several
other kinds.   The Malays consider it to be less sweet
than Tubboo Itam.

2. Tubboo bittong beraboo, the powdery bark cane.

3. Tubboo Merah, a red cane, the juice of which
is considered more acidulous than the two foregoing.

4. Tubboo Rotan, the rattan cane, thin and hard.

5. Tubboo kookoo karban.   Buffalo hoof cane, a
hard cane with a chocolate-coloured rind.

6. Tubboo Itam, a black cane, esteemed by the
Malays; will attain to the height of twelve feet.

The juice of all these canes immediately after it is
expressed will show a strength of 9° to 11° by Baume's
saccharometer.

The first object in sugar-planting is to clear the
ground of all obstructions, not only of jungle but of
undergrowth and old stumps and tree roots; the surface grass, too, must be cleared away and the naked
earth kept clean.   The canes are then set out in long
parallel rows six feet apart, each plant in the row being
about two feet and a half apart.   From April till June
is the season best suited for the planting of the canes;
but this is not strictly adhered to, and ripe canes may
be generally seen at all seasons of the year.   As the
plants grow up trenches of about two feet in depth are
dug between the rows; the canes are manured from
time to time with decayed fish, bat guano, and other
manures which can be obtained in abundance.   Upon

the attention paid to trenching and manuring, the
period of maturity in a great measure depends, but
fifteen months may be taken as the average time
which elapses from planting till the canes are ready
to be cut. They are then fully seven feet in height,
are thick and well filled, and in many respects superior
to the canes of the West Indies. Each acre contains
about 2,500 plants or bunches, each bunch yielding
about eight canes; and the produce of these would
be about a ton of good sugar, with a proportionate
quantity of molasses.

There are now eleven extensive sugar plantations
in Province Wellesley the property of European capitalists and under European superintendence. Of these
no fewer than six—the Caledonia, Krean, Victoria,
Jawee, Golden Grove, and Valdor estates—are the
property of the Right Hon. Edward Horsman, M.P.,
H.M.'s Privy Councillor. Mr. Horsman, who I
believe has never seen these valuable properties of
his, embarked some twelve years ago upon the venture
of sugar-planting solely upon the representations which
were conveyed to him of the productiveness of the soil
and the suitability of the climate. Nor as far as I can
learn have these representations proved exaggerated.
An enormous outlay, larger perhaps than could at first
have been contemplated, was necessary at the outset,
but the returns have already been large, and are likely
to be progressive for a good many years to come, and
this with no commensurate increase of annual outlay.
The other estates are : Batu Kawan, the property of
the Messrs. Brown and Nairne ; Tassek, the property

of Mr. Nairne; Malakoff, the property of Mr. Chasserian; and Juru and Simpang Ampat, the properties of Messrs. Herriot and Co.

To most of these plantations is attached milling machinery of the highest order, in all cases driven by steam power, and an extensive staff of European superintendents and engineers. But to the introduction of fine modern machinery the efforts of the European planter seem to have been confined; for, as I have remarked before, the culture of the cane is left pretty much as it was in the hands of the Chinese and native pioneers. This is probably the result of the character of the labour that must be depended upon, for it would perhaps be a fruitless task and at all events would be an expensive experiment for a handful of Europeans to endeavour to break a whole people off their old method of cultivation in favour of a new one. Besides this, large patches of land remain in the native hands, and no modern intervention could affect the manner of cultivation on these, and they furnish, I have been told, a very considerable proportion of the canes that are crushed at the various mills.

There can be no doubt whatever that in sugar production a large and sure source of wealth will continue to be derived to Province Wellesley; but it is to be regretted at the same time that as long as the boundaries of the British territory remain as they are, this source must be confined within sure but ascertained limits. It appears that beyond the estates already secured every acre of land suitable for the cultivation

of this great staple has already passed out of the hands
of Government. A small portion of what is held by
the planters still remains uncultivated, but the largest
and best tracts are taken up by the Malays and Chinese
for paddy-fields and fruit-gardens, and cannot be
bought from them. So that I rely for the increase
of the sugar returns rather on an improvement of the
estates already in existence than to the establishment
of new ones. There is only one way of overcoming
this obstacle to the full development of this valuable
product in these parts; that is, by the extension of the
territorial boundaries of Province Wellesley, and to
this I am of opinion the British Government should
early direct its serious attention.

On many of the sugar plantations and also on the
slopes of some of the hills in Penang, the cultivation
of coffee has been attempted, but though meeting with
no discouragement its growth has never been more
than experimental; the trees that have been planted
bear a beautiful small blue bean quite equal in flavour
to that of the best Ceylon. Indigo is grown almost
entirely by the Chinese in the province, and only for
local consumption. The plant is in most countries
considered as an annual and renewed every year, but
in the richer soil here it continues productive for two
years. This drug however will never be able to be
produced in the province cheap enough for exportation. Tobacco is grown by the Malays, but it is
badly prepared and never exported. Tapioca has in
late years been cultivated somewhat extensively; it
will flourish upon land unfit for sugar, and several

Europeans have directed their attention to it. In addition to these there are a number of other products of limited growth, and Province Wellesley produces in abundance all the fruits of Singapore and Malacca.

While Penang is almost untenanted by wild animals Province Wellesley boasts a very fair list. Tigers are here in considerable numbers and are very often seen prowling about the outskirts of the native villages; but whether it is that they are less ferocious than their sturdy brethren which swim across from the mainland of the Peninsula to Singapore, or that the people of Province Wellesley are more scattered, and their pursuits and the nature of the country less favourable to a surprise, the loss of life by these monsters is comparatively speaking insignificant. Still however a few victims pass off every year, and it was here that the remarkable case related in the fourth chapter of this book occurred, in which a tiger broke into a house on the outskirts of a village and carried off a man.

Elephants were plentiful in Province Wellesley at the time the British first took possession, and are still to be met with in the bordering forests. They are not nor does it appear that they were more largely used by the Malays in field labour or as beasts of burden, though it is said that the tin from the Patani and Perak mines is chiefly conveyed by these animals to the various depôts. They at one time formed an item of export to British India, the traffic having been carried on by the Coromandel native traders. The vessels used in the transport

were constructed so that the planking of one side
would open out or let down; these vessels were run
some miles up the Prye river and moored in deep
water close to the bank, the side was opened out
and a broad planking sloped from the bank into the
hold. The elephants were enticed on to this planking,
the extremity of which reaching on board was then
suddenly lowered a little and the animals slid down
into the hold. It is many years since this export
stopped, and the demand in Siam is so great as to
absorb all that are now reclaimed from the forests.

The rhinoceros is still plentiful in the bordering
forests, and they not unfrequently make incursions
into the province itself. They are hunted by the
Malays for the sake of their horns and hides. The
wild ox or bison is also in great abundance; its flesh
is sweet and wholesome, and the Malay hunters cure
the meat and bring it into market to be sold to the
Chinese junks and native prahus; these hides are
also valuable, but the great object is to capture them
alive and break them in to be beasts of burden.
Wild hogs and deer abound; the former is a very
powerful animal. A few months ago a planter in
the province shot at one and slightly wounded it,
on which the beast rushed upon him, knocked him
down, and a deadly scuffle ensued, from which the
planter very narrowly escaped with his life. Besides
these that I have enumerated, there is an abundance
of smaller animals, such as monkeys, squirrels, &c.,
also birds, alligators, and snakes; and any one really
bent upon sport, with some good guns in his kit, and

rmined to undergo all the hardships and discom-
s of a ten days' campaign among the creeks and
sts on the borders of the province, would be amply
arded both in the number and variety of the game
ould secure.

(348)

CHAPTER XIII.

MALACCA: ITS ANTIQUITY — TRACES OF ITS EARLIER
DAYS.

How and when it came into European Possession—Its former Great-
ness—Traces of its earlier Days—The Stadt House—St. Paul's
Cathedral—Old Tombs and their Epitaphs—The Ancient Fort—Its
Destruction by the English — Underground Passages and their
Traditions— Curious Discoveries— Evidences of extensive Gold
Mining—Painful Incident—The Modern Church—Practical Spirit
of the East India Company.

MALACCA was founded about the year 1260 by the
Malays who were driven from the Island of Singapore,
as related in the first chapter. By the inherent energy
of these people and by good government, the colony
rose in little more than a century and a half to be a
place of great importance, its rulers claiming equality
with the kings of Siam and Java, and maintaining
friendly relations even with the emperors of China.
The states of Patani, Quedah, Perak, Pahang, Kalantan
and Tringanu, were all under its dominion, besides
several provinces in Sumatra opposite. It continued
in a condition of almost uninterrupted prosperity, until
attracting the cupidity of the Portuguese, it was, after
an unsuccessful assault in 1508, captured by Albuquerque in 1511. During the Portuguese occupation

it appears fully to have maintained its importance; but when it came into the hands of the Dutch in 1642, its onward progress was seriously arrested, for the latter power inaugurated a cruel policy, which drove away the Malays in large numbers to the neighbouring states. In 1795 Malacca was wrested from the Dutch by the English, and remained in our hands till 1818, when it was given back to come finally into our possession seven years afterwards, in 1825, by virtue of the treaty with Holland.

But it had ceased long before British rule to be a point of attraction to the busy adventurers who poured eastward in the search of riches.* Time was beyond doubt, for the impress of enterprise long dead still remains, when Malacca was a great commercial emporium, at least according to the ideas of that time. Nor are there wanting indications to show that its local resources were developed to a degree that has been long forgotten; so much, indeed, is this the case, that the richness of the land we hold is now judged of rather by the knowledge of what it has produced than by our own research and examination. Malacca is a ruin—ruin moral and material; not a moral ruin because its people have become bad, but because they have fallen into that negative state of existence which is most fatal to progress. The people, like the place, gather to themselves glory only from the past, not from what they are and what they do now, but from what they were and what their ancestors

* Here I partly transcribe from notes made by me during a visit to Malacca in 1863.

did before; and with this reflected splendour they are
content to a degree that forbids the hope of reawakened
energy. The material ruin of Malacca is less painful
to behold; in truth it is its most pleasing feature; for
though we can look upon the broken arches and
crumbled walls of the dead works of dead men with
an almost tenderer admiration than we should have
bestowed upon them in their full strength and perfection, if is not so with the broken or wasted spirit
of a people. At the present day, therefore, it is but
seldom that Malacca is approached by Europeans in
search of commercial advantages. Those who may
land there on their passage through the Straits,
examine it as a relic, and those who proceed from the
sister settlements do so generally for pleasure or
from curiosity only.

The appearance of the town from the roadstead
is to say the least pretty. The anchorage for vessels
of any great draught of water is about two miles out
from the landing; and from this, the eye embraces
a view of nearly twelve miles along the coast, extending
from Tanjong Kling on the westward to Water Islands
on the eastward. In front there rises prominently
the old ruined church or cathedral on St. Paul's hill,
where the flagstaff is erected, and where the light-
tower is built up against the wall of the old church:
at the foot of the hill stands the ancient Stadt House,
which is nearly hid among the foliage of the stately
Weringan trees which cluster round the bend of the
hill and are of a size unknown in Singapore. Close
to the Stadt House runs the Malacca river, and this

divides the native part of the town on the westward
from the European to the eastward. The former is not
attractive, though from a distance, the tiled and closely
packed roofs, which gradually lose themselves among
the cocoanut and other foliage, have no bad effect.
The European part of the town is, on the other hand,
very picturesque; for the houses, which line the sea
wall, are tastefully built and in most cases surrounded
by trees and flowers; and these also become gradually
shut in by the foliage on the islands to the eastward.
The background `is composed of a series of wooded
knolls and hills gradually increasing in elevation and
size as they go inland, until abruptly terminated by the
rugged outline of Mount Ophir. Altogether, the view
of Malacca that is presented to the visitor newly arrived
in the roads, is one which invites to a closer inspection.

The Stadt House is probably the place to which
the stranger will first direct his steps; and this not
entirely with a view to commence his researches after
the curious; for though the building is properly
speaking the Government house, it is too large for
any single family, and, except when in the occupation
of the Governor or the Recorder on their periodical
visits, the use of one or two rooms can be obtained by
application to the Resident Councillor. And indeed
the fine old edifice is no bad place where to sit down
and collect and arrange some fragments of the past
history and present condition of the country whose
rulers had for a century and a half dwelt within the
same walls. The palace, for it is still as worthy of
that name as any edifice yet reared in these parts

... Dutch ... and ... is itself not the least
... ... to be examined. The style of its
architecture belongs to an age that has now gone by,
... ... of its construction bears no resemblance to the modern buildings around it. It is
... ... is the best style of the Dutch
architecture of a hundred and fifty years ago. It has
those ... gables and castellated walls and
... together with that prim yet irregular aspect
which is everywhere to be seen in old Holland. Nor is
it merely the ... interior of the old Dutch palaces.
These are ... modern buildings in the East, which
are to often but the pasteboard representations of
their original types, all is solid and substantial. Indeed
with respect to every one of the old buildings at Malacca
there is nothing that will strike the thoughtful observer
more ... than the substantial character of their
... ... it ... almost ... and this con-
... ... by subsequent observation,
that the emigrants of those old days were colonists,
and not birds of passage merely. They must not
have come, as the people of England now flock to the
... ... either to gather so much of the wealth of the
land as they could grasp and then to hurry back and
spend it at home heedless of the after fate of the
country from which it had been derived. Both the
Portuguese and the Dutch appear to have determined
to deal more fairly by their Indian possessions, and to
content themselves with a luxurious life in the east
as the reward of their enterprise and industry. The
flights of stairs, the pavements of all the courtyards

and halls, and also the facings of the building, are of solid blocks of stone, which it is said must have been brought from a great distance, and which is of such a flinty nature as to have required no little masonry labour to have reduced it to shape. The building, which after the capture of Malacca by the English had become slightly dilapidated, was subsequently repaired, and many of its oldest features swept away; but still more than enough remains to tell its date and origin. It would seem too, that an effort has been made in later times, probably by some romance-loving Resident Councillor, to make the inward furnishings of the building have some consistency with its quaint exterior; for the stranger who retires to rest within its dreary chambers, reposes on an antiquated canopied bed of gigantic proportions and sombre aspect, standing four feet and a half high at least off the ground, with the old-fashioned steps on either side; and by a natural process, the mind is carried away in dreams of stately Stadtholders and portly Burgomasters. But, unlike many ancient buildings in Europe, the Stadt-house appears never to have owned any ghostly tenant; and whatever may be the vagaries of the traveller's mind during sleep, he need not fear in his waking moments to encounter the spectres of any of its bygone inhabitants. The mornings in Malacca are cool, and this even in the hotter part of the year, and give time for a fair amount of inspection before the sun becomes uncomfortably strong. St. Paul's Hill, with its ruined Cathedral, its tower and its flagstaff, is the point to which a visitor is most likely to be first attracted; and if he

23

be of a contemplative mind, if he have it in his power with the relics of a past age before him to call back some shadow of its life and manners, he will be amply rewarded. The Cathedral must have been one of the first works of the Portuguese after their occupation of the Settlement, and cannot be much less than three hundred and fifty years old. At the first dawn of the Reformation, while Henry the Eighth was still toying with the great religious revolution, the walls of St. Paul's Cathedral at Malacca were slowly rising by the forced labour of a conquered people under the guidance and direction of the enthusiastic and powerful missionaries of Rome. There can be no doubt that forced labour was employed upon this, and upon most other buildings at the time; the extent of the work would prohibit the possibility of its having been executed by European artisans, and a careful examination of the masonry would rather confirm this opinion; for though the design is faultless and the carving of the stones minute and laboured, still there is the want of that perfect symmetry and regularity which is so remarkable in the contemporaneous works of Europe. But, even if the religious enthusiasm of the emigrants, or the wealth of the church, had secured European stone-cutters, the great bulk of the work must still have been performed by the people of the soil,—and the principle of remuneration adopted in those days is well known. According to the opinion of the present local authorities the procuring of materials, and especially of stone, must have been the heaviest part of the work; for this last, a hard honeycombed iron-stone, it is said cannot be found within many miles of the Cathedral. I scarcely agree, however, in this, or in the Dutch legend that it was built by the Portuguese with the stones of the ancient Malay Kings; for according to my observation, all the large boulders on the beach on the Malacca side of Tanjong Kling bear a very close resemblance to the material which composes the old church.

Whatever may have been the difficulty attending its construction and whatever the skill of its design, they have been unable to rescue it from the inevitable decay of age. But time has dealt gently with it; the roof it is true is gone, and the sun and shower of near a century have wrought their work; yet the walls stand and the plan of the building remains perfect. There are the groined arches of the windows and the doors, the built-up niches which had held saints or martyrs, and the recesses where had stood the holy water and consecrated wine. The Dutch, who in 1642 wrested the settlement from the Portuguese, had done their best to efface all memorials of the Romish worship, for it appears that for some years after their accession this church was used by them for Protestant service. Still, however, they have been more merciful or more enlightened than the reformers of Europe, and when they had built a church for themselves they continued to respect the walls which had been the temporary shelter of their own faith.

It is not to the walls however of this old church that we must look for the story of the past. At our

23—2

feet lie the chronicles of the dead; indeed, the pavement is of tomb-stones, of all sizes, of every variety of stone, and of sculpture of different degrees of fineness. The earlier stones—those marking the resting-places of the Portuguese—are mostly granite and of a plain and simple character. Those set up after the Dutch accession have much finer carving—finer by far than is now to be found in most modern cemeteries; the stone, too, is a something between dark limestone and black marble, and unlike any to be found near Malacca, from which it would appear that the wealthy Dutchmen must have procured these tablets from Europe. Most of the Dutch stones bear crests or armorial bearings, in which the ship and lady of Holland are conspicuous; these crests, together with the limited number of graves which the enclosure of the church walls permits, would favour the conclusion that the influential citizens only of Malacca obtained their last resting-place within the favoured ground. The rules of admission, too, appear to have been calculated with singular foresight, for though every nook of the old ground is now appropriated, still the tenants of no particular generation predominate, but commmencing three hundred years back, the dates come gradually down to within the present age; now, however, the ground is closed to all but two or three families.

The most ancient date that remains legible upon of the tombs is 1568; but the body of the epitaph such effaced to enable anything but a conjecture med of its purport. There are several other stones of the same material and style of inscription as this first, but all worn away to such an extent that neither name nor date is now discernible. The most perfect stone of the time of the Portuguese is that of a Jesuit bishop of the Japan mission, bearing the following inscription :—

HIC JACET DO
MINUS PETRUS
SOCIETATIS
JESU SECUN
DUS EPISCOPUS
JAPONENSIS
OBIIT AD FRE
TUM SINGAPU
RÆ MENSE FEB
RUARIS ANNO
1598.

" Here lies Bishop Peter of the Jesuit Society ; second Bishop of Japan. He died in the Straits of Singapore in the month of February. 1598."

A great deal may be learned from this stone. It tells, in the first instance, of the wonderful extent to which the Roman Catholic religion had been pushed in these days by the powerful, ambitious, yet self-denying followers of the order of Jesus. This man, not the first but the second bishop who had laboured to spread the gospel in Japan, no doubt on his return from that far-off land, that Ultima Thule of the then known world, and probably after many years of ministry, died in the Straits of Singapore. We learn here, too, that the island of Singapore, though not reclaimed to civilization for 250 years afterwards, bore then the same name as it bears now, and gave its title to the narrow straits between it and the coast of Johore—

a channel which, though altogether abandoned within the last 70 years, was until then believed the only safe thoroughfare to China.

Fifty years before this Jesuit Bishop had laid his bones in the old church, the renowned St. Francis Xavier had arrived in Malacca and had directed the great fire which terminated in the entire destruction of the Achinese fleet, whose admiral had sent a defiant challenge to George de Melo, the Portuguese commander. Nor had trouble entirely ceased at the date of the bishop's sepulture; for, according to the old chronicles, from the year 1597 to 1600 the Portuguese garrison at Malacca was subjected to a succession of exhausting attacks both from the Malayan princes in the interior, and from the powerful rulers of Achin in Sumatra, then the most important naval power in these quarters. However, though the times were troublous enough when the grave closed over the good old bishop, no rude hand, raised in local faction or lifted by foreign foe, has disturbed the tablet to his memory, which remains in a singular state of preservation.

There are many other ancient graves, but they only serve to carry the enquirer's mind back to the period of their dates, and leave it there to fill in the life and manners of the age according as his knowledge of history may be more or less perfect. There is one however, which I must notice, for it tells some story of domestic life. As far as antiquity is concerned, it loses by comparison with the grave I have just considered. It is of the Dutch age—when the Portuguese had for nearly

half a century ceased to be rulers of Malacca. It reads
in this way,—

DOM

PIAEQUE MEMORIAE
AGNITAE TRIP
UXORIS CASTAE
FOECUNDÆ DELECTÆ
HOC MONUMENTUM FT.
ARNOLD VAN ALSEM
FISCI ADVOCATUS
14 KALEN FEBRUARIS
M. D. C. XCVII

" To the pious memory of Agnes Trip, a chaste, fruitful, and beloved
wife, this monument was erected by Arnold Von Alsem, Crown Counsel,
14th February, 1697."

Here can be gathered a little of the inner life of
the people of that time. We learn that then as now,
chastity in woman was her chief virtue and ornament;
but when it is specially recorded to the honour of a
wife's memory that she was chaste, we have some
reason to doubt of the general morality of the times
in which she lived. In an age like our own, and
among a people—

" Whose daughters are always virtuous,
Whose sons are always brave."

—a husband would scarcely seek to gain respect for
his wife's memory by recording on her tombstone that
through life she had been chaste. Nor does history
serve to dispel such misgivings. As far back, it is said,
as the time of St. Xavier, that sainted worthy found the
morality of the people of Malacca at such a low ebb,
that, unable to make head against it, he saw no other
course before him but to curse the place and fly from
it. But the grave of Von Alsem's wife tells us that in

addition to her being chaste she was fruitful; and though it is a singular virtue to have piously recorded on an epitaph, yet one cannot but admire the honesty and forgive the pride of the husband who thus tells to future ages that his wife had increased and multiplied according to God's commandment given to our common ancestor. Besides, the husband appears to have been keenly alive to the fact, that to be both chaste, and at the same time fruitful, is a greater virtue than to be chaste and not fruitful. From this stone, too, we learn that at the time the lady died, there was a Crown counsel, or State advocate in Malacca, for so I translate *Fisci Advocatus*. A hundred and seventy years later, Singapore, that has grown to ten times the importance of Malacca in its palmiest days, is behind it in this one respect,—in that, to the present day, though much wanted, there is no office of Crown prosecutor.*

Altogether, the graves within the walls of this old church must continue one of the chief attractions of Malacca. The epitaphs on many are quaint and curious;—some, too, may be simple—and others perhaps faulty; but, strange as it may seem, they stand forth in bold superiority to those of modern times which are to be found in the building now used for Protestant worship. I said that the roof of the old church had fallen in; I must, however, except the chancel, which has, in a spirit of irreverent economy, been appropriated by the English Government for a

* Since this was written a Crown prosecutor has been appointed for the Straits.

powder magazine. Though, whether the roof that
now shelters the gunpowder of her Majesty is the
selfsame as that which sheltered the worship of the
faithful in the time of St. Xavier, is of course a matter
of conjecture only.

There is about the broken walls of this church something far more striking than is to be observed in the ruins
of a similar age at home. Instead of the weird and
sombre surroundings which as it were by prescription
belong to such ancient memorials in Europe, we see
on every side the fresh and lusty growth of tropical
vegetation. Where at home we would look for old
oaks or stately pine-trees, here we find the feathery
cocoa-nut, the werringan, mango and mangoosteen;
though the yellow rice-fields in the distance might,
with no great effort of imagination, be taken for the
corn-fields of Europe. In the very centre of the
eastern wall of the ruin, may be seen a tropical plant
which, having taken root in the basement of the
building, has in the vigour of its upward growth fairly
split the old walls rather than deviate to right or left
of its course. From every chink and crevice, too,
droop a luxuriant profusion of lichens, and some of
those lovely orchids which are but rarely to be seen in
the choicest conservatories of Europe. Altogether, it
is a picture not often to be met with; to see the
reverend old pile, gray with age, surrounded by that
warmth of Eastern scenery, which is associated in the
English mind with everything that is mutable and
transient.

Round the base of St. Paul's Hill, to seaward,

stood one of the strongest forts which had probably
ever been constructed by Europeans in Eastern parts,
either before or for many years after its date.　It was
designed and begun by Albuquerque in 1515, or about
four years after his conquest of Malacca from Mahomed
Shah, its Malayan ruler.　From its size, and from the
durable materials from which it was composed, a considerable number of years must have been devoted to
its construction; old traditions among the Malays
state, that its building occupied thirty-six years and
fourteen days; this period, however, seems too nicely
measured to merit much credence.　It is also stated
that Albuquerque at the same time laid the foundation
of the old church already described, and that he
dedicated it to the " Visitation of our Lady."

　　The fort remained in a tolerable state of preservation till the year 1807, when the British, who had
some time before taken Malacca from the Dutch, caused
it, at an enormous expense, to be razed to the ground.
This was done in anticipation of the abandonment of
the place, and so to prevent its afterwards being occupied as a stronghold by any other European power.
The expense of this destruction, which was close upon
70,000*l.*, will give a very good idea of the extent and
durability of the ancient fort.　All that now remains
is the eastern gateway, which has probably been spared
as a sort of relic of the old work; the material of
which it is built is the same honeycombed iron-stone
as is to be observed in the church on the hill; the
stones have all been well cut and fit perfectly into one
another, and the gate must originally have been orna-

mental in appearance. But the Dutch, with that strong love of plaster and whitewash which has at all times distinguished them, must shortly after their occupation have commenced to renovate the fort after their own style, for though the walls of the gateway have in many places been bared by time, it is evident that at one period they had been well coated over with plaster; and immediately over the entrance, on the plaster that remains, may still be seen the impress of the Dutch coat of arms, and the date 1670 below—a very glaring record of cool appropriation, whereby the Dutch have sought for themselves the credit of a work which had been completed more than 100 years before their accession; it would seem too, that, at the time, they were not unconscious of a measure of effrontery when they wrote on plaster instead of on stone.

It is difficult to imagine any other purpose for which the fort was built than as a protection from an attack upon the town by an enemy's ships; and yet, unless the physical geography of the harbour has considerably altered, and its depth of water was much greater than it is now, the fort must have been entirely useless except to prevent an attack from a landing party in small boats. At the present day, vessels capable of carrying guns heavy enough to be destructive against a fortification, must, unless they would ground at low water, anchor so far out as, even with the superior weapons of modern days, to be safe themselves, and at the same time harmless against the fort. That some material alteration in the depth of water in Malacca Roads has gradually taken place

within the last 350 years, seems a most probable conjecture. In 1508, when the Portuguese admiral,
Lopez de Sequeira, cast anchor for the first time in
Malacca roads, it is recorded that he opened a heavy
fire on the town from all his vessels, and the effects of
which are thus described in the Malay annals. "All
the people of Malacca were frightened when they heard
the sound of cannon; saying, what sound is this like
thunder? And the bullets came and struck the people
who were on the land, and some had their necks
severed, and some had their waists, and some their
hands and their feet. The terror grew constantly
worse and worse, and they said what is the name of
this weapon, which is so round; it is not sharp, yet
will it kill?" And three years afterwards when Albuquerque came to take possession of the place, as soon
as he dropped anchor he commenced a heavy can-
nonade, referring to which the same annals tell us
that "multitudes ran searching for a place to shelter
themselves from the bullets." It is plainly enough to
be inferred from this, that the harbour could in those
times permit tolerably heavy vessels to lie within gun-
shot of the shore, whereas now, at low water, even
a ship's boat cannot approach to within half a mile,
except by following the very narrow channel which the
river has formed for itself through the mud. If the
depth of water was no greater in 1807 than it is now,
the destruction of the fort by the British authorities,
at a cost of 70,000l., must be set down as little else
than a piece of thoughtless Vandalism.

The decay of Malacca has been gradual, and very

little besides bare walls has been left to tell of its past importance. The later poverty of the people had doubtless made them reduce to money every relic that had any intrinsic value; still, however, some of its ancient stores and implements which had escaped their notice or cupidity continue from time to time to turn up. Twelve years ago, while opening out a subterraneous passage at the foot of the hill, two cases of ancient cutlasses were found, which, with a lamentable disregard of their historical value, were distributed by the authorities amongst the convict and sepoy workmen, and we believe not one can now be found. The passage in which these weapons were discovered, is reported to have been some sort of communication leading from the town to the monastery behind the church, and which the old monks availed themselves of when engaged in those scarcely clerical enterprises on which it is said they at times adventured. A more unkind legend prevails, that from the same monastery another subterraneous passage led to the nunnery of " the Mother of God," which was erected on St. John's Hill, about three quarters of a mile distant, but which was afterwards pulled down by the Dutch to build a fort to check the incursions of the Malayan princes. The distance, however, is too great to make such an underground passage possible, and the tradition has probably had for its origin the loose morality into which the people themselves had fallen, and which, as we have seen, made chastity so scarce a virtue as to be specially recorded in favour of those who had practised it.

But however questionable may be the truth of the popular traditions concerning these subterraneous passages, there can be no doubt that underground communications did exist in the neighbourhood of the old hill. Nearly opposite the present landing is the orifice of a stone-built passage which runs directly into the hill a few feet above the level of the road. Not many yards from the entrance this passage is now blocked up with stone; and though it was here that the two cases of cutlasses were discovered, no persistent effort has since been made to clear away the intervening masonry, and ascertain the place to which it leads, or the purpose which it served; a couple of convicts could surely be well spared for this work. In the old church the mouth of another underground entrance has also been laid open, but nothing has been done to follow it up. It is said that in this case the authorities have been deterred from going to work by respect to the prejudice of the old Malacca families, who consider the ground is too holy to be disturbed, either to satisfy curiosity or to afford an additional page to the history of the place. So far indeed was this feeling allowed to prevail, that many years ago, when a coffin was discovered in a recess of the walls of the church, displaying all the indications of great age and of the importance of the individual whose remains it contained, being surrounded by a metallic case, it was returned unopened by the Resident Councillor of the day to the place where it was found, and the recess built up.

But the most curious discovery of late years was

made by Captain Playfair about twelve months ago. A
part of the road that now runs round the base of the
hill had to be straightened and levelled, and in making
the necessary excavations the walls of a cellar or store-
room which had formed part of the old Portuguese
Government buildings were broken down, and in a
small recess were discovered forty or fifty earthenware
pots, many of which were crumbled to pieces, but in
each of those which were whole was found a small
quantity of quicksilver.   Only about four pounds
weight in all was recovered ; but had the pots been full,
as they doubtless were when the light had last closed
upon them, they must have contained considerably
more than a ton weight of this uncommon metal.
There is only one purpose for which such a large
quantity of quicksilver could be required or made
available, and that is for the amalgamating process in
gold mining.   It is well known that the greater portion
of the lands in the interior of Malacca are auriferous.
Ten years ago, when the rich discoveries of Australia
had revived over the world the gold fever which was
fast declining under the reduced returns of California,
prospecting parties, European as well as Chinese,
spread themselves over the jungled valleys around
Mount Ophir, with the hope of striking some rich lead
of the precious metal.   No such lead could be found ;
but it is worthy of remark that in almost every spot
which was tried gold in small quantities was procured,
and though all the sinkings were ultimately abandoned, still some had been worked for nine months or
a year.   But it scarcely required this modern rush to

point to the auriferous locality, for the name Mount
Ophir is sufficiently indicative of the presence of the
precious metal.   No doubt an extensive system of gold
mining was carried on in the time of the Portuguese,
and that whether or not richer fields were than known
than can now be discovered, by forced labour and by
the introduction of European appliances they were
able to make it an important source of revenue; and
if the jungle of 300 years could be cleared away, it is
possible that there might still be seen the abandoned
diggings of the early colonists of Malacca.   But at all
events I think it well here to point to this discovery of
quicksilver as giving rather a startling proof both of
the extent of the auriferous resources of the country,
and of the skill with which they were developed in
olden times.

Before closing these observations in the vicinity of
St. Paul's hill, I should notice the Light Tower which
is built up against the southern gable of the old church.
Its origin is materially different from that of the older
building to which it clings.   It was erected by the
Dutch for the purpose which it now serves, of being a
guide to ships passing to and fro, or approaching the
harbour.   From its elevation and from the superior
character of the light with which in late years it has
been fitted, it has proved of great use to vessels passing the Straits.   A rather singular incident occurred
here, which will serve to impress this tower somewhat
painfully on my memory; for it happened on the
morning of the first arrival at Malacca of the party of
which I was one.   Two fine boys, six years and three

years old respectively, children of the signal-master and light-keeper, obtained by some means a bottle of brandy, and either from playfulness or from the gratification it afforded, drank so deeply that one of them died within half an hour, and the other, after lingering insensible until next morning, also expired.

The building at present used for divine service stands close to the Stadt-house. It had been built by the Dutch as soon after their accession as they could spare the necessary time and expenditure, and is probably 150 years old. It remains in an almost perfect state of preservation, and promises for many years to come to afford ample accommodation for all the Protestant worshippers of the place. Outside it presents a very plain appearance, nor is it of imposing dimensions. It is gable-ended, having the entrance at one extremity and the altar at the other. No attempt has been made at a tower, but the peak of either gable bears a curious ornament in the shape of a large sphere composed of iron bands, which give a somewhat prison-like aspect to the building. The interior is of more pleasing appearance, its furnishings are plain but neat, and are strangely old-fashioned. Immediately over the entrance is a gallery where stands an organ which now discourses very doleful music in somewhat trembling and uncertain voice; it has the merit however of being in keeping with everything else around it.

Like the old Cathedral of St. Paul's, under the pavement of this church lie the bones of some of the old Dutch residents, among whom must have been

24

the fathers of the church. These graves are covered with carefully carved tablets which form a paving right up the centre of the building from the entrance to the altar. Since our time in Malacca, if not earlier, all burials within the walls of the church have been discontinued, but so strong is still the desire of the older residents to keep the names of their dead before the eyes of the living, that though the bodies lie in the burial-ground at the back of the hill, the walls of the church are lined all round by monumental tablets. The inscriptions on these as a rule do not, as I have before observed, compare favourably with those in the old cathedral. In one place some sorrowing friends in the fulness of their esteem for a deceased gentleman have recorded on the tablet to his memory that—

> He was a loving husband and father
> and a *sincere friend to all who knew him.*

And the most conspicuous if not the most ornamental slab around the walls is a huge block of white marble four times the size of any of the other tablets, and from its weight must have been set up in its position with great difficulty, which has nevertheless been erected by a disconsolate husband as a *small* mark of his regard for his amiable and affectionate wife.

The epitaph reads in this way :—

> Beneath this stone is interred
> the remains of ————————
> Her disconsolate husband has caused
> this stone to be placed here as a
> *small mark* of his regard for an
> amiable and affectionate wife.

Unfortunately for the veracity of the tablet, the remains in question do not lie under this stone, but are quietly interred in the burial-ground beyond the hill ; the stone, too, originally marked the place of sepulture there, but has now been removed by the disconsolate husband to its present scarcely appropriate place on the church walls. In the rear of the church are some old buildings which have an interesting appearance, and are said to have formed a monastery, but which are now used as store-rooms and barracks. Indeed it seems to have been a policy inaugurated by the Dutch and faithfully followed up by ourselves, to adapt to some present practical purpose all the old buildings in the place. The sword that rusts in its scabbard will sooner wear away than that which has to do hard fighting, and possibly the British authorities have had some such conviction when originally making their arrangements within their newly-acquired possession of Malacca. Nor except with reference to the chancel of the ruined cathedral which is still used as a powder magazine, can much fault be found with the results of this practical spirit.

CHAPTER XIV.

MALACCA: INHABITANTS—AGRICULTURE—MINING.

Native Division of the Town—The Inhabitants—A Convict's Story—
Internal Resources of the Territory—Fruit Gardens—Paddy Cul-
tivation—Tapioca—Its Growth and Manufacture—" Ayer Panas "
Bungalow—The Hot Springs—The Tin Mines at Kassang—The
Roman Catholic Mission to the Aborigines—Father Borie—The
Jacoons—Tiger Story—Superstition of the Jacoons—Deserted
Nutmeg Plantation.

As I stated at the outset, the European and official is
divided from the native part of the town by the river
Malacca, a turgid water of canal-like appearance,
which at high tide enables tonkangs and small cargo-
boats to come up and discharge opposite the numerous
godowns which line the banks. All the old buildings as yet remarked upon are on the European
or official side of the river, which is both the most
ancient and picturesque part of the town. But the
western or native division, if less interesting, is by
far the most characteristic of the present condition
of the place. A handsome iron bridge communicates
from one side of the town to the other. The western
division is built upon flat ground, no part more than
ten or fifteen feet above the sea level; and it slopes
gradually off towards the beach, the houses running

out on posts or piles considerably beyond high-water
mark. It is strange that the houses thus built out
into the sea in most cases over mud-banks, which
when the tide is out emit a strong repulsive smell,
are nevertheless perfectly healthy; indeed it is said
even more so than those built on firm dry ground.
The same thing may be remarked in most eastern
seaports; and in Singapore not only is the beach
built out upon in this way, but the numberless
mangrove swamps which are filled and emptied by
the river seem to be much more thickly built over
than the adjoining dry land, and yet no evil effects
are believed to result. The selection of these sites
however can scarcely be the consequence of pure
choice, and most likely arises either from the comparative cheapness of the land or from the greater
facility for receiving and delivering goods; as at high
water boats can load and discharge at the very doors
of these houses.

The division of Malacca of which I am now treating,
and which is properly speaking the business part, is
densely peopled; the houses are small and closely
packed together and appear to teem with human life.
The streets are also crowded; but still the entire
aspect is essentially not a busy one. People never
seem to bustle or bestir themselves, but saunter along
in a dreamy, spiritless, and yet apparently contented
manner; and a stranger accustomed to the activity
of any of the great Eastern marts, is at first strongly
impressed with the idea that he is in the midst of some
holiday or religious festival.

Of the varied races who compose its population, there is none whose bearing is more suggestive of this feeling of indolent apathy than the descendants of the founders of the settlement—the Portuguese. They are still called the Portuguese, but they have long ago ceased to deserve to be distinguished, at least favourably so, from the native inhabitants. Indeed they have so intermarried with the Malays and other native people that they would now with great difficulty be distinguished from them, if it were not that, with a strange remnant of ancestral pride, they rigidly adhere to the European style of dress; and more black bell-topped hats—napless and dinged it may be—are to be seen in a morning's walk through this part of Malacca than would be met with during a whole year in any other part of India. A black alpaca jacket, perhaps a shirt, but as often none, and a pair of cotton pants, the legs reaching a little below the knee and the bodies braced up close under the arm-pits, complete their attire. Nor do the minds of these people show any indication of their superior descent; they are not clever or industrious, and not ambitious. It seems that as soon as they accumulate a little money, either by accident or labour, they cease working and either live in indolence until it is spent, or as is more frequently the case—for they are given to good-fellowship among themselves—they have one grand "blow out." They are great musicians, and are prolific to a degree; and at the close of day the married men sit out in the verandahs of their houses fronting the street, discoursing, generally on the violin, some melan-

choly dirge for the amusement of their wives and families
who are gathered around them. Another remarkable
feature connected with these people is, that notwith-
standing the fact of Malacca having passed over two
hundred years ago into the occupation of the Dutch,
and having again been transferred to the English in
the early part of this century, and the fact of their
intermarriage and close contact with the native races,
they have yet managed to preserve their original tongue,
and continue to speak a sort of broken Portuguese.

It is not easy to discover to what pursuits these
people chiefly devote themselves ; for though there are
no European houses of business in Malacca and the
trade of the place passes through native hands, yet
there is, I believe, no Malacca-Portuguese merchants
in Malacca itself, nor in either of the neighbouring
settlements. In Singapore and Penang, to which
large numbers of these Portuguese have flocked, they
fill the positions of copying-clerks in mercantile houses,
head servants in hotels, and generally constitute the
entire strength of the different printing-offices there ;
but these men are or become more intelligent than
the friends they leave behind in Malacca. In Malacca
however there are no hotels and no printing-offices,
so that the Portuguese have not there any of these
vents for their labour. They are fishermen, but not
tillers of the soil to a greater extent than the cultivation of the small patches of ground attached to their
houses; it is probable that a good many of them
inherit means enough to live upon, and that others
eke out an existence upon the profits of occasional

small ventures to or from Singapore; while some few hold subordinate clerkships in the Government offices. Still there remains a large section whose means of livelihood I have been unable to discover.

But the Portuguese though the most interesting inhabitants of Malacca are not the most numerous. Chinese, Malays, Klings and other natives of India (many of these time-expired convicts,) each equal if not outnumber them; and in the country, few but Chinese and Malays are to be met with. Here, as in the other Settlements of the Straits, the Chinese are the most industrious. The Malays are not particularly active; they fish, and grow and sell fruit, but seldom trade. The Klings are chiefly boatmen and road labourers, the better circumstanced being money-lenders and money-changers. The convicts form a strange medley, having a decidedly mixed nationality; many return to their own country when they have served the term of their transportation, but others remain, and betake themselves to whatever turns up. A very singular and remarkable man of this class, but in whose case the majesty of the law, according to his account, had dealt somewhat harshly, is known by the name Tickery Bandah, who has by sheer strength of character made himself a notability of the place. He is a shopkeeper, a scribe, gives legal advice, and is a most useful man to all strangers in the search either of comfort or information. He is a native of Ceylon, and was sent a convict to Malacca for seven years, but as to the cause of his expatriation he is not very clear; he is now a free man, his sentence having expired early this year. He is fond of displaying his law library to all strangers, and shows autograph letters from the King of Siam, with whom he corresponds regularly, and whose royal liberality he has more than once experienced. His acquaintance with the King of Siam is owing to his having when in Ceylon performed a great service for a holy mission which had been despatched there by the King. The story, as Tickery tells it, is not uninteresting :—

When the English took possession of Ceylon, Tickery Bandah and two or three brothers—children of the first minister of the King of the Kandians—were taken and educated in English by the Governor. Tickery afterwards became manager of coffee plantations, and was so on the arrival of the Siamese mission of priests in 1845 in search of Buddha's tooth. It seems he met the mission returning disconsolate, having spent some 5,000l. in presents and bribes in a vain endeavour to obtain a sight of the relic. Tickery learned their story, and at once ordered them to unload their carts and wait for three days longer, and in due time he promised to obtain for them the desired view of the holy tooth. He had a cheque on the bank for 200l. in his hands at the time, and this he offered to leave with the priests as a guarantee that he would fulfil his promise ; he does not say whether the cheque was his own or his master's, or whether it was handed over or not. Perhaps it was the cheque for the misappropriation of which he found his way to the convict lines of Malacca. The Siamese priests accepted his undertaking and unloaded their baggage, agreeing to

wait for the three days. Tickery immediately placed
himself in communication with the then Governor,
and represented, as he says, forcibly, the impositions
that must have been practised upon the King of
Siam's holy mission, when they had expended all their
gifts and not yet obtained the desired view of the tooth.

The Governor, who Tickery says was a great friend
of his, appreciated the hardship of the priests, and
agreed that the relic should be shown to them with
as little delay as possible. It happened, however, that
the keys of the mosque where the relic was preserved
were in the keeping of the then Resident Councillor,
who was away some eight miles elephant-shooting.
But this difficulty was not long allowed to remain
in the way. Tickery immediately suggested that it
was very improbable the Councillor would have included
these keys in his hunting furniture, and insisted that
they must be in the Councillor's house. He therefore
asked the Governor's leave to call upon Mrs. ——,
the Resident Councillor's wife, and presenting the
Governor's compliments to request a search to be
made for the keys. Tickery was deputed accordingly,
and by dint of his characteristic tact and force of
language, carried the keys triumphantly to the
Governor.

The Kandy priests were immediately notified that
their presence was desired, as it was intended to exhibit
the great relic, and their guardian offices would be
necessary. Accordingly, on the third day, the mosque
or temple was opened; and in the building were
assembled the Siamese priests and worshippers with

Tickery on the one side, and the Kandy or guardian
priests on the other, the Recorder and the Governor
in the centre.

After making all due offering to the tooth of the
great deity, the Siamese head priest, who had brought
a golden jar filled with otto of roses, desired to have
a small piece of cotton with some of the otto rubbed
on the tooth and then passed into the jar, thereby to
consecrate the whole of the contents. To this process
the Kandy priests objected, as being a liberty too great
to be extended to any foreigners. The Siamese, however, persevered in their request, and the Governor and
Recorder not knowing the cause of altercation inquired
of Tickery. Tickery, who had fairly espoused the
cause of the Siamese, though knowing that in their
last request they exceeded all precedent, resolved
quietly to gratify their wish; so in answer to the
Governor's interrogatory, took from the hands of the
Siamese priest a small piece of cotton and the golden
jar of oil. "This is what they want, your honour,
they want to take this small piece of cotton—so; and
having dipped it in this oil—so; they wish to rub it
on this here sacred tooth—so; and having done this
to return it to the jar of oil—so; thereby, your honour,
to consecrate the whole contents." All the words of
Tickery were accompanied by the corresponding action,
and of course the desired ceremony had been performed
in affording the explanation. The whole thing was
the work of a moment. The Governor and Recorder
did not know how to interfere in time, though they
knew such a proceeding to be against all precedent;

the Kandy priests were taken aback; and the Siamese priests, having obtained the desired object, took from Tickery's hands the now consecrated jar with every demonstration of fervent gratitude. The Kandy priests were loud in their indignation; but the Governor, patting Tickery on the back, said, "Tickery, my boy, you have settled the question for us,—a pity it is you were not born in the precincts of St. James's, for you would have made a splendid political agent."

Tickery received next morning a douceur of 1,000 rupees from the priests, and ever since has been held in the highest esteem and respect by the King of Siam, also by the Buddhist priests, by whom he is considered a holy man. From the King he periodically receives honorary and substantial tokens of royal favour. He has a *carte blanche* to draw on the King for any amount; but he says he has, as yet, contented himself with a moderate draft of 700 dollars.

The territory of Malacca is now extensive, having been nearly doubled since it came into our hands from the Dutch by the war with Nanning in 1833; and it is to the development of the resources of the inlying lands that we must look for any increase in the prosperity of this settlement. These resources are two in number—agriculture and mining—and though they have occupied undivided attention since Malacca ceased to be resorted to as an emporium, it does not seem that they have attained that progress which latterly, at all events, might have been expected of them. With regard to agriculture, the unsatisfactory nature of the land grants alluded to in a previous chapter, was long thought to be the chief cause of the inactivity that prevailed. But now that the soil is ready to be granted away in fee-simple, reserving only a royalty upon metals, very little improvement is perceptible. The indolent character of the Portuguese population, and its contagious effect upon the other races, added to the aversion entertained by European capitalists to begin extensive cultivation in a new field, have doubtless been, and still are, the chief causes why Malacca has not attained that agricultural development for which its soil and climate are so singularly suited.

The exports of produce are, with the exception of tapioca and sago, confined entirely to what might be termed garden products—chiefly fruits. These are for the most part grown in the gardens of the houses in town, and embrace almost every variety of intertropical growth, besides some that may be considered peculiar to the peninsula. Along many of the streets, drooping over the garden walls of the houses that line them, may be seen rich clusters of mangoes and jambu fruit, and mangoosteen, custard apple, durian, and rambutan trees actually loaded with fruit. Further out of town the fruit gardens though fewer are larger, and stocked with greater variety. Beyond these fruit gardens, however, the products of the soil of Malacca must be viewed at some distance from town, as also must the entire mining wealth of the station.

The road to the tin mines of Kassang serves two purposes very well; ultimately leading to the chief mines now working about eighteen miles inland, it

affords along its length a tolerably perfect insight to
the character of the country and the extent of cultivation. As soon as the straggling houses of the
town and the many mosques and temples that abound
on its outskirts are passed, long prairie-like plains
of waving paddy stretch away from either side of
the road, till they are broken by a belt of jungle or a
range of hills. The fields which compose these plains
are seldom more than an acre or two in extent, and
are marked off by little mud-dikes a foot or two in
height, which, though sufficiently marking the boundaries of each plot, do not interrupt the prairie-like
appearance of the whole. Dotted here and there
over these yellow fields, are little dark green clumps
of cocoa-nut trees shading the homesteads of the
husbandmen, chiefly Malays. The paddy or rice plant
very much resembles corn in its growth and appearance when ripe, but by the Malays, at all events, it is
both planted and gathered in a peculiar manner.
When completely ripe, the women of the homesteads
proceed to the fields with a kind of scissors, and
commence to gather it by clipping off the tops or
ears of each stalk, the stubble being left standing
some eighteen inches high. As soon as the reaper
has a handful of these ears, she ties them firmly
together and places the bundle down with a heap of
others, to be carried to the homestead when the day's
work is over. It is singular how exactly similar in
weight these little bundles are made by practised
reapers; and in disposing of the paddy for husking,
it is never weighed out, but sold at so much the

hundred bundles. The husking is a very primitive
operation in the Straits; the grains are stripped off
these bundles into a bowl-like cavity dug in a large
log of solid wood, and pounded by a long heavy stick
till the husk is gradually loosened, when it is taken
out and winnowed, and again pounded till perfectly
clean. After reaping, when the rains come, the fields
are dammed up and the water allowed to collect.
When a foot or so of the water lies over the surface,
bullocks and other cattle are turned in to tread down
the stubble, which soon rots under water, and forms a
valuable manure for next year's crop. When the rains
dry up and the ground is ready for planting, small
holes are made about a foot apart, and into each of
these a few paddy stalks or seedlings, about forty days
old, which have been reared from the seed in a separate
part of the field, are planted at the depth of four
inches. Though undoubtedly a more laborious method
this than sowing, it is more economical and more
efficacious.

For about four miles inland from the town these
paddy-fields stretch uninterruptedly along. At this
distance belts of jungle and half-cleared land appear,
beyond which very little paddy is grown. Here,
however, commence the tapioca tracts; they scarcely
deserve to be called plantations. There can be no
more slovenly cultivation, I think, than that of tapioca
in the Straits. A piece of jungle is cut down and
fired, and as soon as the brushwood is burned away
the planting commences, amid all the confusion of
fallen, half-charred logs and stumps. The plant is

a bush of eight or nine feet high, and grows in great abundance in any kind of soil. It has a root much like the sweet potato, and it is from this that the tapioca is made. The roots of the young plants only are used, as the older ones get too fibrous; the stalk of the plant is very brittle; it is planted by breaking up a stalk into a number of short pieces and sticking them in the ground, so one can therefore stock a plantation in a day. It is said that the stalk must be put in the ground, lower end downward, and that if this order is reversed the root becomes poisonous; but this is believed by natives only.

When the roots are gathered they are peeled or pared, and then placed in a sort of mill, where they are squeezed, crushed, and ground to a flowery pulp. This pulp is then taken and placed on a sieve of calico, and bucketfuls of water are poured upon it while a man works it backwards and forwards, allowing the water to carry all the substance through the calico into a tub beneath; the rubbing is continued until the fibre only is left on the calico, and this is then laid aside and afterwards used for pig's meat. The water with the substance of the root passes from the tub through a long series of vats, depositing the particles of substance, which, from their specific gravity, seek the bottom, and allow the water in the end to pass off pure. The tapioca first taken from the vats looks exactly like pipe-clay, and until it has undergone several washings, is discoloured; ultimately however it becomes beautifully white, and is then allowed to dry, when it is taken out in a sort of cakey state, but being heavy crumbles into flour on the touch. I do not know how it receives the sort of lumpy form in which it is ordinarily sold; for at the manufactory I examined it was made up into small globules or pearls like sago. The process of thus making it up is exceedingly simple. A sort of hammock of white cloth is hung up with a stick across the centre to distend it; into this hammock the flour or cakey matter is cast while still a little damp, and the hammock is then rocked backwards and forwards; from an adhesive property in the flour, the motion makes it take the form of the small globules, which the longer it is rocked become the larger, something on the principle of snowballs. These small pearls are reduced to a uniform size by being riddled through sieves. The pearl, however, has as yet no solidity, and is reduced to powder on the slightest pressure, and all those that are too large or too small are at once reduced to powder and returned again to the hammock. The pearls of the proper size are rolled about as much as possible and allowed to dry, when, from a sort of affinity in their material, they gradually become hard, and enabled to stand the final process of rubbing with the hand on smooth boards, which gives them a perfect consistency. Sago is made nearly in the same way.

About ten miles from town these tapioca tracts cease, and the road runs then through jungle for some five miles to the hot springs, or *Ayer Panas*, at which stands a small native hamlet, and a Government bungalow. Up to this point the road is identical with that which existed two or perhaps three hundred years ago, and had been constructed by the Dutch or Portuguese. Very little traffic goes over it now, for, with the exception of visitors to the springs and the mines, it is only used by pedestrians; but it must have been a more busy road in olden times, for it has been substantially made. The sides are now for the most part overgrown with tangled brushwood and ferns, and a foot track only laid bare; but at some points where this brushwood is cleared away, can still be seen the hard well-cemented brick coping on the edges of the drains, a precaution to keep the road from being washed away with the heavy rains, which, though it must undoubtedly have been an expensive one, has singularly well served its purpose, for at those points where these copings still remain the road is found indeed almost concrete and beautifully level.

The Government bungalow at Ayer Panas is some 300 yards distant from the hot springs, which lie down in a hollow, and have a shed built over them. There are three separate springs, and they have been cleared out and walled round in a square form, each well being about three feet by three feet, by six feet deep. The hot water comes up to the top of the brick enclosures, and flows over by a small drain. The hottest spring is about 130° and is quite unbearable, scalding the hand or foot if immersed. The other two are cooler, but too hot to bathe in. From the bottom of each of the wells large bubbles of phosphorated hydrogen gas are sent up at intermittent periods, and

the water itself is so strongly impregnated with this
gas as to be highly disagreeable to the smell. Close
to the shed enclosing the wells there runs a rapid
stream of cold water which is used for the irri-
gation of the rice-fields. At the level mark of the
hot water in each well is a deposit of green crystals.
A bath is effected either by taking a bucket of cold water
to the springs and bringing it to the desired heat, or
having the hot water carried up to a large and
convenient bath at the bungalow, and there cooled
down to a proper temperature.

The road from the bungalow to the mining village
of Kassang leads irregularly through the forest for
almost five miles. The inhabitants there are almost
entirely Chinese, numbering several thousands, and
their attap houses are built close together in the
centre of their workings. The mines reminded me a
good deal of some of the abandoned diggings in
Australia, with a difference in the colour of the soil,
which is white and greyish, instead of yellow and
brown as in the gold-fields. A great deal of ground
seems to have been opened up and worked, but the
present sinkings are very few and far between. The
ground is entirely open cast; no attempt that I saw
having been made to get at the washing stuff by the
more economical plan of shaft working; probably the
sandy nature of the soil would render this last plan
impracticable. The wash dirt of those workings that
I saw was about twenty or twenty-five feet from the
surface, and I was informed averages about four feet
in thickness. The miners do not wash out the tin

25—2

as they collect the dirt, but wait until they have
gathered together a good pile and then " wash out "
by means of sluices: the latter operation I did not see.
The ore is smelted on the ground in a very primitive
but quite effective manner. In the shed I saw, there
were two furnaces made of mud, bound together by
saplings. At the bottom of each furnace there were
two small holes of two inches in diameter for the
molten metal to run out, and the draft to be carried
up. One furnace was working while I was there, the
ore was mixed up with charcoal and a light applied,
no artificial draft was created. The metal drops
through the small holes as it melts into a cavity
scooped in the earth, and from this it is ladled up and
poured into the moulds, then sent to town, and there
generally remelted by the exporting merchant.

A very interesting feature in the neighbourhood
of Malacca is the Roman Catholic mission to the
Jacoons, a tribe of the aborigines of the peninsula.
The station is about eight miles out of town; the
road to it for some distance skirts the western sea
beach, and is shaded by a stately double row of augasma
trees, which were planted fifty years ago, and are now
in magnificent foliage having a height of seventy and
eighty feet and a diameter of even more than that.
At two miles from town the road strikes away from
the beach straight inland, and passes through country
similar to that first noticed on the way to Kassang;
a long plain of paddy-fields stretching away to right and
to left, till at almost five miles from the shore cultivation
ceases and the confines of the jungle are reached. Here

too the road becomes choked up with underwood and tiger grass and difficult of passage to a conveyance. The jungle on either side, however, is not dense; many of the larger trees have been cut down, as if an attempt at clearance had at one period been made and abandoned.

About a mile within this jungle where the trees begin to get closer and the undergrowth denser, is the palisade of the priest's homestead. About five acres of ground have been cleared and laid out with fruit-trees. The buildings of the mission comprise a chapel, a school-house, and the padre's dwelling, which are all constructed of wood with attap or leaf roofs, but of neat design. On the borders of the clearing are a number of the huts of the natives, as many as generally constitute a Malay hamlet in the interior. Everything has an aspect of cleanliness and order which at once impresses the visitor favourably.

It was on a Sabbath morning when as one of a party of four, I visited this mission about a year ago. We had chosen that day because the Jacoons, who were for the most part away hunting and fishing in the forests during the week, would then be gathered together in the chapel to offer up their prayers and have their sermon preached to them. The service had just commenced when we reached the chapel, but the priest, Father Borie, suspended it for a moment to come out and welcome us, and procure us seats. The service lasted for about half an hour, and the sermon for probably half that time; in the former there was not much to remark or admire; but the sermon was a good honest simple one delivered in Malay; and I am sure was suited even to the very limited capacities of his hearers. There were probably one hundred and twenty natives, men, women, and children, present in the church, of whom probably two-thirds were Jacoons, and the rest Malays. Great must have been the labour of this lonely missionary before he assembled this crowd of worshippers, for to the Jacoons he must first have had to teach Malay before he could teach them the Gospel; and he must have taught all his lessons in a spirit of love and forbearance, for so timorous and gentle are these people that the slightest exhibition of harshness or unkindliness would have frightened them all away from him.

After the service had closed Father Borie led us to his house close by, a neat little bungalow, where he opened his little stores and freely invited us to partake of his hospitality. He had been eighteen years in the Malay peninsula labouring to convert to Christianity the strange tribe that were now gathered around him. He had met many vicissitudes and many adventures, but had little to complain of the treatment he had received from the aboriginal tribes. His flock now numbered 450 Jacoons, and they were attached to the mission by the strongest tie by which it was possible to attach their simple natures—that of affection. I have heard missionaries of the Protestant church in some parts of the East, when alluding to the spread of the Romish faith among the natives, attribute it to the showiness of the Catholic service as compared with that of our own church. No doubt a service which appeals so much to the senses has its advantages in point of attraction to the simple mind of the native; but I think that this is but a small cause of the success of the Catholic missions in comparison with the laborious devotion of the Catholic missionaries. Here was Father Borie, a man of good parts and education, who had for nearly twenty years withdrawn himself from the world, built his home in the midst of these people, and set himself about their education and conversion to the exclusion of all other ambition; and this on the fat living of some 50*l.* a year, which was itself all shared with his flock. Dried fish and rice, enriched at times by the birds or venison of the jungle brought to him by his flock, was his food, and water with now and then a flask of old French wine was his drink. And there was no rushing back for relief from this seclusion into the presence and excitement of civilization, as we have witnessed with our own missionaries. Malacca was barely eight miles distant from Father Borie's mission, and yet a visit in six months was the most he made to it.

Father Borie gave us many interesting particulars of the Jacoons, of their habits, and of their character and superstitions. As for their appearance we could judge of that ourselves, for about fifty or sixty of them were squatted in a semicircle round the front of the padre's house where we were sitting. They were mostly of very diminutive stature with woolly hair, but wearing an amiable expression on their features. Their wives and children were with them, and I noticed that the little boys came fearlessly up to the padre, and while staring rather timorously at us kept firm hold of his gown. These he took in turn upon his knee, patted and patted them and apparently reconciled them to our presence, when they grew braver and came up to us. We saw an old couple of the Jacoons who could give no idea of their age, but could point to their married grandchildren. They were very small, and old age while it had silvered their woolly locks and shrivelled them up, appeared to have robbed them of little of their activity or liveliness.

The neighbourhood of the mission was more or less frequented by tigers, and the padre told us an adventure he had with one. He had been out in the forests looking for game, and was returning home, having been unsuccessful, with one barrel of his fowling-piece still loaded with small shot. When within a few hundred yards of his clearing he turned round to light his pipe, laying his gun on the ground, and taking his hat to protect the match from the breeze, commenced to strike the steel against the flint. At this moment he was surprised to hear his two dogs each give utterance to a short whining cry, and he noticed that they crept close to him, their hair bristling with terror. Alarmed at these symptoms he removed his hat from in front of him, and standing right in face of him, not more than ten yards distant, was a huge powerful tiger, his tail erect, uneasily pawing the ground, and uttering a sort of low hissing growl. In a moment—as the padre admitted—of great terror, and in obedience rather to instinct than reason, he snatched his musket from the ground and

scarcely waiting to take aim he fired off the contents
of the loaded barrel in the direction of the tiger. Not
waiting to see the result of the shot, but conscious that
he had exhausted his entire means of defence, the
priest turned and fled, followed by his dogs, in the
direction of the mission. Fear lent him strength and
speed, and he reached his clearing in safety, but in an
almost fainting condition. A well-armed party was
formed and went to the spot where the tiger had been
seen, but no sign of him could be obtained. That
night one of the dogs which had been with the padre
in the morning, after a succession of convulsions, died,
as far as could be judged, from the effects of terror
only, and the other one only lingered a few days
longer. About a week afterwards, as the priest was
passing the spot where he had fired at the tiger, he
felt a strong smell of animal decay; and gathering a
party of the natives together a search was made, and
in about half an hour the dead body of the tiger was
discovered. The small shot from the musket had
lodged in the animal's face, and though barely piercing
into the flesh, the pain and irritation had so annoyed
him that he had literally torn himself to death with
his claws, his head and neck being all in strips.

Father Borie told me that the Jacoons have a fixed
and singular superstition concerning tigers, ninety-nine
men out of every hundred believing it, even in face of their
Christian teaching. They believe that a tiger in their
path is invariably a human enemy, who, having sold
himself to the evil spirit, assumes by sorcery the
shape of the beast to execute his vengeance or malignity.

They assert that invariably before a tiger is met, a man has been or might have been seen to disappear in the direction from which the animal springs. In many cases the metamorphosis, they assert, has been plainly seen to take place.

We left the good priest's homestead deeply impressed with the remarkable devotion to the cause of an imperfect religion, which had led a gentleman and scholar of no mean pretensions thus to seclude himself for life in the jungle borders of Malacca. On our way back, we visited a half-forsaken nutmeg plantation, famous for the extraordinary size of the nuts borne by the trees. Some of those which we gathered were fully nine inches in circumference of the fruit or husk, or more than twice the ordinary size. Over the chief entrance of the bungalow which had been erected on this plantation was a large black board with the first lines of the sixth canto of Sir Walter Scott's *Lay of the Last Minstrel.* What sudden access of enthusiasm had caused the proprietor to break out in such rhapsody it is difficult to understand ; it had possibly been induced by the exceedingly fine prospects of the nutmeg crop ; at all events, the patriotic sentiment now reads drearily enough in sight of the whitened branches of the blighted trees which are fast being choked up by tiger-grass and jungle.

APPENDIX I.

LIST OF THE FRUITS TO BE FOUND IN THE BAZAARS OF THE STRAITS SETTLEMENTS.*

(Buah, the Malay term for fruit in general, is always prefixed to the specific name.)

Malayan Names.	Linnean, &c. Names.	Remarks.
Angoor	Vitis vinifera	Grapes. Cultivated occasionally successfully, but not abundant.
Assam gloogoor.. Assam kambing eejoo. Assam kundisun.	Tamarindus indica	Principally used in the composition of curries, for which the Malays are famed. The fruit is also used with water as a cooling laxative drink in fevers.
Babesaram	Morus indica	The mulberry. Used by the natives as a mild emollient.
Bachang	Mangifera fœtida	The horse-mango. A very coarse fruit, of unpleasant odour; much eaten by the lower classes, and producing cholera, diarrhœa, and dysentery.
Bangkudu	Morinda citrifolia	The leaves of this plant are used by the Javanese in various diseases as astringents. " Bontius mentions their use in diarrhœa and cholera. Internally they act as a mild emollient diuretic." — Horsfield in *Trans. Batt. Soc.*, vol. viii., p. 25.
Batee	Papaya	
Beenjai	Mangifera cassia of Dr. Jack.	A very large, oblong, brown-coloured, rather agreeably tasted fruit, like the common mango.
Bidara	Rhamnus jujuba	A subacid fruit of a bright yellow colour, about the size of a cherry, the pulp enclosing an elliptical-shaped seed. " The bark of this tree is possessed of mild tonic virtues; it is recommended in weakness of the stomach, and in diseases of the intestines." — Horsfield loc. cit., p. 23.

* Compiled by Dr. Ward.

Malayan Names.	Linnean, &c. Names.	Remarks.
Bilimbing bisee.. Bilimbing bulu. Brambang...............	Averrhoa carambola Averrhoa bilimbi. (Not ascertained)	Two well-known, pleasant tart fruits, resembling, strongly, unripe gooseberries. A sour fruit, used for making chatnies and curry.
Brangun	Fagi species	In appearance and taste strongly resembling the European chestnut.
Champadoo	Arctocarpus integrifolia	The jack. Farinaceous, mucilaginous, and nutritive.
Chirimi.....................	Averrhoa acida, or Cicca disticha	A pleasant tart fruit. " The root of the Cicca disticha is said to be emetic, and great activity is ascribed to it."—Horsfield, loc. cit., p. 33.
Dalima	Punica granatum	Pomegranate. The rind is used as an astringent, and the bark of the root as an anthelmintic by the natives.
Dookoo	Lansium domesticum, Blume. "Bijdragen tot de Flora van Nederlandshe Indie," 4 de stuk., p. 175.	This delightful fruit is the produce of a large tree. It grows in clusters: each is about the size of a cricket-ball. The brownish thin skin being broken, displays the pulp in six cloves, of a pleasantly acid taste, enclosing a greenish kidney-shaped seed. It is by many reckoned the finest fruit in the peninsula. The month of July is the season at Malacca, in which it is had in greatest perfection.
Doorian	Durio zibethinus	This fruit is well known from the descriptions of travellers. Those who have overcome the prejudice excited by the disagreeable fœtid odour of the external shell, reckon it delicious. From experience, I can pronounce it the most luscious and the most fascinating fruit in the universe. The pulp covering the seeds, the only part eaten, excels the finest custards which could be prepared either by Ude or Kitchener. Bontius says it proves laxative, diuretic, and carminative ; but when eaten in too great quantities, that it predisposes to inflammatory complaints. The natives consider it to possess aphrodisiac qualities. It is certainly in some measure exciting.
Gajook .... Gayer	(Not ascertained) .. Ditto	The seeds used by the Indian boys as marbles.
Jambao merah ..... Jambao ayer Jambao bulu Jambao ayer ma-war Jambao cheelee..	Eugenia Malaccensis Eugenia aquea Eugenia jambos Eugenia rosea Eugenia rosea var	Some of these, when in perfection, have a fine flavour, but in general they are insipid, being in taste something between a good turnip and a bad apple. The first species is commonly called Jamboo Malacca, and is certainly the finest. The fourth goes under the name of rose-apple.
Jambao kling	Myrtus cumini	

Malayan Names.	Linnean, &c. Names.	Remarks.
Jambao irong	Anacardium occidentale	Cashew-nut. Fruit coarse, not much eaten. Nut astringent.
Jambao bijee or portgl.	Psidium pyriferum	Common guava.
Jintue Jintue	(Not ascertained)	A handsome-looking jungle fruit; an orange pulp surrounds a small seed about the size of a pea, and the whole is enclosed in a trilocular capsule of a deep orange colour, hanging in clusters from the branches. Taste sour.
Kadondong	Phyllanthus Chrysobolanum of Marsden Spondias — Horsfield	The bark of this is used by the natives as an astringent.
Kalapa	Cocos nucifera	Cocoa-nut. Of this Rumphius enumerates thirteen varieties.
Kamang	(Not ascertained)	A fruit of the appearance of a mango; sour, used principally in curries.
Kapas	Bombax pentandrum	The fruit of the cotton tree, taste sweetish, much eaten. Seeds occasionally eaten. The gum of the tree is astringent, and sometimes given in bowel complaints.
Karkara	(Not ascertained)	
Kamoonting	Myrtus tomentoso	A very common and rather handsome plant, bearing a dark purple-coloured fruit, about the size of a hip, pleasant in tarts or preserved.
Karta-tanga	(Not ascertained)	A very hard brownish black fruit, about the size of an egg, containing a farinaceous substance, boiled and eaten like yam.
Katapang	Terminalia catappa	A large tree: the fruit and kernel being very like those of the common almond.
Kayoo kolit	(Not ascertained)	A small brown coloured fruit, of sweet taste, common in the jungles.
Khoorma	Phœnix dactilifera	Dates; mostly imported from Arabia.
Kichanee	(Not ascertained)	Resembling the soontool in appearance; pulp sweet, tough.
Kiloor	Guillandinia moringa	Ben-nuts of old authors. The whole tree is esculent; the seeds and leaves are aromatic, and used in curries; the root is an excellent substitute for horse-radish. It is a valuable external stimulant. Rumphius says, in large doses it produces strangury and abortion. "The leaves are recommended in gonorrhœa as a mild diuretic."—Horsfield, loc. cit., p. 20.
Kitapang	Callicarpa japonica	An acid fruit, resembling a machang in shape.
Kledang	(Not ascertained)	A small and very handsome fruit, consisting of an outer shell strongly resembling that of the Rambootan, of a bright red colour, within which is the seed, surrounded by a whitish pulp—the part eaten.

Malayan Names.	Linnean, &c. Names.	Remarks.
Kolit lawang Kolit layoo	Laurus kulit lawan .. (Not ascertained)	Small sweet jungle fruits, eaten by the children, as hips and haws are in England.
Kooseenee	Ditto	A small subacid fruit, of the appearance of a mango, with the same flavour and a very fine scent.
Korinche	Ditto	A small very dark brown fruit, consisting of a hard outer shell, containing a flesh-coloured pulp, hanging in bunches. Sourish taste.
Kras	Camarium cordifolium. The Juglans camirium of Loureiro	A fruit of the size and appearance of the winter apple, resembling, in all its qualities, the walnut of Europe.
Kumbut	(Not ascertained)	The seeds of a large capitate flower, used in curries.
Langoonee	Vitex trifolia	A small greenish subacid fruit, growing in numerous clusters, excellent in tarts. "The root and a bath or cataplasm of the leaves is applied (by the Javanese) externally in rheumatism and local pains in various parts."—Horsfield, loc. cit., p. 16. The leaves are said to cure intermittent fever, to promote urine, and relieve the pain of the colic.—Id.: They are stimulant and aromatic.
Lampanee	(Not ascertained)	Small jungle fruit, eaten by the Malays. Used by infusion by lying-in women.
Langsat	Langsii domestici var.	A very pleasant, subacid, and favourite fruit of the Malays and others. In appearance it is like the dookoo already described. The seeds of it are said to possess anthelmintic properties.
Lanjoot	Mangiferæ species	The oblong, large, coarse-looking, green-coloured fruit of a variety of mango—rather prized by the natives.
Leemoo gadang..	Citrus decumana	Pumpelmoose or shaddock; rind, a very agreeable bitter.
Leemoo manis	Citrus aurantium	Several varieties of orange, both indigenous and imported, are to be met with.
Leemoo kustooree Leemoo jamboa Leemoo japoon Leemoo neepis Leemoo sookoo	Citri variæ species	Different varieties of limes and oranges, the list of which might be greatly increased. Some of them are made into excellent preserves.
Lontar	Borassus flabelliformis	The seeds of the Palmyra tree form very good preserves, and are only used for that purpose.
Malaka	Phyllanthus emblica	A handsome tree and fruit. From its abundance round the site of the town at the first arrival of the Malays, Malacca is supposed to have derived its name. The fruit has astringent properties. The fruit is made into a cataplasm, and applied to the head in cases of giddiness.

Malayan Names.	Linnean, &c. Names.	Remarks.
Mangis or Mangistan	Garcina mangostena	The far-famed mangoosteen. The fruit has been justly praised by all who have ever written upon it. It is too well known to require description. The habitat of it is extremely limited. We believe that it does not extend further to the northward than the old fort of Tennasserim in lat. 11° 40′, and all attempts to cultivate it on the continent of India have failed. The shell of the fruit is strongly astringent, and decoctions of it are used by the natives in bowel complaints.
Mangistan ootan.	Embryopteris glutinifer	Wild mangoosteen.
Manga dodol....... Manga pao	Mangifera indica ... Mangifera amboinensis	Two varieties of mango, the first of which is very excellent, but much inferior to the graft-mangoes at Madras. The common coarse mango is very abundant and much used.
Mata kuching	(Not ascertained) ...	A small fruit growing in thick bunches, consisting of a rough brownish-coloured round shell, containing a deep purple-coloured seed, surrounded with a whitish, opalescent looking pulp like a cat's eye, hence its Malay name; much prized.
Mata plandoq	Ditto	A small sweetish-tasted jungle fruit.
Nam-nam	Cynometra cauliflora	A fruit of the size and shape of a kidney, of a brownish green colour, growing on the stem of the tree; the outer shell is the part eaten, and when good has some resemblance to an apple.
Nanas	Bromelia ananas	Pineapple; very abundant and very cheap. "The unripe fruits are diuretic, and employed as a remedy in gonorrhœa." —Horsfield, loc. cit., p. 27.
Nanka	Arctocarpus integrifolia	A variety of jack fruit—well known.
Nasse nasee	Phyllanthes alba	A small white sweetish fruit in clusters not much prized.
Neebong	Caryota urens	The small flat pulpy fruit of this palm is made into a good preserve for the table.
Nona	Annona reticulata...	The bullock's heart—a much prized fruit.
Pala	Myristica moschata..	Nutmeg. Made into preserve, when in a half-ripe state.
Papaya	Carica papaya	A pleasant, well-known fruit. The seeds are employed by the natives as anthelmintics.
Pinang	Areca catechu..... ...	Common betelnut. Sometimes employed in decoction as an astringent in diarrhœa.
Pisang	Musa paradisea	The plantain. Of this about 40 varieties might be enumerated. The best are the Pisang mas, P. raja, P. oodang, and P. medgi. Decoctions of the root are used as emollient applications.

26

Malayan Names.	Linnean, &c. Names.	Remarks.
Pooksan	Nephelii species	A very delicate and pleasant fruit.
Rambootan	Nephelium lappaceum	Differs from the preceding in size, having long bristle-like processes on outer shell.
Rambei	Lansii species	This pleasantly subacid fruit, about size of a plum, hangs in clusters from the branches of the tree. The pulp surrounding the seed is the part eaten.
Rambaya	Metroxylon sagu	From the pith of this tree sago is pared. The starchy fruit is made into preserves for the table.
Rookam	Carrissa spinarum	A common fruit, of a purplish colour, clustered round the stem, good in tarts or making jellies.
Salak	Calamus salacca	Fruit used as a preserve.
Sattool	(Not ascertained)	A fruit of a yellow-brown colour, the size of a moderately large one, consisting of a thick hard rind, containing five or six cloves, resembling the mangosteen; taste, acidish.
Sappam	Cæsalpinia sappan	Little used.
Seri kaya	Annona squamosa	Custard apple. Well known.
Sika duduk	Melastoma	A common wild fruit, rather astringent, little prized.
Sookoon	Arctocarpus incisa	The bread-fruit. Little used.
Soongool ootan	(Not ascertained)	
Surba rasa	Ditto	A kind of mango, oblong, large, surrounding the seed of a rich sugar.
Soopoom	Ditto	A sour fruit of the mango kind, used in curries and in making chutnees.
Soorboot	Ditto	A jungle fruit.
Sow or sao	Ditto	A handsome deep red jungle fruit, the size of a hen's egg, containing a sweetish pulp, surrounding three brown seeds.
Tampang	Ditto	This fruit exactly resembles an overgrown strawberry; externally it is of a reddish colour mixed with red; inside a fine pink colour. Taste ...
Tanjong	Mimusops elengi	Of little value as a fruit. " The ... a mild tonic; it has been found ... in fevers, and as a general ... used in decoctions."— ... p. 39.
Tampoo-ee	Lansii species	A small subacid fruit.
Tampoonee	Arctocarpo (affinis ?)	A fruit in external appearance like small jack, and like it also ... rows of seeds, but without ... The pulp, of a yellowish colour, ... an agreeably subacid taste, and ... prised both by natives and ...
Tomi tomi	Flacourtia inermis	A small reddish fruit, used in ... tarts and jellies.

APPENDIX II.

LIST OF THE CHIEF FRUIT AND FOREST TREES INDIGENOUS TO THE STRAITS SETTLEMENTS.*

(The Malay term *Kayoo*, wood, or *Pokok*, tree, should be prefixed to each name.)

Dammer Laut .... A very resinous, heavy, and durable wood; does not float in water; very hard; perhaps the most valuable of the woods found here; will remain uninjured for twenty years under ground; beams a foot square, or even much larger, can be had.

Tummoossooh .... Is a very resinous wood, and, although durable, is more disposed to warp than Dammer Laut; it is useful for rafters; its colour is light straw; the tree is high; it is most frequently hollow, but beams from six to ten inches square can be had; this wood will remain uninjured 100 years under ground.

Tampenes .... Is a very hard and durable wood, excellent for house-building; it is of a light-reddish and yellowish colour.

Pinang Pargam . A white wood, fracture yellowish coloured, used for boat-building.

Moon Tapoos .... Is a wood with a loose bark, used for spear shafts, musket stocks, and such purposes; large spars of it may be had; it is chiefly found in Perak and Pulow Trootow or Trotto; it sinks in water.

Fir .... It is found on the upper zones of the hills, at an elevation of about 2,200 feet; large spars may be had.

Maranti .... Of two sorts, red and white; the red is most used; planks may be had three feet broad; it is chiefly used for planking; grows on plains, and river banks and hills; it floats.

Chingei .... A high tree, from 18 to 25 feet in circumference, used for ship and boat building; stands the salt water well; is much used on the Tennasserim coast; the wood itself floats; fracture rather short; it grows in sandy grounds.

Muddang-leber-daun .. Fracture fibrous; used for house building; white colour; broad leaf; large spars may be had.

Gillam Tikoos .... Middle-sized tree, colour brownish-yellow; fracture strong fibrous; used for house building; its red bark is much used to tan fishing-nets; the wood is not prized.

Doongoon .... A large tree which grows on the banks of rivers near the sea shore; colour dark brown; the planks are used for a defence against musketry by Malayan pirates; crooked timber and tough.

Kayoo Laut ... . Used for house posts; lasts five or six years if exposed; colour yellowish; the tree grows in brackish water.

Rummiyah .... High tree; the wood is a light dirty-brown when young, of a dark brown when old, and sinks in water ; cross fracture, splintery; grows on hills; the fruit is eaten ; used as posts for houses.

Api Api............ .... A large tree, has a white wood; is excellent firewood.

Bruss............................ A moderately sized tree, which bears a sour mangoosteen; the wood is used for house building and for making oars ; sinks in water.

Killat ... . Very tough ; very fibrous fracture ; tree high ; timber not durable if exposed to weather; used in house building and for planks; light colour; sinks in water.

Runggas ... . A lofty tree, the juice of which is deleterious to the human frame, creating swellings over the whole body ; the wood is of a reddish-brown colour ; it is used for making furniture; the fracture is cross and splintery; it is often prettily enough veined, and takes a good polish; sinks in water.

Niris Battu . ... A high tree ; the wood is of a dark brown colour ; it is used for house pillars; it grows in mangrove jungle.

Maralilin . ... Used for rafters ; wood straw-coloured ; fracture fibrous ; tree not large.

Babi Kooroos . . .. White wood.

Chindrai .... Firewood, light and white; the tree is not large; the leaves are used in bowel complaints; lying-in females are kept near a fire of this wood; is very inflammable.

Butabuta ... ... The juice is boiled, and the oil collected, and used in cutaneous disorders externally.

Gading .... White wood, white thin bark, used by Malayan women for tambouring frames.

Jumirlang Sittooei .. Cross fracture; used in house and boat building.
Middang Serai . High tree, used in boat-building.
Bongor Ayer Used for boat oars, floats.
Durian and Durian High trees, afford valuable spars, and the latter masts for
Burong vessels; a large mast will cost 120 dollars.
Moratajam .. White wood ; its root and leaves are mashed, and used as a cooling application in cases of brain-fever ; the infusion of this root is drank in cases requiring astringent medicine ; it is not a strong wood.

Boonoot ..... A large tree bearing an acid fruit, edible ; the wood is of a dark chocolate colour ; it is used as house posts and in boat-building.

Pattalung A good-sized tree; the wood is close grained, of a light red or brown colour; used in house building.

Toommoos High tree, grows in mangrove jungles; used for rafters.
Langadei A tree growing in mangrove jungles ; the wood is white, used for firewood.

Bintangor High tree, few branches; used for masts and spars for vessels; floats, and is tough ; it is approved before all others for these purposes—Calophyllum mophyllum, L.

Middang Kunyit Fibrous fracture; used for planks of boats.
Niris Bunga A tree growing in mangrove jungle, used for house-building and fencing ; colour reddish ; its fruit is as large as a cocoa-nut.

Nunka Pipit Is the lightest, perhaps, of the durable woods; its habitat is on high land; it is difficult to saw; it is the sparrow jack ; it is useful for house pillars, as it endures being sunk in the earth; sinks in water.

Barco Its bark is used for making twine, caulking, and other purposes.
Bagu Is another of the same kind.

gi Laut	It is used for wheels, bows, and spear shafts.
....	Different species of the Ficus indicus, with entire leaves; they are planted near temples.
Laut...............	Momordia charantia.
jawi	A species of banian.
au	This is a high tree, affording large planks for making tables, chairs, &c., also for house pillars and boat building; it is durable.
au Etam, or ido, M. Darah, Rengkong	Are varieties.
ang Kamangi	Sassafras apparently; soft and fragrant wood; has a rough bark.
ng Sila	
ang Soory	Is used for planking and in house building.
ang Benar	
, Koolim	Very large tree, and very hard wood; makes good planks for boats; sinks in water.
, Koolit	
ch.................	A high tree, red for about two-thirds of the diameter, 18 ins. diameter, tough, and used for making paddles, oars, &c.
a	Rhamnus jujuba.
, Chicha	Very durable.
, Penaga	A large tree; yields crooked timber for knees of vessels; an infusion of its leaves and roots is applied to the eyes to allay inflammation; on the Malabar coast this tree is called Alexandrian laurel, and in Bengal, poorlange; it grows only on the sea-shore, in sandy places; its wood is used for ribs of boats.
, Kamooning	Apparently the Chakas paniculata of Lin.; Astronia of Batavia Transact.; it is an ornamental wood, and the roots, which are large, and flat, and twisting, are formed into kris handles, and take a fine polish; there are several kinds, such as the Kayoo Kamooning amas, K. K. kunyit troos, K. K. tei karban, K. K. angin, and K. K. battu; the tree prefers rocky places.
ang	Is a tall tree; inhabits swamps; it is used for planks.
a	Is a hard and durable wood, much in request by native boat-builders, who are good judges of the best kinds of timber; it sinks in water, and resists the salt water insects a long while.
i	Is another, used for the same purpose; a sacred tree, very scarce here.
oo	A high tree; grows in marshy places; fawn coloured; sinks in water; does not resist the worm or beetle.
o	Is a high tree, with a succulent fleshy leaf, and has a poisonous sap; has an edible acid fruit; the branches grow in shape of an umbrella.
....	A slim tree, used in house building.
' Arrow	A graceful tree, somewhat tapering, and resembling some species of the fir; it has small cones and fibrous leaves, Casuarina littorea; the wood is hard; not prized.
n	Is a small tree.
oos ..	Its bark is used by the Chinese to dye their sails and lines of a brownish red.
dei	For rafters and firewood.
;	A species of mimosa, resembling a chestnut; the fruit is edible, but has a repulsive smell.
ig ..	Large tree, used for boat-building; that growing on high grounds is best for making tables.
i ...	Iron-wood.

Brangan	Is a large tree, with a broad leaf; light wood, and not subject to dry rot; has an edible fruit; cultivated.
Kayoo Singam	This tree grows in mangrove tracts; it is approved for boat and house building.
Gharoo	Agila wood.
Tinkaras	From this tree gharoo is also, it is said, obtained.
Krooing	This tree yields a valuable oil called miniak kooing or krooing.
Kalookoob	Thorny tree; has an acidulous edible fruit.
Kammiyan	The tree which yields the benjamin.
Ipel	Is a large tree, having a reddish coloured wood; the natives use it in house-building; very fibrous fracture; planks for boat-building are cut from it; it is reckoned equal to Merbus; sinks in water; the diameter is sometimes two feet.
Matati	Very brittle wood.
Tatati	For house posts.
K. Tampang Bloace	Hard iron wood, used in some places instead of betel-nut along with betel-leaf; used in house-building.
K. Benar	Used in house-building.
K. Boonga	Ditto ditto
Kananga	A large tree.
Babuta	Is a low shrubby tree; its bark contains a very viscous juice; an oil is extracted from this, which is used in cutaneous affections by the Burmans; great care is required in cutting the tree down, for if the sap reaches the face of the wood-cutter, it will be swelled in a hideous manner, and his sight will be endangered.
To Joak	A dark-leaved small tree, to which superstition affixes a sacred character; most old and isolated trees are held to be kramat, and small white flags are stuck up near them, and often propitiatory offerings made to the spirits supposed to reside on the spot.
Sudoo soodoo	The Euphorium; the Malays use it as a drug for cattle.
Kranji	Large tree; does not float; fibrous fracture; it is a valuable wood; the Chinese use it for masts and rudders to the junks; the Malays for house posts; less durable than Tampenes or Tummassoo; the bark is astringent, and is used by Malays instead of betel-nut when the latter is scarce; the fruit is edible; the wood is not very buoyant.
Kayoo arang, or Siam wood	A black wood, which takes a high polish; it may be had, but does not grow here.
Chumpada Ayer	High tree, growing in marshes; the wood floats; it is yellowish; it is used in making boats; its bark is very flexible and strong, and is used in making walls for native houses, granaries, &c.
Nipis Kulit	Is a moderate-sized tree, about 1½ feet diameter; the bark is very thin, and vertically striated; colour fawn; hard, used to make mortar pestles, and as it sinks in water is used to make anchors.
Seeat	A tree having a red bark, which is called by the Burmese "Chekha," and is used to eat along with betel-leaf; it is sold at Junkeeylon, at 8 drs. the picul; it is a very scarce tree here.
K. Srayan	A hard wood used for house-building.
Nunka or Jack	Is well known; its wood is not much used here.
Bittaot	Grows in mangrove jungle; fawn-coloured; of little use.
Middang Bunga	Fawn-coloured wood; not durable if exposed.
K. Maralilin.	
Kranam.	A creeper; medicinal.
Tumpang	High tree; grain yellowish; good for house-posts; very durable; next to Tummassoo for this purpose.

Bayor .... Used for boat-building; not very much prized.

Tampenes putih ..... Not so good as the dark Tampenes.

Chirmei Burong .... Small tree; its leaves are used in medicine, and given to lying-in women, and externally in certain cutaneous affections; birds are very fond of its seeds.

K. Tamak bukit .... For planks, boat-building; good white.

Mengroopoos .... Reckoned nearly equal to Tampenes; it is dark-coloured.

Pulei .... White wood, for planks only.

Juhtong .... Very white; these woods are chiefly used by undertakers.

Langadei .... For firewood; sinks in water.

K. Kaledang................ Large tree, used in boat-building; dark-coloured.

Nibong .... Caryota urens; is a species of palm; the wood is valuable for house-posts and rafters, laths, &c.; grows in marshy places; it is very hard and fibrous, as is its fracture.

Tummak .... For ships' planks.

Maroonggei .... The Guilandina moringa of Lin. and Bengal.

Sajina or Ramoongei. A tree having a root of a pungent flavour, resembling horse-radish, for which it is substituted; the natives eat both the leaves and pods; the latter form a good table vegetable.

Bayas .... Is a tree of the palm tribe, which grows on the hills, and is put to the same purposes as the Nibong, and is reckoned stronger.

Bintaro........................ Carbera of Lin.; yields a deleterious milky juice.

Pangkap .... A species of palm; its fibre is used to tie on thatch.

Pussat Linga .... A tree, the outer coats of wood white, the heart red; is easily worked into planks, and is durable.

Assam Jawa.............. The tamarind tree; it is scarce, and cultivated for its fruit.

K. Pisang Pisang...... High tree; useful for ships' masts; very tough; colour yellow.

Ipoh .... Is the long-dreaded poison tree of Java; with the inspissated juice the Samangs, or wild tribes in the interior, poison their arrows; but this juice, which is prepared over a fire, must be used soon after the process, or it loses much of its virulence.

Babuta .... A high tree, the juice of which, or even the exhalations from it, cause swelling in the face, eyes, and body of the wood-cutter, who is careful, therefore, to peel the bark before using the axe.

Dammar meniah .... Not equal to Dammar laut. Its oil is mixed with Kruing oil for paying prahus.

Dammar etam .... Heavy wood.

Ballong Ayam and Used for house-building.
&ream

Tummak .... For boat-building.

Meddang kuning........ Yellow sassafras.

Tabangow battu .... A hill tree.

Tumpayan amas .... A fine-grained yellowish wood, used for furniture.

Rotan .... The rattan, a generic term; there are many varieties of the Rotan:—

   R. Sigga .... Knotted; used for chair-bottoms.

   R. Tiga sagi .... Three-sided.

   R. Kawat .... Used for rigging.

   R. Tawar .... It grows on the banks of rivers, and drops in strong tendrils armed with crooked thorns; these will pull a man out of a boat.

   R. Mannan .... Used for walking-canes.

   R. Samamboo ..... Also for walking-canes, dark-coloured and glossy, with joints far apart; grows to many hundred feet in length.

   R. Dhannau .... A very long and thick cane, perhaps the largest species; the gatherers of the edible birds'-nest make their ladders for scaling precipices of this species.

   R. Sinnee .... Long and delicate, colour white; it is used by the Malays for cables and rigging of prahus.

R. Ligor benar..... True rattan.

R. Jomang .... Produces the " dragon's blood."

R. Salak .... Produces an edible fruit; the Calamus zallacca.

R. Bumban .... Grows about seven or eight feet long; is used for tying on thatch; it is a ground rattan, growing straight up.

R. Saboot .... Is made into cables and rigging for native prahus.

R. Binni or Dinni Its leaves are poisonous.

R. Oodang .... Red rattan; the cane of which the Samangs and other tribes make their blowpipes for poisoned arrows.

Buluh Bamboos:—

B. Bittang .... The large bamboo; it is used for house-building and for ladders; a section forms a water-pitcher; fishing weirs, &c are constructed of it.

B. Trimiang......... Used by the wild tribes to make their blowpipes for poisoned arrows.

B. Bitting.. .... A large bamboo; its root is pithy; it is used by the wild tribes to make bows.

B. Duri...... .... Thorny bamboo, used for high fences; it grows 60 or 70 feet high.

B. Gading .... Yellow bamboo.

B. Siggei .... Used for ladders to scale precipices.

THE END.

London: Printed by SMITH, ELDER AND Co., Old Bailey, E.C.

509

569

Lightning Source UK Ltd.
Milton Keynes UK
UKOW06n0701270416

273020UK00001B/49/P